# Maury County, Tennessee

# Marriages

# 1852 – 1867

**Byron and Barbara Sistler**

JANAWAY PUBLISHING, INC.
2013

*Maury County, Tennessee, Marriages 1852-1867*

Originally printed, Nashville, 1985

Reprinted
by

Janaway Publishing, Inc.
732 Kelsey Ct.
Santa Maria, California 93454
(805) 925-1038
www.JanawayPublishing.com

2007, 2013

ISBN: 978-1-59641-127-2

*Made in the United States of America*

# MAURY COUNTY, TN MARRIAGES

## 1852-1867

Where two dates appear on an entry, the first one is the date license
was issued, the second (in parentheses) the date marriage was solemnized.  If only one date, it usually means that the date of execution
was the same as the date of license issuance.

Sometimes the execution of the marriage was not reported to the
courthouse, and occasionally the clerk failed to note in the marriage
book that the license was returned.  We would usually make a notation
in the entry to indicate the non-execution of a marriage if the book
so revealed.

We transcribed these marriage records directly from a microfilmed
copy of the original county marriage books, so error, where it occurs,
will usually be ours.  However, it should be remembered that entries
in the books themselves were copied from the licenses by clerks, and
it is obvious from examining the pages that many of them were not
prepared with great care.  Sometimes, for example, the date of
execution will appear in the book as a date prior to license issuance.
In such cases, as well as where we had to guess in deciphering the
handwriting, a question mark or "sic" is inserted on the entry.

The notation (col) after a name means Colored (Black).

Byron Sistler
Barbara Sistler

Abernathy, C. B. to Mary K. Wilkers 11-15-1866
Abernathy, Wm. J. to Margaret A. Fitzpatrick 6-29-1858
Adams, Fred to S. C. Rickman 7-29-1865 (7-30-1865)
Adams, Nathan to Susan L. Pankey 1-9-1854 (1-10-1854)
Adams, Thomas C. to Lizzie T. Caughran 2-17-1866 (2-18-1866)
Adcock, Allen to Amanda Douell 1-20-1855 (1-21-1855)
Adcock, Houston to Margaret L. Peyton 6-30-1859
Adcock, Jesse to Martha Ann Willaford 6-4-1859 (6-5-1859)
Adkerson, Benjamin F. to Beckey Ann Dockery 3-5-1866 (3-6-1866)
Adkins, John to Elizabeth Farmer 3-16-1854
Adkins, Lewis M. to Musadorah P. Jackson 7-20-1854
Adkinson, John G. to Sarah J. Wilson 11-24-1859
Adkison, William F. to Lucy A. Thompson 12-19-1866 (12-20-1866)
Adkison, William M. to Martha J. Church 11-29-1860
Adkisson, Jas. Cinc. to Nancy Ann Dockery 12-22-1866 (12-31-1866) *
Adkisson, John to W. Ann Fitzgerald 2-10-1858
Adkisson, Joseph J. to Aramitta M. Robertson 9-3-1862 (9-7-1862)
Agnew, James F. to Amanda P. Turner 9-4-1862 (9-18-1862)
Agnew, John T. to Molley L. Sewell 1-15-1866 (1-16-1866)
Agnew, Joseph M. to Sarah L. Murphey 4-29-1864 (no return)
Aigius?, John to Elizabeth A. Green 2-13-1854 (no return)
Akers, Robert to Eliza Nickens 2-16-1864 (2-18-1864)
Akin, A. N. to Sarah Jones 8-29-1867
Akin, Anderson J. to Melissa J. Ricketts 12-17-1866 (12-18-1866)
Akin, E. F. to Norveline Miller 2-21-1862 (2-23-1862)
Akin, Eli E. to Elizabeth J. Young 12-19-1859 (12-22-1859)
Akin, Green M. to F. C. C. Neely 5-7-1863 (5-10-1863)
Akin, James H. to Marinda W. Cecil 10-31-1859 (11-2-1859)
Akin, John W. to Virginia A. English 11-29-1865 (11-30-1865)
Akin, John Williamson to Mary Ann Grimes 8-18-1856 (8-19-1856)
Akin, Nathaniel B. to Elizabeth A. Blakely 8-18-1852
Akin, Nathaniel B. to Elizabeth A. Blakely 8-18-1852 (no return)
Akin, Robert to Addie G. McLemore 11-19-1866 (11-20-1866)
Akin, Samuel W. to Martha Jane English 11-21-1859 (11-23-1859)
Akin, Walter to Mary J. Frierson 6-18-1867
Alderson, Robert J. to Rebeca A. Pigge 10-21-1865 (10-24-1865)
Alderson, Robert to Elizabeth Ragsdale 8-19-1861 (8-20-1861)
Alderson, Thomas E. to Jennie L. Gantt 1-3-1861
Alderson, William S. to Nancy Jane Alderson 7-3-1855 (7-4-1855)
Alderson, William to Sarah F. Wilkes 6-24-1857
Aldridge, Aaron to Louisa B. Carigan 3-21-1864 (3-22-1864)
Aldridge, David B. to Malinda Adkins 10-8-1856
Aldridge, Edmund H. to Matilda L. Tanner 6-26-1852 (6-27-1852)
Aldridge, James to Elmyra J. Graves 5-20-1865 (no return)
Aldridge, William to Mary Tanner 11-22-1858 (11-24-1858)
Alexander, A. F. to Sue C. Fuzzell 2-15-1860
Alexander, Abdon J. to Susan C. McConnico 12-12-1857 (12-13-1857)
Alexander, Albert C. to Amanda H. Roy 2-16-1853
Alexander, Ebenezer P. to Eliza J. Gaither 11-26-1866 (11-27-1866)
Alexander, James H. to Eliz. M. McLemore 9-26-1865 (9-28-1865)
Alexander, James M. to Jane E. Campbell 3-12-1855 (3-15-1855)
Alexander, Jerome to Elizabeth Cook 8-30-1865 (9-3-1865)
Alexander, S. R. to Ellen J. O'Nell 5-14-1852 (5-16-1852)
Alexander, Thomas to Susan H. Bailey 10-25-1865 (10-26-1865)
Alford, James W. to Martha F. Jenkins 2-5-1856
Alford, Lambert M. to Lucy A. Baughan 4-23-1859 (4-24-1859)
Alford, Madison M. to Mary C. Norman 9-10-1859 (9-14-1859)
Alfrod, Tristam B. to Emely Clendennin 2-20-1856 (2-21-1856)
Allen, James M. to Susan Sargeant 2-22-1858 (2-23-1858)
Allen, Joseph C. to Delila Lawson 10-17-1857 (10-18-1857)
Allen, Thomas J. to Isabella C. Crawford 4-8-1861 (not executed)
Allen, Valantine to Sarah Holt 4-20-1863 (no return)
Allen, William J. to Mollie E. Adkisson 7-29-1861 (7-30-1861)
Alley, Henry C. to Eliza J. Nevils 1-11-1853 (1-12-1853)
Allford, Monroe to Salley Berry 10-10-1867
Allmond, Thomas to Frances Pickett 9-1-1856
Allmond, William T. to Susan F. Fogleman 12-9-1861 (12-11-1861)
Allred, James L. to Josephine T. Tyler 7-15-1865 (7-20-1865)
Alston, John to Lavinia W. Martin 6-7-1859
Altmeyer, Frederick to Isabella Dunham 2-27-1865 (3-2-1865)
Amick, Chris. C. to Mariah L. Stamps 10-20-1864 (11-20-1864)
Amis, John D. to Margaret D. Hardison 10-19-1854
Amis, John D. to Margaret H. Daniel 6-8-1852 (6-10-1852)
Amis, John D. to Margaret H. Daniel 6-8-1852 (6-10-1865)
Amis, John E. to Rebecca Thomas 10-12-1857 (10-13-1857)
Amis, Jonathan to Catharine Farley 11-28-1863 (12-2-1863)
Anderson, James M. to M. E. Dickson 11-14-1859 (11-15-1859)
Anderson, James M. to Margaret C. Nelson 11-8-1852 (11-9-1852)
Anderson, John G. to Sallie P. Helm 3-11-1861 (8-18-1861)
Anderson, John to Ellen Baker 10-17-1866 (10-24-1866)
Anderson, Newton J. to Roxana A. E. Grimmett 8-9-1867 (8-14-1867)
Anderson, Richard B. to Nancy E. Huey 10-9-1867 (10-8?-1867)
Anderson, Richard to Josephine Cathey 7-19-1859 (7-24-1859)
Andrews, J. A. to Mary Jane Haynes 10-22-1853 (10-25-1853)
Andrews, James K. P. to Hannah A. Harris 4-22-1864 (no return)
Andrews, James M. to Permelia J. Derryberry 4-27-1852
Andrews, Jessee to Martha A. Turner 10-24-1860 (10-25-1860)

Andrews, Michael P. to Nannie E. Harris 6-13-1865 (6-15-1865)
Andrews, Robert W. to Permelia R. Hill 2-28-1867
Andrews, William B. to S. E. F. Bridgeforth 12-2-1856
Armstrong, Alphonso J. to Fannie G. Edmondson 4-27-1859
Armstrong, Elias J. to Elizabeth Walker 12-20-1865 (12-21-1865)
Armstrong, Frank C. to Mariah P. Walker 4-23-1863 (4-27-1863)
Armstrong, Moses G. to Catharine F. Dickey 9-13-1854 (9-14-1854)
Armstrong, Samuel H. to Mary Odil 12-7-1863 (12-8-1863)
Armstrong, William J. to Sallie C. Martin 5-6-1857 (5-7-1857)
Armstrong, William to Martha Jane Gilbreath 3-2-1858
Arnell, Samuel M. to Cornelia C. Orton 11-15-1855
Arnold, William D. to Martha Rock 3-24-1857
Ashton, John to Clara C. A. Parish 6-24-1852 (7-1-1852)
Ashton, John to Clara C. A. Parish 6-24-1852 (7-7-1852)
Atkin, Joseph W. to Jinsey L. Guin 1-31-1867
Atkinson, John G. to Ruth H. Burkett 12-14-1864 (12-15-1864)
Atkinson, Robert D. to Celia P. Walker 10-4-1866
Atkisson, James H. to Sarah Dickey 8-24-1865
Autry, William T. to Sophia Cannon 1-17-1860 (1-18-1860)
Aydelotte, William C. to Sallie L. Polk 11-19-1866 (11-21-1866)
Aydolette, C. D. to Emely Hair 3-9-1861 (no return)
Babbitt, Benjamin F. to Margaret Underwood 1-25-1860 (1-26-1860)
Bagley, William L. to Milley Ann Haley 9-13-1854 (9-14-1854)
Bailess, Charles L. to Emily C. Graves 3-21-1866 (3-22-1866)
Bailey, A. M. to Mary F. Cheairs 9-3-1866 (9-5-1866)
Bailey, George W. to Keezee McKennon 8-25-1865 (no return)
Bailey, Joseph M. to Eliza Brown 7-2-1866 (7-4-1866)
Bailey, Joshua G. to Mary C. Hendley 3-7-1859
Baily, Willis A. to Parthena C. Boaz 12-1-1855 (12-3-1855)
Bain, Francis M. to Susan M. Stephenson 10-12-1853
Bain, Frederick W. to Susan B. Caskey 4-3-1859 (4-12-1859)
Baird, Thos. L. to Laura C. Briggs 1-7-1861 (ret,not exec.)
Bakenbach, Peter to Elizabeth Altmyer 10-13-1859 (10-16-1859)
Baker, Berry H. to Frances O. Carrigan 3-2-1866 (3-11-1866)
Baker, Edward D. to Sacha Bradshaw 3-15-1865 (3-16-1865)
Baker, Fielding H. to M. M. Fly 12-27-1853 (12-29-1853)
Baker, George W. to Sarah M. Harbison 10-9-1860 (10-14-1860)
Baker, John A. to Darcus J. Harbison 1-11-1858 (1-17-1858)
Baker, Narman? to Mary A. Callins? 12-7-1857
Baker, Perry G. to Mary Ann Oakley 11-7-1853 (11-9-1853)
Ballard, Levi G. to Talitha Bishop 3-21-1866 (3-22-1866)
Bard, Robert H. to Martha L. Mooney 11-9-1858
Baright?, Edward P. to Sophia W. Newcomb 2-15-1858 (2-17-1858)
Barker, Elisha to Corintha A. Brazier 10-28-1858
Barnes, Claudius F. to Mrs. Mary J. Frierson 11-15-1859
Barnes, J. E. to S. A. Henderson 1-6-1854 (1-10-1854)
Barnett, James to Elizabeth Deal 4-29-1857
Barnett, Marcus L. to Fanney Chaffin 10-26-1863 (10-28-1863)
Barnette, William P. to Mary Jane Spain 1-31-1855 (2-1-1855)
Barr, Algernon A. to Mrs. Rachel J. Gill 12-5-1855
Barr, Isaac G. to Susan S. K. Coffman 2-9-1852 (2-2?-1852)
Barracks, John to Manerva Nance 11-23-1854 (no return)
Barrett, James to Mary A. Rumbo 8-26-1867 (no return)
Barton, Thomas to Mary D. Irvine 4-16-1853 (4-7-1853)
Basham, Freeman J. to Charlotte Moses 3-24-1860 (3-25-1860)
Batton, George W. to Lucy Hobson 3-19-1853 (no return)
Baty, John J. to Maria Calahan 8-16-1852 (8-26-1852)
Baucom, Elijah to Cyntha Huey 8-11-1855 (8-12-1855)
Baucome, Elisha J. to Mary A. Sowell 1-13-1853
Baugh, J. C. to Mary J. Carrigan 9-5-1866 (9-7-1866)
Baxter, A. J. to Maria J. Farmer 8-14-1866 (8-16-1866)
Beales, William to Nancy Ann Green 3-29-1855 (no return)
Bean, Curtis Coe to Mary Margaret Bradshaw 10-16-1864
Bean, George H. to Roxana McDonald 9-19-1866 (9-20-1866)
Beard, Thomas L. to Laura C. Briggsa 7-31-1861 (8-4-1861)
Beard, William C. to Elizabeth Green 7-3-1855 (no return)
Beasely, Wm. H. to Elizabeth Robertson 12-22-1852 (12-23-1852)
Beasley, William H. to Elizabeth Robertson 12-22-1852 (12-23-1852)
Beasly, William to Mary T. White 3-24-1858
Beaty, J. J. to Mary M. Brown 12-10-1866 (12-25-1866)
Beaves, Spencer D. to Mary C. True 12-23-1865 (12-24-1865)
Beck, Calvin to Rutha Gardner 3-17-1865 (no return)
Beecher, John Sloan to Mary E. Armstrong 2-13-1862
Begly, William L. to Mary Haley 3-9-1857
Bell, Lucius M. to Elizabeth Walker 9-26-1853
Bendamin, John to Frances J. E. Douglass 1-2-1860 (1-5-1860)
Bendamin, William F. to Mary E. Hackney 8-22-1859 (8-25-1859)
Bendermand, William D. to Mary J. Gilbreath 12-20-1864 (12-27-1864)
Bennett, Jacob to Mary Frances Richardson 10-1-1867 (10-2-1867)
Bennett, John D. to Lucinda J. Hunt 6-20-1865
Bennett, John D. to Lucretia A. Hunt 4-8-1861 (4-9-1861)
Benton, Wm. R. H. to Margaret A. Egnew 2-23-1853 (3-1-1853)
Berry, William to Sophia Amanda Wahl 7-11-1859 (7-14-1859)
Bethel, William D. to Cyntha S. Pillow 6-27-1860 (6-28-1860)
Bieard?, Chas. H. to Nancy A. E. Galloway 6-25-1866 (6-27-1866)
Bigger, William E. to Lucinda E. Hackney 3-8-1867 (3-10-1867)

Biggers, John L. to Amelia A. Williams 12-19-1866 (12-25-1866)
Bigham, James to Elizabeth Hart 10-18-1852 (10-21-1852)
Bigham, James to Elizabeth Hart 10-18-1852 (no return)
Bills, W. J. T. to Unis P. Andrews 12-14-1853
Bingham, Alexander to Evaline A. Hart 11-24-1859
Bingham, John T. to Jane L. M. Jones 1-11-1862 (1-14-1862)
Bingham, John T. to Virginia V. Cyrus 11-17-1860 (11-20-1860)
Birdsong, J. R. to Dicey K. Bruce 9-22-1866 (no return)
Birkeen, Joseph S. to Eliza J. Tindle 10-26-1854 (11-1-1854)
Birney, William L. to Mary V. Reynolds 6-21-1865 (6-22-1865)
Bishop, Andrew J. to Earsley M. Pannell 10-5-1866 (10-7-1866)
Bishop, Francis M. to Mary Ann Laws 8-12-1865
Black, David S. to Margaret Hall 5-22-1865 (5-23-1865)
Black, Luther W. to Fannie L. Moore 9-1-1865 (9-4-1865)
Black, Samuel to Sarah Jane Reed 3-27-1855 (3-29-1855)
Blackbern, Alexander to Emarintha Mayes 3-23-1857 (3-26-1857)
Blackburn, Dr. Thos. B. to Alabama S. Mayes 1-10-1853 (1-13-1853)
Blackburn, George W. to Margaret C. Bingham 8-2-1856 (no return)
Blackburn, L. C. to Martha P. Johnson 5-5-1856 (5-6-1856)
Blackburn, Rob. S. to Sarah Finch 11-29-1856 (no date)
Blackburn, Robert M. to Helen M. Ayres 7-26-1861
Blackburn, Wm. S. to Susan A. Sellar 5-7-1855 (no date)
Blackwell, John M. to Martha E. Patton 9-13-1865 (9-14-1865)
Blair, George H. to America P. Hardin 4-20-1852 (5-4-1852)
Blair, J. H. M. C. to Ellen A. Scheltier 12-22-1858 (12-30-1858)
Blair, James D. to Margaret M. Harrison 5-3-1861 (5-12-1861)
Blair, Joseph to Martha Buckner 12-22-1852 (12-30-1852)
Blair, Thomas W. to Susan J. Blanton 5-8-1866 (5-13-1866)
Blake, Frank D. to Sallie H. Polk 4-23-1866 (5-1-1866)
Blakeley, John D. to Portia T. Howard 3-25-1863 (3-26-1863)
Blakeley, Robert D. to Mary S. Frierson 10-18-1858 (10-20-1858)
Blakely, John D. to Harriett W. Pettillo 4-7-1852 (4-8-1852)
Blankenship, A. T. to Lucy J. Smith 5-6-1853 (5-10-1853)
Blankenship, Thomas J. to Nancy Jane Dodson 10-9-1863 (10-28-1863)
Blanton, James O. to Bettie E. Caldwell 4-20-1867 (4-24-1867)
Blanton, William C. to Virginia F. Miller 12-7-1858 (12-8-1858)
Blocker, Alexander C. to Arzilia Anderson 9-1-1866 (9-6-1866)
Blocker, Elijah to E. A. Wilkes 7-7-1862 (7-8-1862)
Bohananan?, J. V. to Nancy Crawford 2-14-1863 (2-15-1863)
Bolton, Benjamin to Rosanah McClain 10-10-1854
Boman, John to Kissirah J. Bain 3-14-1853
Bond, Arstead to Julia Jordan 8-18-1856
Bond, Henry C. to Mrs. Mary McBride 1-23-1866 (1-25-1866)
Bond, James L. to Mary V. Watkins 12-17-1858 (12-19-1858)
Bond, John H. to Sarah E. Williams 11-14-1854 (11-15-1854)
Booker, Carter J. to Sarah J. Dowell 9-8-1859 (9-11-1859)
Booker, G. M. to Mary A. P. Owens 12-23-1865 (12-24-1865)
Booker, James P. to Mary Jane Mills 1-29-1861
Booth, Sam to Frances Cunningham 7-1-1858
Borum, J. B. to Eve M. Dobbins 1-22-1867
Boshear, Andrew J. to Frances Bell 1-23-1867 (1-26-1867)
Boshears (Beshears?), James R. to Honor C. Weaver 8-21-1852 (8-22-1852)
Boshears, James R. to Honor C. Weaver 8-21-1852 (8-22-1852)
Boshears, Jason to Honor Boshears 8-31-1861 (9-1-1861)
Box, Stephen M. to Elizabeth A. Kirks 3-14-1859
Boyd, Leonida A. to Sallie Ann Priest 10-13-1859
Boyd, W. Calvin to Angeline E. White 12-25-1861
Bracheen, John H. to Eliza A. Hayes 9-23-1863
Brackenridge, David to Nancy Overstreet 9-15-1852
Brackenridge, Davis to Nancy Overstreet 9-15-1852
Braddon, John to Louisa Rail 10-10-1859 (10-11-1859)
Bradley, Vivaldy to Nancy Clark 7-19-1856 (7-20-1856)
Bradon, Thomas to Louisa Sneed 5-3-1862 (5-12-1862)
Bradshaw, Hugh to Cynthia C. Ford 1-21-1863 (1-23-1863)
Bradshaw, James N. to Mary E. Ramsey 2-10-1866 (2-11-1866)
Branch, Joseph to Mary Jones Polk 11-27-1858 (11-29-1858)
Branch, Reuben E. J. to Prisc. E. Craig 12-25-1865 (12-26-1865)
Branden, John L. to Izora Hall 3-16-1852
Brandon, John L. to Izora Holt 3-17-1852
Brashear, James to Julia M. E. Rains 2-4-1861 (2-5-1861)
Bratton, S. H. to Mary W. Conner 2-17-1866 (2-20-1866)
Brazier, William E. to Laura B. Huey 9-18-1867
Brazier, William E. to S. E. Barker 8-5-1852 (8-7-1852)
Brien, Carlton D. to Emily Jane Johnson 3-14-1854 (3-15-1854)
Brien, Fines E. to Caledonia Revier 11-25-1858 (11-28-1858)
Briggs, John C. to Felicia A. Stephenson 10-20-1863
Briggs, William J. to Frances H. Beard 6-2-1862 (no return)
Bright, John M. to Yurildia B. Bucker 6-3-1857 (6-4-1857)
Briley, S. E. to Caroline Noles 1-3-1865
Briley, Seaton P. to Delia Frances Noles 2-6-1865 (2-7-1865)
Brims, John J. to Julia R. Hudspeth 1-30-1858 (1-31-1858)
Brock, James to Lucindy Davis 6-7-1852
Brooks, Abner to Sarah C. P. Sowell 7-16-1856 (no return)
Brooks, Elisha A. to Ellen J. Grimes 9-4-1866 (9-6-1866)
Brooks, Henry Clay to Lizie G. Cook 10-26-1864 (10-27-1864)
Brooks, James H. to Virginia T. Jordan 1-16-1860 (1-19-1860)
Brooks, James T. to Sidney A. Brickle 7-23-1866 (7-26-1866)

Brooks, James to Sarah J. Whittaker 11-28-1865 (12-29-1865)
Brooks, John A. to Lucy A. Jordan 10-2-1856
Brooks, John to Anne P. Smith 2-25-1861 (2-26-1861)
Brooks, Lish to Sarah Mosley 3-24-1860 (4-10-1860)
Brooks, Thomas B. to Mary B. Worley 10-16-1854 (10-17-1854)
Brooks, Wm. T. to Henrietta S. McBride 12-22-1862 (12-23-1862)
Brown, Allen to Martha Scott 1-2-1854
Brown, Campbell to Lucie? R. Polk 9-11-1866
Brown, David C. to Louisa M. Hill 10-3-1859 (10-4-1859)
Brown, David F. to Rachael Hart 11-27-1865 (no return)
Brown, Ephraim to Celia Burrass 5-22-1852 (5-23-1852)
Brown, Ephram to Celia Burass 5-22-1852 (5-23-1852)
Brown, Gabriel B. to Margaret J. Moreen 6-14-1860
Brown, Gabriel to Hariet J. Miller 12-20-1852 (12-23-1852)
Brown, George H. to Mary N. Hughes 2-24-1858 (2-25-1858)
Brown, George W. to Leemy Amich 4-7-1864
Brown, George to Louisa Carter 9-1-1865
Brown, Irvin to Lucy Johnson 7-7-1866 (7-8-1866)
Brown, John A. to Paralee Amick 2-15-1864 (no return)
Brown, Joseph J. to Eliza S. Vestal 5-29-1852 (5-30-1852)
Brown, Joseph W. to Maggie L. Judkins 8-30-1859 (8-31-1859)
Brown, Martin V. to Sarah E. Cooper 2-2-1865 (3-2-1865)
Brown, Richard to Sarah L. Ragan 7-15-1861 (7-16-1861)
Brown, Robert P. to S. E. Nichelz 11-17-1857 (11-18-1857)
Brown, Robert to Elizabeth Collins 6-4-1852 (6-6-1852)
Brown, Samuel T. to Medora E. Bledsoe 1-15-1866 (1-17-1866)
Brown, Thomas J. to Mary Amanda Pillow 4-20-1859 (4-21-1859)
Brown, W. F. to Elizabeth M. McManus 2-23-1853 (2-24-1853)
Brown, Wiley B. to Henrietta A. Phelps 5-16-1866 (5-17-1866)
Brown, William H. to Sarah E. Porter 1-16-1866
Brown, William R. to Lucinda Shires 10-17-1856 (10-19-1856)
Brown, William to Eliza Jane Robertson 7-16-1864 (7-17-1864)
Browning, Clincey to Martha Ann Finch 1-8-1856
Browning, William H. to Mary E. Smith 10-8-1853 (10-10-1853)
Bryant, A. S. to Jane W. Gresham 1-8-1855 (1-11-1855)
Bryant, Andrew D. to Sarah W. Hill 1-3-1852 (1-4-1852)
Bryant, David F. to Rutha A. Andrews 10-16-1862 (no return)
Bryant, James E. to Judith C. Cheatham 10-14-1856 (10-15-1856)
Bryant, Lucius R. to Martha E. Branch 11-15-1865 (11-16-1865)
Bryant, Thomas H. to Emily J. Howard 1-3-1866
Bryant, Thomas S. to Nancy J. Bryant 3-15-1852 (3-18-1852)
Bryant, W. D. to Hanna M. Scott 7-6-1853
Bryson, James H. to Emily F. Morgan 3-15-1854 (3-16-1854)
Buch, Americus B. to Sarah A. Stockard 7-14-1856 (7-15-1856)
Buchanan, Andrew H. to Malinda A. Alexander 7-9-1855 (7-10-1855)
Buchanan, William J. to Mary E. Moore 3-9-1858 (3-?-1858)
Buford, Spencer W. to Tennessee Stephenson 9-12-1865 (9-13-1865)
Bugg, John R. to Ann M. Richarson 11-18-1865 (11-23-1865)
Bugger, Robert to Eliza Stinson 6-22-1867 (6-23-1867)
Bullard, George A. to Sarah E. Gill 7-12-1865 (7-13-1865)
Bullock, Jason Lee to Laura Voorhies 9-13-1860
Bumpass, Augustine to Lety D. King 11-22-1855 (11-25-1855)
Bumpass, Augustus to Malinda Collins 7-31-1852
Bunch, John B. to Mary A. E. Sanders 3-2-1853 (3-3-1853)
Bunch, Solomon H. to Ruth D. Jones 10-6-1858
Burditt, John to Sarah Hargrove 1-6-1865 (1-7-1865)
Burkett, Absolum to Valeria Wright 4-9-1864 (4-12-1864)
Burkett, James M. to Martha Frances Spain 10-16-1855 (10-17-1855)
Burkett, Samuel H. to Viana Estes 7-15-1862 (7-16-1862)
Burlison, Martin to Cynthia Waldron 3-11-1861
Burney, Alfred M. to Martha M. Davis 1-6-1858 (1-8-1858)
Burney, John Milton to Molly J. Alexander 12-6-1859 (12-8-1859)
Burnham, Ira E. to Elizabeth Farless 4-12-1858 (4-15-1858)
Burns, Jesse to Nancy S. Fitzgerald 2-22-1852 (1-29-1852)
Burpo, Abner T. to Esther Furlow 7-13-1855 (7-14-1855)
Burpo, George W. to Margaret Ann Gibson 8-1-1855 (8-2-1855)
Burr, William to Malinda L. Stricklin 10-23-1860
Butler, Thomas E. to Rebecca E. Faris 6-5-1867
Byers, Abijah to Martha Jane Potts 1-31-1856 (no return)
Bynum, Andrew J. to Catharine J. Nevils 12-15-1863 (12-17-1863)
Byrd, Dabney C. to Mary C. Ladd 7-5-1860
Cabler, James B. to Sarah E. Forsyth 2-15-1858
Cabler, James B. to Sarah E. Kellam 10-13-1863 (no return)
Cabler, John M. to Eliza J. Moore 10-22-1852 (date not given
Caldwell, Alexander J. to Mary E. Caldwell 8-5-1853 (8-?-1853)
Caldwell, Andrew W. to Mary M. Watson 12-29-1863 (12-30-1863)
Caldwell, David A. to Fannie Everett 3-8-1856 (3-9-1856)
Caldwell, Edward T. to Julia Watson 5-4-1861 (5-5-1861)
Caldwell, Samuel S. to Sarah P. Peery 3-19-1855 (no return)
Caldwell, Thomas J. to Nancy J. Gist 9-27-1859 (9-29-1859)
Caldwell, William J. to Margaret Gist 4-10-1860 (4-12-1860)
Callahan, David M. to Sarah Scott 12-22-1857
Callahan, William F. to Priscilla Trigg 1-17-1866 (1-25-1866)
Calvert, Robert W. to Sarah Ann Coffee 4-18-1867
Campbell, Colin M. to Sallie E. Young 10-10-1853 (10-11-1853)
Campbell, John to Mary E. Gwinn 12-13-1854 (12-17-1854)
Campbell, McCoy C. to Alice L. Bauguss 2-7-1866

Campbell, Richard C. to Elizabeth P. Tanner? 2-11-1867 (2-12-1867)
Campbell, Samuel S. to Tennessee C. McGolrick 9-26-1862 (9-30-1862)
Campbell, William to Mary Charlotte Miller 9-26-1865 (9-27-1865)
Cannon, Michael to Mary E. Jones 3-7-1860 (3-8-1860)
Cannon, William M. to Nancy J. Gilbreath 12-9-1854 (11?-10-1854)
Caperton, Samuel B. to Mary J. Childress 8-7-1854 (8-8-1854)
Caperton, Thomas H. to Mary E. Hardgraves 7-18-1853 (7-22-1853)
Carothers, J. H. to D. M. Hassell 8-17-1859
Carpenter, James N. to Martha C. Lane 5-30-1855 (5-31-1855)
Carter, B. Frank to Cynthia Rivers 4-6-1852
Carter, Henry to Maria E. Briggs 9-29-1865 (10-1-1865)
Carter, T. P. to Mrs. Nancy Coleman 10-30-1858 (10-31-1858)
Carthel, Thomas J. to Mary M. Frierson 7-12-1859 (7-13-1859)
Cartwright, Mark T. to Mary P. Lester 10-4-1860 (no return)
Caruthers, Thos. J. to Sallie J. McEwen 10-30-1866
Caskey, John T. to Sarah E. Davidson 9-28-1867 (10-2-1867)
Casky, James R. to Laura C. Sowell 7-25-1867 (7-28-1867)
Cates, Greenberry to Henrietta J. Buckner 11-30-1857 (12-1-1857)
Cates, William G. to Martha F. E. Akin 9-22-1857 (9-24-1857)
Cathey, Alexander B. to Tennie E. Smith 9-26-1859 (9-27-1859)
Cathey, Alexander to Mary Holden 2-28-1867
Cathey, Alfred to Callie Holden 8-29-1864 (9-1-1864)
Cathey, James A. to Elizabeth Worley 9-19-1866 (9-20-1866)
Cathey, James to Effee Bullock 12-3-1861
Cathey, William H. to Martha S. Kennedy 12-9-1852 (12-14-1852)
Cathey, William to Martha S. Kennedy 12-9-1852
Cavender, James H. to Lucinda Baker 11-10-1859
Cavender, John C. to Eliza A. Ricketts 1-2-1854 (1-5-1854)
Cavender, Stephen C. to Helena Kirk 11-13-1857 (no return)
Cavin, Robert W. to Eliza A. Moore 8-12-1863 (8-20-1863)
Cawsey, William R. to Ann Eliza Edwards 5-30-1864 (5-31-1864)
Cawsey, William R. to Sarah Jane Edwards 9-15-1855 (9-16-1855)
Cayce, Geo. Marshall to Mary Ann Killingsworth 12-5-1855 (12-6-1855)
Cecil, Samuel R. to Melindar Howard 11-1-1866
Chaffin, Green T. to Mrs. Sarah J. Kincaide 8-15-1867
Chaffin, James B. to Ophelia M. Peyton 1-9-1861 (1-10-1861)
Chaffin, William B. to Margaret C. Martin 11-27-1855 (11-28-1855)
Chaffin, William M. to Eliza S. Payton 3-23-1855
Chagle, H. D. to Paralee Brown 12-27-1864 (12-28-1864)
Chambers, John to Jane Curry 8-22-1853
Chambers, Joseph to Medea Ann Hines 10-13-1855 (10-16-1855)
Chaney, J. A. J. to Martha R. Fitzgerald 4-27-1864 (5-1-1864)
Chaney, Marcus L. to Amanda Slayden 1-16-1865 (ret,no endors.
Chapman, Baxter C. to Eliza K. Fussell 2-13-1862
Chapman, James to Alfreda Davis 6-22-1852
Chapman, James to Alzada Davis 6-22-1852
Chapman, Jos. Rob. to Margaret M. Thomas 8-6-1859 (no return)
Chapman, William F. to Sarah Hammox 4-27-1866 (4-29-1866)
Chapman, William to Ann Thomason 1-22-1866 (1-23-1866)
Chappell, Sandie to Belle Dooley 11-14-1865 (11-16-1865)
Chappell, Sandy to Maggie Bullock 12-8-1857 (12-10-1857)
Charter, William to Alabama D. Johnson 11-8-1852
Cheatham, Fletcher H. to Martha Ann Martin 4-30-1856 (5-1-1856)
Cheek, Jesse A. to Sarah Jane Durham 9-17-1862 (no return)
Cheek, Jesse to Mary Ann Hardison 5-4-1859 (5-5-1859)
Cheek, Orean P. to Susan J. Huey 8-17-1854
Cheek, Robert L. to Nancy J. Craig 6-9-1865 (6-20-1865)
Cherry, William W. to Maria W. Polk 4-6-1858
Childery, Albert to Julie A. Cruise 12-27-1858 (12-29-1858)
Childress, William J. to Amanda J. Adkins 12-29-1853
Childrey, Nathaniel T. to Mary Crews 11-27-1865 (12-7-1865)
Choate, Joseph M. to Mary Stallings 2-10-1857 (no return)
Christian, Lorenzo D. to Mariana Turnage 3-8-1865
Christly, Frederick to Nancy W. Warren 11-21-1854 (11-23-1854)
Christopher, Towns? to Agness Brown 1-1-1855 (1-2-1855)
Chumbly, A. M. to Sarah E. Sprinkles 7-18-1862 (7-27-1862)
Chumbly, James N. to Juda A. Harmon 2-29-1864 (3-1-1864)
Chumbly, John E. to Sarah E. Robinson 10-7-1867 (10-13-1867)
Chumbly, Thomas S. to Nancy Hargrove 11-1-1855 (11-4-1855)
Chunn, Henry T. to O. J. Jones 6-6-1865 (6-7-1865)
Church, Charles M. to Dolley Ann Mullens 8-18-1859
Church, David J. to Parthena Walters 10-16-1856
Church, Edmund F. to Sarah P. Satterfield 9-24-1860 (9-26-1860)
Church, J. P. to S. S. Oakley 8-20-1866 (8-21-1866)
Church, John M. to Sarah Younger 7-16-1853 (7-17-1853)
Church, Joshua P. to Mary J. Vestal 10-27-1852
Church, Joshua P. to Mary J. Vestal 10-27-1852 (no return)
Church, William J. to Tennessee Walter 3-12-1857 (no return)
Clanton, Abraham to Mary Williams 1-16-1854
Clanton, George W. to Nancy C. Renfro 10-12-1865 (10-15-1865)
Clanton, William to Rachel Moore 10-20-1864 (10-23-1864)
Clark, James to Mary Russell 5-30-1864
Clark, Robert D. to Mary Frances Meece 12-20-1866
Clark, Thomas to Eliza Hereford 11-19-1855 (12-31-1855)
Clark, William H. to Tabitha E. Isbell 1-12-1857 (1-20-1857)
Clear, Charles to Amanda A. Hodge 2-6-1860 (3-8-1860)
Clemons, Andrew J. to Nancy J. London 10-22-1856 (no return)

Clendenan, Thomas to Elizabeth Dorton 2-11-1857 (no return)
Clopton, B. Drake to Mary T. Booker 11-25-1858
Clouston, William G. to Eudora P. Sewell 9-25-1865 (9-28-1865)
Clymer, Joseph H. to Narcissa Fox 12-13-1865 (12-17-1865)
Clymore, J. M. to Amanda Jordan 9-10-1866 (9-13-1866)
Clymore, James M. to Adaline M. Mullins 11-24-1856 (11-27-1856)
Cobler?, John M. to Eliza J. Moore 10-22-1852
Coburn, Theophilus to Naomi Howard 9-28-1852 (9-29-1852)
Cochran, James A. to Sallie E. Wilkes 12-16-1865 (12-19-1865)
Cochran, James T. L. to Susan E. Kittrell 9-22-1853
Cockrell, Anderson J. to Eliza J. Howard 12-26-1860 (12-29-1860)
Cockrell, N. G. to Mary M. Box 3-9-1853
Cockrill, Jasper B. to Nancy E. Wright 1-14-1857 (1-15-1857)
Cockrill, M. G. to Mary U. Freeland 4-3-1856
Cockrill, Newton G. to Mary M. Denham 12-20-1865
Coffee, George W. to Nancy L. Morrow 8-4-1857 (no return)
Coffee, Green B. to Sarah A. Sutton 5-8-1854
Coffey, Felix G. to Catharine Greenhorn 2-28-1866 (3-1-1866)
Coffey, Felix G. to Mary J. Davis 5-9-1863 (no return)
Coffey, John A. to Mary W. Gresham 11-21-1865
Coffey, John A. to Nannie S. Gresham 2-3-1862 (2-4-1862)
Coffey, Samuel M. to Mattie A. Compton 12-18-1865 (12-19-1865)
Coffy, Davis N. to Mary E. B. Morrow 11-1-1855 (11-8-1855)
Cole, Peter C. to Mary Elizabeth Roy 12-14-1865
Coleburn, Thomas L. to Pemelia Parkison 10-6-1866 (10-12-1866)
Coleman, Thomas to Ellen Anderson 11-5-1866 (11-8-1866)
Coleman, Wilson to Sarah Isbell 10-18-1853 (10-20-1853)
Collier, A. W. to Mary A. B. Bostick 9-14-1859
Collier, William M. to Mary Alderson 12-28-1853 (1-3-1854)
Collins, Armstrong R. to Mary Ann Newcomb 12-13-1859 (12-5?-1859)
Collins, Charles F. to Lulie M. Hamner 2-10-1857 (2-11-1857)
Collins, James to Mary Morris 3-7-1863 (no return)
Collins, Lycurgus to Helen A. Rucker 7-25-1864 (no return)
Collins, Lycurgus to Margaret Young 5-18-1852 (5-19-1852)
Colquitt, George D. to Martha Jane McKey 1-28-1858
Compton, Elihu S. to Mira Ann Rust 10-21-1852
Compton, Elisha S. to Mira Ann Rust 10-21-1852
Compton, Richard to Caledonia Strayhorn? 7-21-1866 (7-25-1866)
Comstock, Clark M. to Mrs. Mary E. Hilliard 12-13-1858  *
Conkey, Z. to S. H. Thomas 5-24-1852 (5-25-1852)
Conn, Jesse to Lousa J. Waddle 9-3-1857
Connelly, Michael G. to Margaret J. Alderson 12-29-1865
Conner, James H. to Amanda V. Love 6-29-1858
Conner, William R. to Martha Blocker 6-14-1852
Cook, James W. to Golden Alexander 8-12-1865 (8-17-1865)
Cook, Patrick A. to Sarah E. Jones 11-30-1857 (12-1-1857)
Cook, R. S. to Elizabeth M. Bond 2-6-1857
Cook, Sidney C. to Mary E. Witherspoon 3-13-1856
Cook, Watson P. to Mary L. Johnson 8-3-1866 (8-5-1866)
Cook, William K. to Mary Eliz. Robertson 3-31-1855 (3-4?-1855)
Cooper, Abner W. to Louisa Tidwell 10-10-1864 (10-11-1864)
Cooper, Abraham H. to Eliz. Jane Dortch 11-21-1855
Cooper, Charles D. to Elizabeth Grimes 1-10-1853 (1-11-1853)
Cooper, Duncan B. to Florence Fleming 10-19-1865
Cooper, Edmund S. to Sarah Ann G. Putman 3-23-1867 (3-24-1867)
Cooper, Edmund to Lydia M. Denham 8-27-1856 (8-28-1856)
Cooper, J. H. to Frances E. Howell 11-22-1866
Cooper, James C. to Emarintha C. Kinzer 9-11-1856 (no return)
Cooper, James O. to Mary A. Underwood 8-22-1863 (8-27-1863)
Cooper, John H. to Ruth A. Vaughn 12-12-1857 (12-13-1857)
Cooper, John R. to Sarah E. Knowles 12-24-1858 (12-26-1858)
Cooper, John to Polly Bynum 4-24-1866
Cooper, Thomas S. to Lavonia McClain 8-21-1860
Cooper, Thomas S. to Sarah E. McKennon 11-23-1863 (no return)
Cooper, W. J. to Helen M. Ridley 3-11-1854 (3-15-1854)
Cooper, William B. to George Ann McFadden 1-15-1866 (1-17-1866)
Cooper, William F. to Mary J. Alderson 5-28-1853 (5-29-1853)
Cooper, William F. to Sarah M. Robertson 1-14-1858
Cooper, William J. to Nancy J. Smith 11-6-1861 (11-7-1861)
Copeland, Alexnader to Elizabeth A. Coffey 9-27-1866 (9-29-1866)
Copeland, John B. to Susan P. Martin 10-25-1854
Corlett, David R. to Martha H. Warren 11-8-1858 (11-10-1858)
Cosby, Druz Smith to Sallie A. Sims 3-21-1860 (3-22-1860)
Cothran, Alexander to Mary Jane West 3-14-1860
Cothran, Eli to Ann E. Johnson 3-4-1867 (3-6-1867)
Cothran, John to Mary E. Holden 11-4-1864 (11-6-1864)
Cotton, Emandus C. to Mary Lester 4-10-1854 (no date)
Cournell, Thomas B. to Levina Aydelotte 2-18-1867
Covey, Levin E. to Martha A. Wilson 8-18-1860 (8-19-1860)
Cowsert, Isaac K. to Mary J. McKenzie 12-19-1859 (9?-20-1859)
Cowsert, John J. to Mary J. Kerr 12-5-1860 (12-6-1860)
Cowsert, Robert S. to Sallie A. Kerr 11-11-1857 (11-12-1857)
Cox, Dr. Henry S. to Rebecca Martin 12-4-1866
Cox, Jackson to Susan Smith 1-30-1863 (2-1-1863)
Cox, James W. to Susan J. Davis 1-18-1859
Cox, Jesse J. to Rebecca A. C. D. Pogue 2-11-1852 (2-12-1852)
Cox, John to Caraline M. Denham 10-26-1857 (10-27-1857)

Cox, John to Margaret Noles 12-22-1857 (2-5-1858)
Cox, Joseph to Nancy E. Baker 12-9-1856
Cox, William E. to Sarah F. Gibson 9-29-1864
Cox, Wm. E. to Sarah F. Gibson 9-27-1864 (no return) *
Craig, James M. to Nancy Jane Watson 3-18-1861 (3-21-1861)
Craig, John B. to Susanah R. Long 3-31-1864
Craig, R. E. to Maggie A. Matthews 11-27-1866
Craig, Robert B. to Minerva J. Morrow 1-1-1856 (1-2-1856)
Craig, Robert to Martha A. McCandless 6-11-1866 (6-12-1866)
Craig, Rufus F. to Lucy Ann Purgerson 8-30-1865 (8-31-1865)
Craig, Samuel M. to Felicia E. Bailey 2-10-1866 (2-11-1866)
Craig, Samuel M. to Mary M. Goad 4-7-1865
Craig, Stephen S. to Mary Ann Sharber 1-24-1859 (1-26-1859)
Cram, James N. to Alesey J. Graves 10-12-1858
Crane, Stephen B. to Mary E. Minor 11-23-1863
Cranford, Arthur H. to Hester Ann Journey 6-23-1859
Cranford, Charles D. to Eliza K. Barr 3-8-1855
Crawford, Andrew to Permelia E. Ray 1-17-1855
Crawford, Charles T. to Sallie A. Wood 12-16-1857 (12-17-1857)
Crawford, Francis M. to Mary S. Davis 12-3-1856
Crawford, Hardin to Angeline Crawford 5-25-1854
Crawford, Henry to Rebecca Norriss 6-1-1857
Crawford, Robert S. to Emely P. Aldridge 7-22-1854 (10-29-1854)
Crawford, Thomas C. to Harriet F. Wood 5-5-1863
Crews, John s. to Sarah Flowers 8-2-1858 (8-3-1858)
Crews, Joseph L. to Malinda Caroline Wright 7-13-1864 (7-14-1864)
Crews, William A. to Martha Donelson 10-25-1858 (10-28-1858)
Crews, William P. to M. E. J. Ashton 3-10-1866 (3-11-1866)
Criswell, William T. to Helen Amanda Smithson 1-1-1867
Cross, John g. to Marilda E. Kernell 11-22-1864 (no return)
Cross, Richard to Phoebe White 10-12-1858 (10-13-1858)
Cross, Robert to E. C. Hill 3-15-1855
Cross, Stephen S. to Nancy C. Crews 7-19-1860
Cross, William J. to Mary J. Winn 4-5-1854 (4-6-1854)
Crowder, Robert B. to Nancy E. Curry 7-18-1867
Crowe, John M. to Martha R. H. McRae 10-7-1865 (10-10-1865)
Crowell, Peter to Mrs. Emily Groves 3-22-1866
Crowell, William H. to Elizabeth Ivey 8-16-1865
Crump, Dr. Charles C. to Mrs. Louisa A. Baily 6-17-1858
Crutcher, Americus R. to Anna E. Williamson 2-27-1865 (3-1-1865)
Crutcher, Edward M. to Maria L. Handy 2-11-1854
Crutcher, Henry L. to Magie E. Williamson 7-27-1863 (7-28-1863)
Crutcher, James P. to T. K. McConnico 7-1-1867 (7-4-1867)
Crutcher, William M. to Mary L. Hays 3-5-1866 (3-20-1866)
Cummings, Franklin B. to Gillacy A. E. Stewart 3-12-1867 (3-14-1867)
Cummons, William to Mrs. Susan Fulks 3-5-1856 (3-6-1856)
Cundiff, James C. to Amanda P. Liggett 1-29-1856 (1-30-1856)
Cuney, James N. to Sarah L. Kirkpatrick 1-25-1853
Currey, George H. to Martha Carrigan 1-9-1867 (1-10-1867)
Currey, N. W. to Frances S. Hines 6-18-1867 (6-20-1867)
Currey, Samuel W. to M. P. Flanigan 7-25-1866 (7-26-1866)
Curry, James L. to Martha A. Beard 10-5-1853 (10-6-1853)
Cutran, John to Joanna Fitzgerald 12-1-1866 (12-5-1866)
Dabbs, John to Margaret Weaver 2-17-1865 (2-20-1865)
Dale, Wm. J. Jr. to Margaret M. McLean 11-20-1866 (11-24-1866)
Damewood, Samuel W. to Annie E. Burton 1-7-1867 (1-9-1867)
Daniel, F. O. to Harriet F. Holland 9-9-1858 (9-14-1858)
Daniel, James P. to Mrs. Nancy C. Hardison 1-24-1866 (1-25-1866)
Daniel, Robert A. to Robina C. Caldwell 5-16-1865 (5-18-1865)
Daniels, Samuel M. to Martha A. Fry 1-18-1862 (4-18-1862)
Dannelley, Swain G. to Palmira Ann Thomas 8-2-1865 (no return)
Darton, Gaskill to Annie Wall 5-11-1857 (no return)
Daugherty, G. W. to Mary E. Garrett 4-24-1854 (4-25-1854)
Daugherty, William E. to Jennie Ann Hill 3-26-1866
Daughtry, Richard M. to Ann R. McCrady 2-6-1858 (2-7-1858)
Davidson, Daniel A. to Jessee S. Dobbins 1-15-1861 (1-16-1861)
Davidson, George E. to Tempy A. Reaves 7-23-1856 (7-24-1856)
Davidson, James C. to Fannie T. Crunk 4-12-1867 (4-17-1867)
Davidson, William A. to Margaret J. Crunk 9-9-1867 (9-12-1867)
Davis, Alexander O. to Ann E. Tucker 11-1-1864 (11-2-1864)
Davis, Benjamin F. to Susan E. Holman 3-6-1856
Davis, Henry B. to Fannie Henderson 11-21-1866 (11-22-1866)
Davis, Henry William to Betsey Jane Green 12-23-1865
Davis, James K. P. to Laura B. Haley 8-6-1867 (8-8-1867)
Davis, James L. to E. Frances Kinzer 12-22-1859 (no return)
Davis, John C. to Emily O. Derryberry 8-8-1865 (9-7-1865)
Davis, John T. to Fannie West 3-26-1863
Davis, Johnson to Amanda Gantt 2-19-1861
Davis, Johnson to Dilla E. Jagger 10-16-1855
Davis, Joseph J. to Margaret E. McIntosh 12-26-1859 (12-27-1859)
Davis, Robert E. to Nancy Wright 10-12-1867 (10-13-1867)
Davis, Samuel H. to Whig C. Kirk 8-12-1863 (8-18-1863)
Davis, Sterling to Rebecca S. McAlister 9-6-1855
Davis, W. H. to M. E. Cannon 3-25-1857 (3-27-1857)
Davis, Wm. H. to Elizabeth J. Mathews 9-13-1858 (9-14-1858)
Davis, Wm. L. to Sarah Perry 6-5-1860
Davis, Wootson D. to Eliza M. Hall 8-29-1855

Daws, Isaac to Emma Dean 4-7-1863 (4-8-1863)
Dawson, Andrew J. to Martha J. Vestal 11-2-1854
Day, John to Mary Hill 7-29-1865 (7-30-1865)
Deal, Henry to Sarah A. Hubble 3-7-1865 (3-12-1865)
Dean, John A. to Mary E. Huckaby 11-14-1854
Debow, John R. to Caroline E. Stockard 10-13-1856 (exec. no date)
Delk, Wm. D. to Candis M. Williams 10-11-1865 (10-12-1865)
Demastew, Wm. N. to Ann Crews 1-19-1867 (1-22-1867)
Denham, Thomas to Nancy Mills 2-7-1852
Denton, Elijah C. to Mary Ann Wood 4-5-1866 (4-8-1866)
Denton, George to Martha Ann Gibson 4-9-1867
Denton, James W. to Matilda J. Dycus 11-24-1866 (11-26-1866)
Denton, John E. to Lucinda V. Whitworth 2-8-1865 (2-9-1865)
Derryberry, Barclay M. to Sophronia C. Cox 2-2-1864 (2-11-1864)
Derryberry, James D. to Malissa E. Hardison 9-1-1856 (9-3-1856)
Derryberry, Joseph H. to Sarah J. Collins 10-8-1866 (10-15-1866)
Derryberry, Milton B. to Nancy A. McClure 4-4-1867
Derryberry, Newton C. to Grizilla A. Davis 8-3-1866 (8-5-1866)
Derryberry, Wm. A. to Eugenia F. Hardison 12-19-1865 (12-24-1865)
Dew, Joseph H. to Margaret E. Johnson 4-25-1866 (4-26-1866)
Dew, Latchlin T. to Sarah D. Madden 12-10-1853
Dew, Wm. T. to Sarah E. Wiltsher 10-8-1857
Dial, Robert to Nancy J. Barnett 7-24-1852 (7-25-1852)
Dial, Robert to Nancy J. Barrett 7-24-1852 (7-25-1852)
Dicken, Hugh to Betsy Emler 11-23-1855 (11-25-1855)
Dickey, B. M. to Sarah J. Cathey 10-4-1866 (10-17-1866)
Dickson, Thomas J. to Margaret A. Ramsey 9-6-1853
Dicus, J. W. to Frances Cox 3-24-1852
Dillaha, Thomas J. to Marian Brown 12-26-1866 (12-27-1866)
Dillahay, James P. to Eliza A. Dial 12-14-1857
Dillehay, John W. to Louisa Murphey 3-31-1852 (3-4?-1852)
Dillin, Wm. E. to Roxie J. Benner 6-10-1864 (6-12-1864)
Dillon, Edward to Fannie A. Polk 11-27-1866 (11-29-1866)
Dillskey, Joseph W. to Susan E. Pinkston 8-30-1854
Dinwoody, A. G. to Rachel J. Odel 11-18-1861 (11-19-1861)
Dishough, George B. to Mary E. Perkinson 5-4-1858 (no return)
Dixon, George C. to Drucilla Gaskill 12-1-1853
Dixon, George C. to Eliza R. Frierson 12-18-1860
Dixon, John W. to Nancy P. Underwood 6-23-1863 (6-24-1863)
Dixon, Joseph E. to Emily C. Watkins 11-7-1860 (11-8-1860)
Dixon, T. J. to Kate C. Kinnard 5-7-1855 (5-8-1855)
Dobbin, Wm. A. to Sarintha H. Andrews 7-22-1857 (7-23-1857)
Dobbins, Albert N. to Mary White Fleming 10-18-1865 (10-19-1865)
Dobbins, David W. to Eliza Shannon 2-28-1865 (3-2-1865)
Dobbins, Wm. W. to Emely J. Turner 12-11-1863 (12-15-1863)
Dockery, James M. to Amarintha Alderson 2-12-1861 (2-21-1861)
Dockery, John C. to Rachel J. Pigg 10-6-1859 (10-9-1859)
Dodson, Beverly A. to Pheba Ann Dowell 1-2-1856 (1-24-1856)
Dodson, George B. to Mahalla S. Lawhorn 7-19-1854 (exec. no date)
Dodson, George H. to Leasey P. Skelly 4-1-1865 (4-20-1865)
Dodson, George to Caroline Lawhorn 6-8-1861 (6-9-1861)
Dodson, Hiram H. to Rachel J. Stephenson 2-5-1856 (2-16-1856)
Dodson, James A. to Elizabeth F. Jones 2-15-1864 (2-18-1864)
Dodson, John H. to Lucinda Carrigan 4-27-1861 (4-29-1861)
Dodson, Joseph M. to Mary E. Kinzer 9-30-1867 (10-3-1867)
Dodson, Joseph R. to Hannah Wells 11-16-1858 (11-?-1858)
Dodson, Joshua W. to Martha R. A. Stevens 8-27-1857 (9-1-1857)
Dodson, Marion L. to Martha Fitzgerald 9-24-1852 (9-25-1852)
Dodson, Riley W. to Caledonia F. Kerr 5-17-1854 (5-18-1854)
Dodson, Robert B. to Sarah L. Clendenan 4-3-1858 (4-4-1858)
Dodson, Rolley N. to Nancy C. Skelley 10-19-1858 (no return)
Dodson, Thomas A. to Virgina E. Humphrey 9-26-1854 (10-4-1854)
Dodson, W. D. to Sirena P. Fitzgerald 6-21-1852 (6-22-1852)
Dodson, W. D. to Sirena P. Fitzgerald 6-21-1852 (6-24-1852)
Dodson, Wm. D. to Sue Denton 3-10-1864
Dodson, Wm. H. to Sarah D. Whitaker 2-5-1856 (2-13-1856)
Dodson, Wm. H. to Susan M. Hart 5-20-1853 (5-22-1853)
Dodson, Wm. T. to Lydia D. Fitzgerald 2-1-1858 (2-8-1858)
Donahar, Thomas to Catarine Bargain 7-31-1858
Donaldson, Alfred R. to Martha Perry 6-19-1852 (6-20-1852)
Donly, John to Mary Garner 4-7-1862
Dooley, Alexander to Sarah J. Hargrove 10-27-1865 (10-29-1865)
Dooley, Peter J. to Mary Loftin 7-19-1866 (1-19-1867)
Dooley, Thomas J. to Martha Huckaby 2-22-1865 (2-26-1865)
Dooley, Wm. M. to Ann E. Little 5-21-1864 (6-6-1864)
Dooley, Wm. McKinney to Fannie A. Brazier 7-24-1866 (7-25-1866)
Dooly, Francis M. to Sarah A. Luna 12-22-1855 (exec. no date)
Dortch, David R. to Elizabeth Dodson 2-8-1854 (2-9-1854)
Dortch, John R. to Rosina S. A. Fitzgerald 12-20-1858 (12-23-1858)
Dorton, H. J. to Lucinda J. Humphrey 8-29-1855 (no return)
Dotson, Beverly R. to Frances Clinch 11-16-1858
Douglas, Charles A. to Lizzie Cross 12-20-1865
Douglas, James O. to Mariah P. Underwood 3-6-1862
Douglass, James to Martha Jane Johnson 8-15-1859 (8-18-1859)
Douglass, John R. to Nancy L. Coffey 8-29-1853 (8-30-1853)
Douglass, Thomas Jr. to Mary Booker 2-13-1867 (2-14-1867)
Dowell, James B. F. to Mary J. Casey 12-26-1866 (12-27-1866)

Dowell, John R. to Louisa A. Powell 10-1-1858 (10-5-1858)
Doxey, Martin to Malinda Hall 10-17-1855 (10-18-1855)
Doyle, Samuel J. to Sarah A. Shires 9-18-1857 (no return)
Drake, James L. to Mary D. Patterson 10-6-1852 (10-7-1852)
Due, James W. to Sarah J. Weaver 2-11-1861 (2-12-1861)
Due, John B. to Margaret E. Erwin 11-19-1857
Dugger, David A. to Mary Baldridge 12-1-1853 (12-3-1853)
Dugger, Jonathan H. to Elizabeth J. Moore 4-24-1852 (4-25-1852)
Duke, James to Elizabeth Nolen 12-18-1855
Duke, Joseph H. to Ann M. Whitehead 9-29-1859 (10-1-1859)
Duke, Squire H. to Adaline Carigan 10-16-1854
Duke, Thomas to Adaline Montgomery 11-10-1856 (no return)
Duke, Thomas to Adaline Montgomery 6-18-1858
Duke, Wm. D. to Nancy R. McDoudd 5-21-1864 (not endrsd)
Duke, Wm. G. to Mary A. Bailey 1-28-1865 (no return)
Duke, Wm. G. to Nancy J. McFall 12-24-1853 (12-26-1853)
Duke, Wm. J. to Alice L. Mareen 11-23-1865 (11-25-1865)
Duncan, John to Mary H. Oliphant 4-4-1856 (4-6-1856)
Duncan, Robert A. F. to Martha L. Granberry 7-24-1856 (7-28-1856)
Dunlap, John L. to Mary A. Paschael 11-8-1854 (11-9-1854)
Dunn, Poindexter to Mary Ella Patton 6-13-1855 (6-14-1855)
Duram, John to Mary Harris 8-16-1859
Durham (Denham?), Thomas to Nancy Mills 2-7-1852
Durham, John to Nancy Durham 1-18-1865 (1-26-1865)
Duvall, Hartwell to Mary E. Jones 8-21-1857 (8-26-1857)
Dycus, Andrew J. to Eliza Ann Perkins 1-12-1867 (1-13-1867)
Dycus, David to Cassandra P. Pogue 4-3-1858 (4-4-1858)
Dyer, James to Eliza C. Wilkins 12-20-1858 (12-21-1858)
Easley, Francis M. to Lusy A. M. Kinzer 5-11-1854
Easley, Stephen G. to Lucretia M. Williams 4-21-1860 (4-22-1860)
Easom, Wm. H. to Sarah A. Davis 1-18-1859 (no return)
Eddleman, John F. to Mary M. Vernon 10-11-1865 (10-17-1865)
Eddy, Marvin L. to Annie Bregester 11-13-1865 (11-15-1865)
Edgin, Soloman to Polly Adams 5-22-1856
Edgin, Soloman to Rebecca Jane White 4-19-1860 (4-22-1860)
Edwards, Charles M. to Mary W. Raines 6-24-1857 (7-5-1857)
Edwards, Henry L. to Sarah Crowell 11-3-1866 (11-4-1866)
Edwards, John S. to Parthenia E. Hankins 12-24-1861 (12-26-1861)
Edwards, Thomas H. to Martha J. Edwards 12-6-1865 (no return)
Edwards, Titus M. to Mary Hoofman 6-6-1853 (6-9-1853)
Edwards, Wm. T. to Mary E. Caperton 10-1-1866 (10-2-1866)
Elam, Robert S. to Nancy J. Gray 2-5-1866 (2-8-1866)
Elam, Wm. J. to Julia Ballard 9-4-1865 (9-5-1865)
Elam, Wm. R. to Sallie E. Andrews 8-14-1865 (8-16-1865)
Ellett, John H. to Ophelia A. Kindel 8-14-1861 (8-15-1861)
Ellison, David F. to Elizabeth Polk 3-17-1855 (3-21-1855)
Embler, Henderson to Lucretia Green 1-15-1857 (no return)
Embler, Wm. to Joice Lovell 8-25-1855 (8-17?-1855)
Embry, Lucian J. to Nancy S. Kannon 2-15-1854 (2-16-1854)
Embry, Lucien J. to Lucretia P. Kennon 12-14-1855 (12-28-1855)
Embry, Merrill W. to Frances J. Frierson 12-16-1854 (no return)
Emby, Wiley S. to Nancy P. Wells 10-9-1852 (10-10-1852)
Emby, Wiley S. to Nancy P. Wells 10-9-1852 (10-10?-1852)
Emler, Hellman to Mary Sellars 10-16-1856 (10-26-1856)
Engle, John A. to Margaret E. Frierson 11-10-1852 (11-11-1852)
English, Addison S. to Annie Williams 12-8-1864 (12-9-1864)
Epperson, Thomas E. to Martha A. Epps 4-8-1856
Erwin, George K. to Mary H. Tankersly 11-21-1861
Erwin, James to Orena Ann Harbison 11-19-1855 (11-22-1855)
Erwin, John F. to Matilda N. Pillow 9-28-1854
Erwin, Jonas H. to Margaret Dew 10-16-1861
Erwin, Jonas N. to Codelia P. Pillow 5-15-1856 (5-18-1856)
Erwin, Martin P. to Louisa Blackman 5-6-1852
Erwin, W. T. to Virginia C. Gant 12-20-1854 (12-21-1854)
Erwin<, Martin P. to Laura Blackman 5-6-1852
Eskew, Thomas P. to Salina R. White 5-6-1857 (5-7-1857)
Estes, Enon T. to Hester J. Lawson 5-5-1853
Estes, Henderson to Mary Rich 11-19-1857
Estes, John to Elizabeth Sparkman 12-22-1855 (exec. no date)
Estes, Wm. H. to Mary Whitley 11-27-1860
Estes, Wm. to Martha Huckely 10-31-1857 (11-1-1857)
Evans, Barrett M. to Cornelia T. Dooley 12-31-1866
Evans, John R. to Judith E. Brown 7-20-1865
Evans, Samuel F. to Louisa J. Kerr 5-29-1858 (5-30-1858)
Everett, Ephraim F. to Ellen J. Douglass 11-17-1857
Ewing, Flavius M. to Mary J. Akin 7-5-1859
Exum, J. F. to Nannie P. Cheatham 6-13-1863 (6-16-1863)
Fain, George S. to Margaret E. Wilson 12-17-1857
Fain, John A. to Maria W. Yancy 8-20-1857
Fargo, David to Lucinda Fester 5-25-1864 (5-26-1864)
Fariss, Hugh F. to Mary E. Brooks 4-14-1866 (4-15-1866)
Fariss, Wm. H. to Mary H. Wilson 5-21-1866 (5-22-1866)
Farley, John H. to Mary Jane Holden 5-3-1852
Farney, J. T. to Judtina Baldridge 11-1-1853
Farris, Alexander to Maria Moore 9-14-1857
Farris, Wm. D. to Sarah W. McCrory 2-20-1866 (2-21-1866)
Farriss, C. A. to Elizabeth R. Allen 2-20-1867

Faulkner, Thomas to Sarah A. Bradshaw 7-4-1859 (7-10-1859)
Faulkner, Thomas to Sarah Bradshaw 2-3-1858 (not solemnized)
Ferguson, Benjamin W. to Mary Frances McDonald 10-30-1861
Fielder, Benjamin F. to Mary Ann H. Estes 10-5-1855 (10-7-1855)
Fields, William P. to Jinnie Gantt 12-19-1860 (not endorsed)
Finch, Richard to Mary A. C. Skillerton 8-8-1867 (8-12-1867)
Finch, Silvester to Nancy R. Evans 7-24-1856 (no return)
Fitzgerald, Abel to Amanda Slayden 6-27-1865
Fitzgerald, Bluford H. to Amanda C. Shelly 6-3-1858
Fitzgerald, Bluford H. to Tennessee Thurman 9-27-1867 (not exec.)
Fitzgerald, Carroll G. to Nancy A. McMeen 11-28-1857 (11-29-1857)
Fitzgerald, Cornelius P. W. to Marg. Jane Bailey 5-17-1855 (no return)
Fitzgerald, David J. to Sarah J. Sellars 6-21-1854 (6-22-1854)
Fitzgerald, Dolphin L. to Cerena A. Walker 8-31-1852 (9-1-1852)
Fitzgerald, Edmund P. to Elizabeth Riggins 2-8-1865 (no return)
Fitzgerald, Francis M. to Caroline Chandler 10-1-1857 (10-2-1857)
Fitzgerald, George W. to Gustavus D. Brown 6-23-1852 (6-24-1852)
Fitzgerald, George W. to Gustavus D.? Brown 6-12-1852 (6-24-1852)
Fitzgerald, Green T. to Mary Jane Vestal 8-2-1864 (8-3-1864)
Fitzgerald, James E. to Patsey A. Carrigan 1-13-1859
Fitzgerald, Morgan E. to Martha L. McMeen 12-13-1865 (12-14-1865)
Fitzgerald, Pleasant to Nancy Wilks 5-18-1858
Fitzgerald, Rufus P. to Martha Jane Godwin 2-1-1858 (2-3-1858)
Fitzgerald, W. P. to Margaret Sellars 9-27-1853 (9-28-1853)
Fitzgerald, William D. to Louisa Johnson 9-25-1861 (9-28-1861)
Fitzgerald, Wm. H. to Cynthia A. Alderson 12-20-1858 (12-24-1858)
Fitzgerrald, Dolphin L. to Cerena A. Walker 8-31-1852 (9-1-1852)
Fitzpatrick, Mortimore to Caroline Moore 2-22-1866 (no return)
Flanigan, George B. to Margaret H. C. Erwin 9-6-1852
Flanigan, George B. to Margaret H. Erwin 9-6-1852
Flanikin, Harvey M. to Nancy A. Johnson 8-9-1854
Fleming, John J. to Cornelia C. Gee 9-27-1855 (no return)
Fleming, Robert J. to Bettie T. Glenn 6-17-1867 (6-18-1867)
Fleming, William S. to Mary W. Frierson 1-12-1854
Flemming, Augustus to Addie Oatman 2-14-1867 (2-18-1867)
Flemming, William S. to Mrs. Ruth A. Booker 2-8-1860
Fly, Ben F. to Catharine E. Kinzer 2-4-1861 (2-5-1861)
Follis, John T. to Francesa Kellum 5-12-1859
Foly, John to Mary Shal 12-24-1857 (12-27-1857)
Ford, James A. to Nancy A. Hervey 3-10-1865
Ford, James to Mary Ann Holloway 5-13-1865 (5-17-1865)
Forguson, Henry to Ann Bell 8-30-1866 (8-31-1866)
Forguson, Thomas to Eliza J. Nelms 9-17-1867
Forgy, Swinford B. to Sarah D. Adkins 10-8-1857 (10-11-1857)
Forsche, Elijah J. to Frances J. Hines 7-31-1865
Forsythe, D. M. to Mary Elizabeth Johnson 4-17-1867
Foster, Andrew J. B. to Nancy S. Jones 9-14-1852 (9-15-1852)
Foster, Andrew J. B. to Nancy S. Jones? 9-14-1852 (9-15-1852)
Foster, Cornelius N. to Celia Edgins 2-9-1854 (2-12-1854)
Foster, Ed. A.H.T. to Mrs. Eliz. H. Lockridge 1-15-1855 (1-17-1855)
Foster, Isaac M. to Harriet S. Killcrease 11-11-1862 (11-12-1862)
Foster, James H. to Martha Jane Hickman 10-18-1866
Foster, John R. to Nancy D. Morrow? 9-28-1866 (9-31?-1866)
Foster, John to Margaret Ann Ellis 4-12-1867
Foster, Joseph M. to Talitha R. Jameson 7-20-1865
Foster, Josiah H. to Josephene V. McConnico 9-28-1859
Foster, Robert H. to Sallie H. Potter 1-15-1862 (1-16-1862)
Foster, Thomas to Mary H. Duke 9-30-1856
Foster, W. T. to C. N. Vestal 12-21-1858 (12-22-1858)
Foster, William C. A. to Sallie A. Polk 12-18-1854 (12-21-1854)
Fotty, John W. to Victoria B. Hogwood 9-25-1866 (9-30-1866)
Fox, James M. C. to J. M. Gardner 12-17-1860 (12-20-1860)
Fox, John E. to Sallie J. Emerson 10-19-1864 (10-27-1864)
Fox, Joseph A. to Mrs. Olley Gardner 10-30-1865 (11-2-1865)
Fox, Pervinus Jr. to Eliz. L. Hayes 10-2-1856
Foxall, William K. to Martha E. Mangrem 1-27-1855 (1-28-1855)
Frail, James to Mrs. Bridget McCormick 8-4-1866 (8-5-1866)
Frank, Aaron B. to Sarah L. Adams 7-28-1865 (7-29-1865)
Franklin, Reuben to Sarah E. Turnage 1-18-1865
Fraser, John A. to Amantha Butts 3-25-1852
Frazier, Edmond A. to Amanda Butts 10-10-1855
Frazier, William D. to Martha Ann Harris 5-6-1859
Freeland, Lucius S. to Jenevia Tenn. Park 1-7-1867 (1-8-1867)
Freeman, Hampton M. to Eliz. Howell 1-16-1856 (2-1-1856)
Frierson, James A. to Mary J. Dooly 12-15-1856 (12-16-1856)
Frierson, John M. to Mrs. Mary B. Erwin 10-15-1859 (10-18-1859)
Frierson, John W. to Alice E. Stephenson 4-15-1852
Frierson, John to Martha Ann Mayes 4-21-1857
Frierson, Rev. Jno. S. to Martha M. Jordon 1-9-1855 (no return)
Frierson, Theodore to Harriet A. Frierson 11-28-1860
Frierson, Wm. J. to Rebecca M. Frierson 11-21-1866 (11-22-1866)
Frith, Archibald D. to Martha Bond 9-17-1856 (9-18-1856)
Frost, Joseph to Trissa Ann Thomason 3-31-1865 (4-2-1865)
Fry, Henry H. to Margaret Hogans 11-30-1865 (12-7-1865)
Fry, J. M. to Lilli R. Foster 12-5-1866 (12-6-1866)
Fry, Nimrod P. to Missouri C. Sands 5-28-1863 (no return)
Fry, W. B. to Mary A. Hogan 9-4-1866 (9-5-1866)

Fryer?, George W. to Ruth McDougal 12-27-1865
Fuller, George C. to Sarah Fulp 12-22-1855 (12-23-1855)
Fuller, Henry H. to M. A. Bradley 9-6-1865
Fuller, John to Elizabeth Smith 9-18-1860
Funderburke, James J. to Mary E. Parish 10-8-1853 (10-9-1853)
Furlow, David to Margaret L. Biggers 11-21-1864 (11-22-1864)
Furlow, James C. to Melvina C. Newcomb 3-21-1859 (3-22-1859)
Gabriel, Ferdinand to Nancy Bonharner 8-4-1864 (8-6-1864)
Gale, William A. to Laura Bingham 9-15-1856 (9-16-1856)
Galloway, John B. to Margaret Ann Hanna 12-19-1855 (12-20-1855)
Galloway, William T. to Elizabeth R. Smith 2-3-1866 (2-6-1866)
Gambill, E. W. to Dora Roberts 8-29-1865 (9-4-1865)
Gant, William P. to Laura A. Young 4-29-1857
Gardner, Alfred to Sarah D. Gray 9-24-1858 (10-31-1858)
Gardner, John to Ann E. Wood 3-8-1858
Gardner, Samuel B. to Martha E. Bird 9-16-1865 (9-17-1865)
Gardner, Sylvang to Sarah Hendricks 11-21-1857 (11-22-1857)
Garnder, Andrew to Olly L. Gray 4-3-1858 (4-7-1858)
Garnder, George W. to Narcissa Miller 12-28-1864
Garner, George to Laura Holden 11-4-1865 (11-5-1865)
Garner, James T. to Martha Jane Partett 4-9-1860
Garner, N. D. to Elitha Delk 12-8-1866 (not solemnized
Garner, N. D. to Molley J. Whiteside 1-14-1867 (1-17-1867)
Garner, Nathan to Elizabeth Ramsey 3-12-1864 (3-20-1864)
Garner, Renfro to Sarah J. Byrd 11-3-1852 (11-5-1852)
Garner, Renfro to Sarah Y. Byrd 11-3-1852 (11-5-1852)
Garner, Rufus L. to Elizabeth A. Easley 9-1-1860 (9-2-1860)
Garner, Samuel L. to Mary A. Walker 12-29-1866 (12-30-1866)
Garratt, G. C. to Narcissa J. E. Mathews 7-7-1856 (7-9-1856)
Garrett, Gabriel E. to Mary E. Lamb 12-25-1866
Garrett, Lucius C. to Frances C. Branch 2-17-1865 (2-19-1865)
Garrett, Martin to Nancy J. Ingram 3-5-1856
Garrett, Milton to Mary Tarwater 12-3-1852 (12-4-1852)
Garton, Jacob to Penelope E. Rainey 7-12-1855 (7-15-1855)
Gaskill, Henry to Mary A. M. Herrington 7-25-1853 (7-26-1853)
Geddens, James to Mollie F. Howard 1-21-1867 (1-24-1867)
George, Flower to Louisa Cooper 12-13-1856 (12-14-1856)
Gibbs, Thomas S. to Elizabeth Thompson 11-3-1866 (11-4-1866)
Gibson, Anderson N. to Mary Duke 6-27-1864 (6-28-1864)
Gibson, J. C. to Lena C. Vick 5-4-1867 (5-5-1867)
Gibson, James A. to Sarah E. Cox 10-29-1864 (10-30-1864)
Gibson, James H? W. to Louisa M. Caldwell 9-20-1861 (9-22-1861)
Gibson, John to Mary E. Grimes 8-13-1857 (no date)
Gibson, Joseph to Mary Denton 8-31-1867 (9-22-1867)
Gibson, Mark C. to Elizabeth McDougle 5-25-1867 (5-26-1867)
Gibson, Mark to Elizabeth Tune 1-4-1854 (1-6-1854)
Gibson, William G. to Nelly C. Pugh 7-30-1853 (7-31-1853)
Gidcomb, Thomas C. to Margaret Hood 2-2-1852
Gifford, Gideon W. to Sara M. Hughes 1-15-1866 (1-16-1866)
Gilbreath, Absalom M. to Emily E. Morrow 11-27-1852 (12-1-1852)
Gilbreath, Isaiah R. to Mary L. Coffey 8-12-1862 (8-19-1862)
Gilbreath, John to Mary Jane Brown 3-8-1861 (3-10-1861)
Giles, Wm. to Nancy V. Walker 10-27-1853
Gill, A. G. to Sarah L. Bauguss 12-24-1856
Gillespie, Blackburn W. to Josephine Cherry 6-30-1857 (7-1-1857)
Gilliam, Harrison O. to Mary J. Pinkston 12-19-1856 (12-23-1856)
Gilliam, James M. to Nancy Jane Denham 2-19-1866 (3-7-1866)
Gilliam, John H. to Julia C. Jones 1-5-1867 (1-6-1867)
Gilliam, Newton C. to Harriet E. Kirk 11-6-1865 (11-16-1865)
Gilliam, Thomas J. to Viney T. Pinkston 8-21-1856 (8-26-1856)
Gilliam, Washington to Margaret E. Watson 3-2-1861 (3-7-1861)
Gilmer, John P. to Margaret M. Adkisson 11-6-1854 (11-8-1854)
Gilmon, Richard to Mary Jane West 12-18-1859 (no return)
Gist, John J. to Rachael Williams 4-28-1866 (4-29-1866)
Givens, Andrew J. to Gennette Willis 10-16-1854 (10-27-1854)
Glenn, Archabald to Sarah A. Birney 1-5-1853 (1-6-1853)
Goad, James E. to Sarah E. Vestal 10-29-1864 (11-3-1864)
Goad, Joel to Lucy C. Haywood 9-4-1865 (9-12-1865)
Goad, John C. to Saccie W. Passmore 7-7-1864 (7-8-1864)
Goad, Joshua to Emily A. Grant 6-15-1853
Goad, Neuton to Hester Ann Estes 6-27-1857 (6-29-1857)
Goad, Robert to Cynthia Fitzgerald 1-27-1858 (1-28-1858)
Goad, Wiley T. to Fanney A. Carrigan 6-13-1857 (1?-14-1857)
Goad, Wiley to Caroline Ivey 5-31-1866
Goad, William M. to Nancy C. Godwin 12-8-1866 (12-9-1866)
Godwin, John A. to Narcissa W. Sparkman 1-12-1854
Godwin, John J. L. to Rachael L. B. Church 11-23-1852 (11-25-1852)
Godwin, John J. S. to Rachel L. B. Church 11-23-1852 (11-25-1852)
Godwin, Kinchen to Mrs. Frances Fox 6-6-1855 (6-10-1855)
Godwin?, S. K. P. to Paralee E. Church 7-18-1866 (7-26-1866)
Goodloe, Henry G. to Mary E. Cecil 10-25-1852
Goodloe, James M. to Martha A. Long 10-26-1857 (10-27-1857)
Goodman, Gideon L. to Mahaley Richardson 11-3-1856
Goodman, Henry D. to Silia S. Edwards 1-26-1858 (1-27-1858)
Goodman, Marshall A. to Martha E. Crowell 1-5-1867
Goodman, Wm. E. to Elvira White 12-16-1862 (12-18-1862)
Gordon, John C. to Fannie A. Gillespie 10-26-1865

Gordon, Richard C. to Mary Camp Webster 8-20-1863
Gordon, Wm. W. to Elizabeth J. Stewart 2-4-1853 (2-6-1853)
Gracey, James F. to Martha E. Hanna 12-12-1864 (12-13-1864)
Gracy, Andrew R. to Henrietta Chaney 9-25-1867 (9-29-1867)
Graham, Henry E. to Ellen E. Cox 1-29-1858 (1-31-1858)
Granberry, Joseph J. to Sue A. Brown 11-29-1860
Graves, Powell P. to Sallie Keer 11-30-1865
Graves, Thomas M. to Eliza K. Gray 9-1-1854 (9-2-1854)
Gray, America to Harvey H. Hill 1-30-1865 (2-2-1865)
Gray, J. M. to Elvira D. Pillow 2-12-1867
Gray, James H. to Sallie Lee Harris 10-22-1867 (no return)
Gray, John F. to Mary Williams 4-27-1857 (4-29-1857)
Gray, Pinkney C. to Mary A. Cook 1-14-1852 (1-15-1852)
Gray, Thomas W. to Leanna W. Jackson 10-19-1852
Gray, Thomas W. to Leavina W. Jackson 10-19-1852
Gray, Wm. B. to Parthenia C. Gardner 2-9-1860
Gray, Wm. C. to Rebecca J. Gates 3-22-1859
Green, Burzella M. to Frances Whitworth 7-12-1856 (7-13-1856)
Green, David C. to Allice A. Kennedy 9-6-1865 (9-8-1865)
Green, George F. to Leana P. Thomasson 12-10-1866 (12-29-1866)
Green, George S. L. to Emily J. Jacobs 1-18-1854
Green, James H. to Manerva Gordon 7-2-1854 (no return)
Green, John C. to Martha J. Watkins 8-15-1860 (8-21-1860)
Green, John S. to Mary Luncinda Coffey 9-4-1855
Green, John S. to Mary T. Phillips 7-29-1867
Green, Lucretus to Mary Frances Brown 9-17-1859
Green, Nathaniel to Eliza A. Purty 5-6-1858 (5-9-1858)
Green, Peter to Narcissa Norman 8-11-1865 (8-14-1865)
Green, William B. to Mary A. E. Jacobs 1-29-1852
Greenlaw, Eugene to Nannie R. Cheairs 10-30-1865 (11-1-1865)
Greer, Thompson to Catharine Grigg 12-19-1856 (no return)
Gregory, Abraham to H. Francis Hall 12-19-1853 (no return)
Gregory, David G. to Mary E. Roberts 11-28-1855
Gregory, James A. to Nancy S. Caker 4-18-1857 (4-22-1857)
Gregory, James H. to Susan E. McEwen 5-30-1860
Greiz, George to Pauline B. Farney 3-17-1857
Gresham, Asa A. to Frances L. Campbell 3-8-1854
Gresham, Isaac to Martha F. Cooper 8-1-1857 (8-2-1857)
Gresham, Wm. R. to Mary D. Cochran 12-3-1866 (12-6-1866)
Griffin, Hugh H. to Mary J. Reeves 3-29-1860
Griffin, John to Martha E. Reaves 12-28-1853 (12-29-1853)
Griffin, Wm. A. to Paulina L. Harris 6-2-1866 (no return)
Grimes, George L. to Rowena Hawkins 10-12-1854 (no return)
Grimes, Henry A. to Mary A. Shaw 11-23-1853 (no return)
Grimes, James A. to Mary E. Thomason 11-6-1858 (11-7-1858)
Grimes, James K. to Elizabeth Stewart 4-4-1867
Grimes, John A. to Mildred A. Moss 5-14-1866 (5-17-1866)
Grimes, John F. to Eliza Williams 9-24-1862 (9-25-1862)
Grimes, John H. to Martha A. Davis 11-14-1853
Grimes, Lewis G. to Elizabeth Donaldson 11-1-1865
Grimes, Luther A. to Sarah Moore 12-18-1865 (12-19-1865)
Grimes, Nathaniel W. to Martha J. Craig 1-24-1852 (1-29-1852)
Grimes, Samuel W. to Elizabeth Dean 3-9-1867 (3-14-1867)
Grimes, William P. to Rachal Gibson 7-30-1853 (7-31-1853)
Grimes, William to Ann Dodson 10-4-1860 (10-5-1860)
Grines, Isaac P. to Martha A. Grines 1-1-1855 (1-2-1855)
Grines, William P. to Elizabeth M. Gibson 7-14-1854 (7-16-1854)
Grissom, Isaac to Sarah L. Jones 12-12-1857 (12-13-1857)
Groves, Jacob R. to Susan P. Roche 10-14-1856 (10-15-1856)
Grubb, John A. to Ann Eliza Leftwick 7-26-1865 (7-27-1865)
Guest, David to Martha Watson 8-2-1852
Guest, David to Martha Watson 8-2-1852 (no return)
Guest, David to Martha Wilson 8-2-1852
Guest, W. F. to Mary E. C. Ham 4-18-1854 (4-19-1854)
Gullett, Benjamin W. P. to Hetty A. Keltner 7-15-1864 (7-17-1864)
Gunning, James to Elvira Bowes 9-17-1863
Gustine, Frederick W. to Sallie W. Smith 1-20-1852
Hackney, Humphrey C. to Ann Cartright? 11-15-1866
Haddox, John to Laura A. Brown 3-6-1854 (3-7-1854)
Hadly, Christopher B. to Rebecca Hill 6-18-1856
Haggard, James K. to Martha H. Davis 2-24-1863
Hale, George A. to Darcas C.? Peyton 1-29-1867 (1-30-1867)
Haley, Andrew J. to Malvina Cook 11-17-1853
Haley, George W. to Rebecca A. Cook 11-16-1854
Haley, Henry V. to Frances T. Mangren 1-16-1856 (1-17-1856)
Haley, James to Bridget Fagan 11-22-1857
Haley, John F. to Pernecia C. Morgan 2-28-1867
Haley, Josephus M. to Mariah F. Hubble 7-29-1857
Hall, F. S. to Ann Hall 10-3-1855 (no return)
Hall, John to Melissa Doxey 7-11-1854
Hall, Woodruff P. to Mary McDaniel 10-30-1858 (10-31-1858)
Halls, Adam R. to S. Poca Helm 10-11-1854 (10-12-1854)
Haly, William N. to Jane B. Mangrum 2-3-1852 (2-4-1852)
Ham, Henry to Mary Chapman 3-4-1861
Ham, Marion to Susan Latta 2-24-1866 (2-25-1866)
Ham, N. G. to Sallie Ann Worley 12-6-1859
Ham, William M. to Sophia Ann Latta 9-10-1859 (9-11-1859)

Hamilton, Alexander C. to Ann Oakley 2-12-1864
Hamilton, Andrew to Semantha Payton 7-6-1853
Hamilton, David to Mary E. Wilson 9-16-1854 (9-17-1854)
Hammer, George W. to Virginia A. Hammer 10-5-1858
Hammonds, Gabriel to Mary C. Chandler 1-20-1864 (1-21-1864)
Hand, James to Johanna Fitzgerald 10-24-1865 (10-25-1865)
Hanks, Elijah N. to Sarah Jane Wisener 4-19-1855
Hanks, Elijah to Esther L. Miller 7-17-1855 (7-19-1855)
Hanks, Elisha W. to Mary M. Scott 12-22-1853
Hanna, Dewitt C. to Margaret E. Goodrum 1-17-1854
Hanna, James R. to Sarah A. Walker 9-14-1854
Hanna, Thomas to Nancy M. Dixon 9-6-1853
Hannah, John to Deanna F. Ramsey 4-21-1853
Hansell, J. D. to Sarah Braden 1-11-1858 (1-12-1858)
Harbison, Alexander to Dorcas A. Harbison 8-16-1854
Harbison, James M. to Margaret Dodson 10-30-1866 (11-1-1866)
Harbison, John D. to M. H. Bobbitt 9-2-1867 (9-6-1867)
Harbison, Joshua T. to Mary C. Fly 10-10-1853
Harbison, Matthew M. to Eliz. G. Wreem 7-28-1855 (8-2-1855)
Harbison, Thomas A. to Leanne McGraw 11-3-1853 (11-10-1853)
Harbison, Thomas S. to Mary T. Oakley 9-30-1867 (10-1-1867)
Harbison, William M. to Desdemoa A. Bibb 12-23-1865 (12-31-1865)
Harden, George W. to Eliza J. Willis 2-10-1866 (2-11-1866)
Harden, William C. to Charlotte S. Blagg 7-12-1860
Hardin, Alexander E. to Susan Gaither 8-27-1855 (8-29-1855)
Hardin, Jeremiah to Sarah Jane Ritchie 10-16-1865 (11-6-1865)
Hardison, Hampton J. to Martha E. Cheek 8-7-1865 (8-10-1865)
Hardison, Ira to Mary G. Gullett 11-29-1862 (12-4-1862)
Hardison, Marshal E. to Eliza A. Ikd 10-24-1853 (11-2-1853)
Hardison, Richard B. to Nancy C. Sowell 12-13-1853
Hardison, Robert H. to Mary C. Hardison 9-25-1855 (no date)
Hardison, Samuel L. to Huldy Fox 10-12-1853 (10-13-1853)
Hardison, William H. to Susan G. Nicholson 11-6-1862
Hargrove, Joseph F. to Mary A. J. Wilson 10-12-1867 (10-13-1867)
Harlan, Henry C. to Josephine Z. Porter 3-19-1867 (3-20-1867)
Harman, Charles W. to Sarah F. Cox 5-4-1867 (5-8-1867)
Harman, James A. to Margaret Jane Robason 12-27-1858 (12-18?-1858)
Harman, Thomas A. to Olivia C. Orman 12-19-1865 (12-24-1865)
Harmon, Frederick C. to Kitty C. Blair 2-11-1867 (2-13-1867)
Harris, Andrew C. to Mary E. Hunter 12-5-1865
Harris, Andrew J. to Margaret S. Wollard 12-17-1853 (12-18-1853)
Harris, David to O. J. Harris 5-24-1867 (6-2-1867)
Harris, Edward to Martha Haywood 4-3-1858 (4-4-1858)
Harris, Edward to Mary J. Hough 4-3-1865 (4-4-1865)
Harris, Edward to Salina Harris 12-30-1852
Harris, Edward to Sarah A. Fuller 12-10-1866 (12-16-1866)
Harris, Edwin to Mattie E. Trousdale 3-14-1860
Harris, Eli to Frances J. Bynum 7-13-1853
Harris, Elis to Elizabeth Haywood 12-22-1859
Harris, Ira T. to Dillie E. Estes 4-10-1867 (4-11-1867)
Harris, James B. to Mary J. T. Murphy 9-27-1862 (no return)
Harris, James M. to Martha J. Gray 2-21-1852 (2-22-1852)
Harris, James P. to Mary M. Orr 7-15-1856 (7-17-1856)
Harris, James R. to Mary E. Caldwell 9-27-1866 (10-2-1866)
Harris, Jesse S. to Sallie W. Webster 12-23-1858
Harris, Jesse to Mira Shires 2-21-1854 (no return)
Harris, John W. to Mary J. Henley 3-26-1866 (3-25?-1866)
Harris, M. M. to Cynthianna Gray 1-6-1859 (1-9-1859)
Harris, Robert G. to Martha J. Neeley 9-13-1862 (9-14-1862)
Harris, Thomas A. to Elizabeth J. Stockard 12-6-1858 (12-?-1858)
Harris, W. H. to Josephine Williams 9-8-1866 (9-9-1866)
Harris, Wiley to Paladira Butts 7-19-1852 (7-22-1852)
Harris, Wiley to Palatira Batt 7-19-1852 (7-22-1852)
Harris, William A. to Regina E. Howard 10-31-1853 (11-3-1853)
Harris, William B. to Malinda C. Fly 9-3-1863
Harris, William L. to Rachel A. Blakely 12-12-1855 (12-13-1855)
Harris, William to Esther Knight 10-12-1859
Harris, William to Jane Haywood 12-8-1859
Harrison, Thomas to Nancy Wigington 10-3-1865
Harrison, Wyatt C. to Eugenia B. Neeley 12-18-1865
Hart, William C. to Sarah J. Hanna 10-24-1854 (10-25-1854)
Hartly, Laban to Mary Brayman 6-29-1855
Hartman, George to Betty Bess 8-23-1859
Harvey, Robert to Margaret E. Lush 7-11-1867 (7-12-1867)
Harwell, Brinkly to Arabella M. White 12-2-1865 (12-3-1865)
Haslen, Stephen M. to Emma Ritchell 2-23-1860
Hastings, Duncan to Mrs. Eliz. N. Thomas 6-7-1858
Hatcher, William to Mrs. Sarah Cook 8-4-1864 (8-5-1864)
Hathaway, Snowden K. to Eliza J. Smith 7-22-1865 (7-31-1865)
Hawkins, Lionel to Frances P. Dale 5-22-1855
Hawley, Isaac B. to Allice M. Hardin 12-24-1858 (12-27-1858)
Hawthorne, James E. to Mrs. Eliz. E. Wilson 8-30-1866 (9-4-1866)
Hay, Henry B. to Nancy M. Litton 12-22-1866 (12-23-1866)
Hay, Henry B. to Sarah E. J. Litton 12-28-1858
Hayes, James L. to Mrs. Mary J. Sharber 5-30-1864 (6-1-1864)
Hayes, James P. to Eliza Jane Smithson 12-26-1857 (12-27-1857)
Haynes, John C. to Sarah F. M. Tanner 10-26-1854

Haywood, Atlas W. to Susan L. Pewett 5-11-1866 (5-15?-1866)
Haywood, Edmund P. to Jemimal H. Boles 3-17-1853
Haywood, Richardson to Mary Ann Haywood 1-4-1858 (1-14-1858)
Haywood, Richardson to Sarah E. Harris 5-4-1864
Hazlewood, John J. to Frances E. Fonville 5-20-1854 (5-25-1854)
Head, Alexander to Amanda Slate 6-11-1859 (6-13-1859)
Head, George S. to Henrietta Finch 10-11-1855
Hearn, Granville T. to Lizzie Thomas 11-1-1865 (11-2-1865)
Helm, Dewitt C. to Ella Young 1-1-1858 (1-12-1858)
Helmick, Thomas H. to Susan E. Jackson 3-3-1854 (3-4-1854)
Henderson, Edward F. to Euphemia P. Flemming 7-24-1867 (7-25-1867)
Henderson, George W. to Susan A. Mills 10-15-1864 (10-16-1864)
Henderson, George to Leecy Ann McClure 9-20-1858 (9-23-1858)
Henderson, J. C. to Rena Harris 7-12-1865
Henderson, James F. to Martha J. P. Hill 4-28-1859
Henderson, James T. to Jane C. Davidson 6-10-1852 (6-11-1852)
Henderson, Thomas H. to Margaret A. Hill 2-5-1866 (2-7-1866)
Henderson, Wm. L. to Mary H. Hanna 4-25-1861 (4-26-1861)
Hendley, Flavius J. to Elizabeth A. Jones 10-31-1859 (11-1-1859)
Hendley, Hiram L. to Addie A. E. Guest 1-29-1861
Hendrick, J. Tilman to Mary Frances Mayes 1-13-1859
Hendricks, John B. to Elizabeth Brown 8-29-1866 (9-16-1866)
Henley, John S. to Mary E. Holder 9-24-1857 (9-28-1857)
Henry, Wm. to Ellen Barrick 1-2-1854
Henshaw, John F. to Susannah Ellis 3-4-1867
Hensley, Arthur S. to Cinthia E. Pogue 6-20-1866 (no return)
Heraldston, Benjamin F. to Martha R. Watson 7-15-1856 (no return)
Herring, James to Rachael J. Brinn 12-20-1865 (12-21-1865)
Hess, John to Martha E. Coffey 10-13-1852 (10-14-1852)
Hewatt, Wm. F. to Minerva E. Tarpley 1-30-1866 (2-7-1866)
Hickey, A. C. to Jennie Cheairs 10-24-1866 (11-24-1866)
Hickman, Andrew J. to Martha C. Weatherford 10-27-1858
Hickman, D. R. to Eliza J. Chaffin 9-19-1867 (9-20-1867)
Hickman, Hugh L. W. to Eveline Taylor 8-15-1855
Hickman, Joseph H. to Nancy C. Chaffin 1-3-1855 (1-4-1855)
Hickman, Noah S. to Nancy Hogan 8-19-1858
Hicks, Wm. to Sarah Roan 12-23-1865
Hiett, James M. to Mary Crawford 8-10-1863 (8-12-1863)
Hight, Richard B. to Emily N. Fitzgerald 12-1-1857
Hight, Rufus H. to Mary E.? Wright 10-8-1857 (10-10-1857)
Hill, Alonzo to Mary A. F. Dugger 1-25-1865 (1-27-1865)
Hill, Green B. to Mary Jane Sprinkles 12-29-1866 (1-1-1867)
Hill, Harvey H. to America Gray 1-30-1865 (2-2-1865)
Hill, James B. to Elmira Lancaster 10-25-1854 (10-26-1854)
Hill, James W. to Susan Anglin 11-1-1855 (no return)
Hill, James to Mollie T. Howser 8-11-1866 (8-15-1866)
Hill, Jesse B. to Amanda C. Hill 5-3-1865 (no return)
Hill, Thomas B. to Rebecca E. Thomas 8-4-1865 (8-5-1865)
Hill, Thomas P. to Elizabeth Butler 3-8-1860
Hill, Wm. D. to Manerva A. Simmons 8-12-1853
Hill, Wm. N. to Louisa M. Dobbin 10-8-1855 (no return)
Hill, Wm. R. to Nancy M. Hudspeth 7-17-1856
Hilliard, Frank B. to Amanda Lewis 10-11-1866
Hilliard, J. W. T. to Mollie Estes 6-22-1863 (no return)
Hines, James P. to Mary Donaldson 12-30-1865 (12-31-1865)
Hines, John W. to Anna Love 12-13-1860
Hines, Samuel H. to Mary Jane Bell 2-22-1865
Hite, Rufus H. to Lucy Ann Reaves 12-20-1854 (12-21-1854)
Hobbs, Benjamin F. to Susan J. Jackson 10-22-1857
Hobbs, John M. to Julia A. Adkisson 12-19-1866 (no return)
Hobbs, Joshua to Martha Jane Taylor 8-20-1853 (8-25-1853)
Hobbs, Thomas J. to Jane C. Coffey 10-30-1852
Hobbs, Thomas J. to Jane C. Coffey 10-30-1852 (11-3-1852)
Hobson, Wm. B. to Mary Ann Kessell 1-8-1855
Hockeday, T. H. B. to Maria E. Kerr 1-12-1858
Hodge, Andrew S. to Rebecca E. Lawhorn 11-28-1865
Hodge, James R. to Mary L. Mackey 7-19-1864 (7-20-1864)
Hodge, James to Margaret Smith 6-20-1857 (6-21-1857)
Hodge, Lewis J. to Margaret Myers 6-19-1865 (6-20-1865)
Hodge, Samuel to Evaline Buie 7-17-1856
Hofman, E. C. to Mary J. Russell 11-23-1852
Hofmann, E. C. to Mary J. Russell 11-23-1852
Hoge, James H. to Lucretia A. Jones 10-14-1856 (exec. no date)
Holcomb, Simpson to Ellen Job 11-8-1853
Holcomb, Wm. to Nancy Holcomb 2-15-1854 (2-19-1854)
Holden, Charles to Elizabeth Covington 9-20-1865
Holden, David to Louisa Gilmore 7-2-1866 (7-19-1866)
Holden, James K. to Sarah E. Willis 10-8-1862 (no return)
Holden, James to Eliza Long 6-6-1860 (6-7-1860)
Holland, John T. to Frances Jane Allen 7-15-1861
Holly, Jesse B. to Susan B. Finch 6-4-1856 (6-5-1856)
Holman, Nathaniel to Eliza Gooding 11-27-1862
Holman, Wm. F. to Jessie A. Bynum 2-14-1866 (2-15-1866)
Holmes, John to Parthena Thomason 11-29-1853 (no return)
Holmes, John to Sarah W. Jones 8-29-1865 (8-31-1865)
Holmes, Robert to Nancy Thomason 10-31-1862 (10-3?-1862)
Holmes, Titus to Ann Andrews 3-22-1853 (3-24-1853)

Holt, Isaac A. to Amanda Cheatham 9-16-1862 (9-25-1862)
Holt, Isaac to Elizabeth L. Crews 12-29-1857 (12-30-1857)
Holt, John H. to Marietta Ida Sheppard 4-30-1856
Hommel, William to Sarah Batin 8-3-1852 (8-5-1852)
Hommel, Wm. to Sarah Baton 8-3-1852 (8-5-1852)
Hood, James to Martha Anderson 4-12-1861 (4-13-1861)
Hood, John T. to Henrietta Allen 8-11-1863 (8-16-1863)
Hood, Wm. C. to Mary Foster 1-7-1861 (1-10-1861)
Hood, Wm. to Catharine Mahala Greer 3-7-1859 (no return)
Hood, Wm. to Margaret J. Stricklin 1-7-1854 (no return)
Hooks, Curtis to Lucy C. Hobson 1-1-1858
Hoosford, Peter to Caladonia Agent 9-19-1866 (9-21-1866)
Hopper, James H. to Sarah M. Dugger 12-18-1862 (12-23-1862)
Horner, John J. to Bettie R. Tully 4-14-1857
Horseley, John G. to Martha H. Bradshaw 6-12-1861 (6-13-1861)
Horsford, Boling H. to Mary White 11-28-1861 (11-29-1861)
Horton, Wm. E. to Mary Jane Barrett 3-13-1859 (no return)
Hosea, L. M. to Fannie Polk Smith 7-20-1865
Hough, Martin to Mary Peyton 1-9-1861 (1-10-1861)
House, G. J. to N. J. E. Garrett 11-21-1860 (11-22-1860)
House, Wm. to Tempe Pipkin 8-9-1855
Howard, John A. J. to Mary M. Denham 11-23-1853 (11-24-1853)
Howard, John W. to Mary E. Cecil 7-19-1865 (7-20-1865)
Howard, Thomas R. to Eliza Kincaid 5-19-1863 (5-20-1863)
Howell, George W. to Elizabeth R. Davis 3-25-1852
Howell, Jesse C. to Frances E. M. Law 10-30-1866 (11-6-1866)
Howell, John B. to Lovidy J. Thomason 6-2-1863 (6-4-1863)
Howell, Major to Clarissa A. Thomas 1-13-1857 (no return)
Howell, Wm. A. B. to Minerva E. Weatherford 1-20-1866 (1-23-1866)
Howell, Wm. B. to Margaret E. Cox 4-9-1866 (4-10-1866)
Howlett, Isaac J. to Mary Ruth Howard 3-27-1861 (3-28-1861)
Howser, Francis O. to Alice E. McBride 1-24-1861 (no return)
Howser, James F. to Mary Jane Mayberry 2-27-1861 (2-28-1861)
Howser, John F. to Johanah Amelia Hauser 12-30-1857 (exec. no date)
Hoy, John H. to Louisa A. Brown 2-28-1864
Hubbard, Robert M. to Mary Ann Duke 9-29-1862 (9-30-1862)
Hubbard, Wm. A. to Nancy A. Tomlinson 3-26-1867 (3-27-1867)
Hubble, Daniel J. to Louisa J. Goad 12-6-1858
Huckaby, John A. to Martha L. Sealey 2-14-1866 (2-15-1866)
Huckaby, John C. to Lavina Woodward 8-5-1865 (8-6-1865)
Huddleston, L. J. to Nancy Latta 1-11-1862 (1-12-1862)
Hudson, Charles C. to Sallie J. Whitehead 10-6-1858
Hudson, Columbus to Nancy Dean 4-15-1867
Hudson, James W. to Emily J. Hill (Mary J.?) 1-18-1854 (1-19-1854)
Hudspeth, Christopher C. to Elizabeth A. Scott 1-1-1866 (1-7-1866)
Hudspeth, Josephus F. to Tabitha J. Anderson 1-13-1860 (1-15-1860)
Huey, James H. to Sarah J. Caugham 1-12-1853 (1-13-1853)
Huey, Wm. G. to Ann E. Wooldridge 9-18-1854 (9-13?-1854)
Huggins, Luke to Mary Ann Gibson 8-29-1859
Hughes, Charles M. to Sarah Bryant 1-9-1867 (no return)
Hughes, James H. to Virginia Bryan 7-12-1858 (7-28-1858)
Hughes, James K. to Sallie E. Parish 4-4-1865
Hughes, Patrick H. to Fannie L. Trousdale 6-12-1865 (6-14-1865)
Hughs, A. B. to Mary P. Bunch 12-4-1854 (12-7-1854)
Hullins, Wm. J. to Tennessee A. Roan 3-29-1863
Hunt, Fountain D. to Mary P. Cooper 9-2-1855
Hunt, James t. to Louisa D. Howard 12-12-1855
Hunter, David M. to Roxina V. Porter 9-10-1859 (9-13-1859)
Hunter, Edward A. to Harriet C. Winn 8-31-1858 (9-1-1858)
Hunter, George to Sallie Anderson 10-6-1866 (10-7-1866)
Hunter, Granville to Martha K. Dodson 9-10-1855
Hunter, John S. to Fanny A. Weaver 5-25-1859 (5-26-1859)
Hunter, Jordan M. to Fannie Hackney 12-25-1865
Huntt, George W. to Joanna Adcock 10-4-1866
Hurt, Wm. S. to Mary E. Fogleman 6-22-1857 (6-24-1857)
Hutcheson, Lewis J. to Mary E. Latty 10-11-1858 (not exec.)
Hutchinson, George M. D. to Sarah P. Fields 8-14-1865 (8-15-1865)
Hutchinson, James K. P. to Margaret R. White 4-14-1866 (4-16-1866)
Hutchinson, Wm. H. to Nancy E. Pigge 1-24-1865 (1-25-1865)
Hutchison, Miles L. to Sarah E. Moore 3-12-1861
Hywood, Wm. H. to Ophelia E. Hood 11-22-1864 (11-24-1864)
Ingram, James F. to Helen K. Wilmott 1-27-1863 (no return)
Ingram, John M. to Sallie Davis 3-12-1863
Inman, John H. to Mary C. Holt 10-30-1866 (11-1-1866)
Irvine, Charles C. to Nancy V. Dortch 2-7-1865 (no return)
Irvine, Crawford W. to Annie E. Witherspoon 8-15-1864 (8-16-1864)
Irvine, G. W. to Sallie A. Sedberry 5-7-1867 (5-9-1867)
Irvine, Joseph A. to Mary D. Davis 9-25-1866
Irvine, Simpson to Volucia B. Craig 1-13-1857 (1-16-1857)
Irvine, Wm. T. to Mary E. Warren 12-19-1866 (12-20-1866)
Irwin, John S. to Fannie E. Church 9-4-1860
Irwin, Simpson H. to Susan E. Gillespie 5-12-1864 (5-17-1864)
Irwin, William M. to Frances A. Moss 11-30-1852
Irwin, Wm. M. to Fracnes A. Moss 11-30-1852
Isbell, Daniel J. to Mariah C. Clark 3-9-1864 (3-10-1864)
Isbell, Lawson J. to Nancy J. Hinson 7-30-1859 (7-31-1859)
Isbell, Wm. B. to Nancy B. Riggins 12-29-1863 (12-30-1863)

Jack, Samel E. G. to Martha D. J. Fitzgerald 9-30-1854 (10-1-1854)
Jackson, John to Cynthia A. Miles 2-3-1864 (2-7-1864)
Jackson, Mark L. to Leannah Wright 1-5-1858 (1-6-1858)
Jackson, Robert to Martha Jane Fox 8-16-1864 (8-18-1864)
Jackson, Rufus C. to Annie M. Granberry 12-20-1860
Jackson, Wm. D. to Lucinda P. Cranford 8-27-1859 (8-30-1859)
Jaco, John J. to Sallie E. Roller 5-15-1866
Jacobs, Thomas H. to Margaret E. P. Fitzgerald 4-12-1867 (4-18-1867)
Jacobs, Wm. J. to Ann E. Parham 10-13-1860 (10-14-1860)
Jaggers, Joseph S. to Clarissa J. Blocker 1-16-1860 (1-18-1860)
Jaggers, Wm. C. to Lucy E. Pillow 12-14-1853
Jameson, James A. to Martha A. Campbell 10-30-1865 (11-30-1865)
Jameson, T. E. to Naoma A. Campbell 1-15-1859 (1-16-1859)
Jamison, James H. to Emely F. Tucker 3-15-1864 (3-16-1864)
Jamison, Robert C. to Margaret R. McMeen 12-19-1866 (12-20-1866)
Jamison, Robert H. to Sarh M. Hilliard 10-31-1855
Jarnagan, Wm. L. to Sarah B. Thomas 3-9-1866 (3-28-1866)
Jarrett, John N. to Mary C. Fly 1-1-1852
Jarrett, Obadiah A. to Maria A. Fleming 12-24-1852
Jarrett, Obadiah A. to Maria A. Fleming 12-24-1852 (no return)
Jarrett, Robert to Alabama Mays 1-15-1866 (1-18-1866)
Jeffreys, J. F. to Harriet Hinson 7-3-1865 (7-23-1865)
Jenkins, George W. to Mary P. Culberson 11-12-1853 (11-13-1853)
Jenkins, James P. to Sarah E. Hutchison 1-21-1858 (1-23-1858)
Jennings, James W. to Jane Nelson 9-21-1852
Jennings, James W. to Sallie E. Alderson 11-26-1860 (11-27-1860)
Jennings, Walter S. to Cordelia M. Kindle 12-1-1866 (12-4-1866)
Johnson, Alexander to Sue A. Carr 10-30-1866
Johnson, Anderson F. to Mary T. Walker 1-3-1856
Johnson, Ashburn to Martha Hord 8-18-1855 (8-19-1855)
Johnson, Barcly Martin to Mary E. Johnson 4-22-1867 (5-5-1867)
Johnson, Cader P. to Nancy E. Oakley 9-15-1860 (9-16-1860)
Johnson, Carrol M. to Elizabeth Seaton 8-1-1867 (8-2-1867)
Johnson, David W. to Nancy M. Duke 8-1-1854
Johnson, Henry to Mary Roan 12-26-1857
Johnson, James E. to Margaret E. Oatman 7-2-1860 (7-3-1860)
Johnson, James M. to Martha Ann Taylor 11-23-1858
Johnson, James T. to Callie J. Brooks 9-23-1858
Johnson, James to Maria Barnes 8-30-1854 (8-20?-1854)
Johnson, John A. to Susan E. Rummage 2-10-1866 (2-15-1866)
Johnson, John L. to Julia Gray 5-22-1856 (5-23-1856)
Johnson, John L. to Martha Norman 2-21-1860
Johnson, John L. to Mary E. Forsyth 5-29-1863
Johnson, John W. to Margaret A. F. Lee 11-14-1855
Johnson, John to Elizabeth Pigge 9-15-1863 (9-16-1863)
Johnson, Joseph to Melissa Bishop 9-16-1865 (9-20-1865)
Johnson, Marshall to Catharine Holcem 6-26-1852 (6-27-1852)
Johnson, Marshall to Catherine Holcum 6-26-1852 (6-27-1852)
Johnson, Nimrod to Caroline Booker 12-16-1854 (12-17-1854)
Johnson, Norvell S. to Nancy Ann Pigge 2-22-1864 (2-25-1864)
Johnson, Robert M. to Victoria Collins 3-3-1858
Johnson, Simeon to Martha Rumage 8-4-1857
Johnson, Thomas H. B. to Jane Jague 9-19-1860 (9-20-1860)
Johnson, W. T. to Sarah J. Thurmond 3-5-1855 (3-8-1855)
Johnson, Willis T. to Mary Ann Oakeley 4-20-1853
Johnson, Wm. B. to Phoeba A. Westmoreland 11-19-1863
Johnson, Wm. H. to Ellen F. Sealey 8-22-1866
Johnson, Wm. J. to Mary F. Davis 2-28-1862 (3-4-1862)
Johnson, Wm. R. to Martha A. E. Franklin 10-25-1852 (10-26-1852)
Johnson, Wm. R. to Martha J. Burnes 2-18-1853
Johnson, Wm. to Amanda Miller 9-27-1860
Johnson, Wm. to Elizabeth Roan 2-4-1861
Johnson, Wm. to Lotty Talley 6-30-1855
Johnson, Y. H. to Mary E. Whitehead 4-3-1854
Johnson?, B. M. to L. D. J. Pigg 9-24-1867 (9-28-1867)
Johnston, A. F. to Emma P. Dickson 5-27-1865 (6-1-1865)
Johnston, George D. to Mariah Barnett 8-30-1865 (8-31-1865)
Johnston, William R. (Dr.) to Martha A. E. Franklin 10-25-1852 (10-26-1852)
Johnstone, Absalom F. to Elizabeth Gray 2-22-1853
Jones, Beverly W. to Ann Eliza Miller 9-23-1867 (9-26-1867)
Jones, David B. to Margere Woody 10-24-1866 (10-25-1866)
Jones, David B. to Margeret Woody 10-24-1866 (10-25-1866)
Jones, David S. to Annie C. Sharp 10-20-1863 (10-21-1863)
Jones, David to Ruth A. Fox 11-2-1853 (no return)
Jones, Felix to Mary J. Davis 11-30-1859
Jones, George W. to Mary E. Moore 4-26-1854
Jones, James L. to Julia E. Blair 2-15-1860
Jones, James L. to Mary Jane Jones 7-27-1861 (7-28-1861)
Jones, James T. to Mary E. Vaughan 12-12-1854 (12-14-1854)
Jones, James to Rebecca A. Satterfield 8-6-1853 (8-7-1853)
Jones, James to Sarah Ann Woody 3-6-1867 (no return)
Jones, John F. T. to Talitha A. Delk 12-29-1866 (12-30-1866)
Jones, John J. to Harreit P. Ramsey 2-10-1866 (2-11-1866)
Jones, John R. to Margaret Sutton 4-25-1859 (no return)
Jones, Richard B. to Frances H. Hardwicke 10-10-1860
Jones, Robert C. to Elizabeth A. Denton 12-9-1857 (12-10-1857)
Jones, Robert C. to Sarah R. Polk 4-24-1855 (no return)

Jones, Robert to Nancy Nicholson 12-29-1862 (12-31-1862)
Jones, Samuel W. to F. F. Miller 2-5-1866 (2-8-1866)
Jones, Thomas H. to Nancy R. Sharp 5-20-1863 (5-21-1863)
Jones, Thomas N. to Cornelia Frierson 10-9-1860 (10-10-1860)
Jones, Thomas to Indiana V. Coleman 4-22-1856 (no return)
Jones, Willie to Martha A. Gidwin 9-25-1861 (9-26-1861)
Jones, Willis C. to Annie E. Bledsoe 9-30-1867 (10-1-1867)
Jones, Wm. D. to Amanda E. Leftwick 4-16-1866 (4-17-1866)
Jones, Wm. H. to Mary F. Mills 4-5-1864 (4-22-1864)
Jones, Wm. J. to Lucinda C. McConnico 1-17-1859 (1-19-1859)
Jones, Wm. J. to Sarah M. Williams 4-23-1856 (4-24-1856)
Jordan, Benjamin F. to Mary A. Kirks 10-13-1863 (no return)
Jordan, James B. to Ann Wood 5-29-1852 (5-30-1852)
Jordan, John Y. to Eliza B. Sanford 5-21-1857
Journey, Elijah F. to Rebecca C. Dark 3-20-1865 (3-21-1865)
Journey, Flavius J. to Eliza A. Foster 2-11-1852
Journey, Francis to Virginia Goad 7-17-1867 (7-18-1867)
Journey, James P. to Amanda J. Gillian 1-27-1865 (1-29-1865)
Journey, Samuel R. to Cordelia A. Campbell 4-29-1867 (6-20-1867)
Joyce, Peter R. H. to M. L. Foster 3-14-1854 (3-16-1854)
Joyce, Wm. C. to Alice Colier 12-7-1865
Joyce, Wm. W. to Elvira F. Jones 9-9-1853 (9-11-1853)
Kannon, James to Minerva B. Smith 3-11-1862
Kelley, J. W. to Jeanie Oakley 2-17-1864 (2-21-1864)
Kelley, John C. to Sarah Humphrey 3-15-1867 (3-16-1867)
Kelley, Wilbott to Caroline Humphrey 3-10-1854 (no return)
Kelley, Wiley to Nancy P. Kelley 5-7-1860 (5-8-1860)
Kelly, Alfred to Emaline Kelly 11-5-1862 (no return)
Kelly, Joseph to Mary N. Nall 11-24-1862 (11-25-1862)
Kelly, Neil S. to Caroline Perry 1-29-1857 (2-3-1857)
Kennedy, James to Martha W. Thomas 10-23-1854 (10-24-1854)
Kennedy, John H. to Josephine Noles 10-24-1866 (10-25-1866)
Kennedy, Robert G. to Susannah Majors 11-6-1858 (11-7-1858)
Kernell, Wm. to Sallie Burkett 2-4-1867 (2-7-1867)
Kerr, Andrew H. to Sallie E. Harrison 11-9-1858 (exec. no date)
Kerr, George W. to Clotilda E. Kerr 12-21-1858 (12-22-1858)
Kerr, J. W. to Sallie E. Scott 3-15-1859 (3-17-1859)
Kerr, John to Nancy Smith 3-6-1857
Kerr, Robert S. to Minerva A. Nichols 6-19-1863 (6-25-1863)
Kerr, Samuel J. to Madora Sanford 5-1-1858 (5-3-1858)
Kersey, James H. to Elizabeth A. Robinson 5-31-1866
Kidd, Jamas B. to Frances Ann Johnson 1-30-1855 (1-31-1855)
Killingsworth, John W. to Nancy R. Fitzpatrick 9-29-1857 (9-30-1857)
Kincaid, Calvin to Martha Chumbly 4-17-1852 (4-18-1852)
Kincaid, Radford M. to Elizabeth J. Lunn 12-15-1862 (12-18-1862)
Kincaid, Wm. T. to Myra Dodson 2-9-1867 (2-17-1867)
King, Eli to Caledonia Thomason 11-6-1865 (11-10-1865)
King, Evander to Elizabeth Moore 1-12-1860 (1-13-1860)
King, James to Sarah Dickson 11-16-1857 (11-17-1857)
King, Meredith D. to Catharine Smith 10-8-1867 (10-9-1867)
King, Napoleon to Frances N. Harris 2-16-1858 (2-17-1858)
King, Thompson H. to Martha L. Allen 10-28-1853 (10-30-1853)
King, Wm. to Eliza Hain 7-8-1865 (7-9-1865)
King, Wm. to Isabella J. Kellum 8-23-1853
Kingcade, Henry to Lydia Hargrove 11-25-1853
Kingston, Samuel M. to Emma White 11-23-1852 (11-21-1852)
Kingston, Samuel W. to Emma White 11-23-1852 (11-21?-1852)
Kingston, Thomas E. to Sabra Owens 3-24-1853 (3-31-1853)
Kinnard, J. W. to Betty Whittaker 2-18-1867 (2-21-1867)
Kinsey, Wm. J. to E. A. Davis 7-31-1861 (8-1-1861)
Kinzer, George M. V. to Anna M. Williams 11-18-1865 (11-23-1865)
Kinzer, George to Malinda Smithson 2-18-1862 (2-20-1862)
Kinzer, Henry H. to Elizabeth J. White 2-6-1861 (2-7-1861)
Kinzer, John A. to Anna Ledbetter 9-14-1867 (9-16-1867)
Kinzer, S. B. to Edna Sparkman 9-30-1854 (10-1-1854)
Kirby, Enoch C. to Martha E. Roberts 12-23-1858
Kirby, Leonidas P.? to Sue H. Bordus 3-21-1866
Kirf, Hugh C. to Mary A. Bynum 11-2-1857 (no return)
Kirk, George O. to Clarinda C. Worley 8-28-1866 (8-29-1866)
Kirk, Robert B. to Rosina Noles 9-12-1865
Kirk, Samuel P. to Harriet E. Box 10-11-1859 (10-12-1859)
Kirk, Williamson Y. to Eliza A. Williams 1-19-1866 (no return)
Kirkpatrick, Robert W. to Sarah T. Davis 1-22-1856 (1-24-1856)
Kirkpatrick, Thomas E. to Sarah N. Wright 5-29-1861 (not endrsd)
Kitchen, F. M. to Martha E. Mays 9-12-1866 (9-16-1866)
Kitrell, John M. to Charity A. Dawson 5-31-1859 (6-1-1859)
Kittrell, George M. to Ann W. Fleming 10-15-1855 (10-16-1855)
Kittrell, John H. to Sarah A. Dobbin 12-14-1854 (no return)
Kuhn, Edward to Flora D. Smith 4-9-1866 (4-10-1866)
Kuhn, Edward to Sallie Smith 1-16-1856 (1-17-1856)
Ladd, Wm. H. to Margaret E. Hudspeth 9-8-1866 (9-9-1866)
Lamar, Wm. B. to Catharine R. Emmerson 10-11-1859 (10-13-1859)
Lamb, Drury to Elizabeth J. Rustin 7-6-1852
Lamb, Drury to Elizabeth P. Rustin 7-6-1852
Lane, David R. to Mary E. Shelby 2-17-1865 (no return)
Lanier, Lewis G. to Nancy Jame Wiltshon 10-16-1855 (10-18-1855)
Lanier, Robert P. to Margaret A. Benderman 1-12-1858 (1-13-1858)

Laniere, Thomas A. to Mary A. Graves 2-8-1866 (2-9-1866)
Lankford, Thomas S. J. to Seleta Kite 2-22-1866 (2-23-1866)
Lanoon, John to Judea Frowly 2-27-1858
Lansdown, Edward L. to Matilda J. Wilson 1-2-1866
Lantham, J. J. to Angeline Babbett 3-20-1860 (3-25-1860)
Lassiter, Jesse C. to Sarah Jane Ellis 2-8-1865
Latta, Sims to Mary C. Hackney 11-10-1860 (11-11-1860)
Latta, Wm. W. to Elizabeth A. Dockery 10-21-1867 (10-24-1867)
Latta, Wm. H. to Rachel Caughron 11-18-1854 (11-21-1854)
Lavender, Jerome to Mary Jane Beard 2-11-1865 (2-16-1865)
Lavender, John to Mary Potts 1-5-1867 (1-8-1867)
Lavender, Nicholas to Mary Potts 3-30-1852
Lawless, John H. to Tabitha Fraly? 4-10-1866 (5-12-1866)
Lawrence, Thomas to Lucinda Phillips 1-28-1860 (1-29-1860)
Lee, Edward F. to Jane Virginia Hayes 12-26-1854
Lee, Joseph to Eliza Cockrell 8-1-1866 (8-2-1866)
Lee, Wm. G. to Mary E. Reaves 12-25-1854 (12-26-1854)
Lee, Wm. H. to Mary H. Hardeman 12-7-1858 (12-8-1858)
Leel, Wm. to Mary A. Williamson 12-22-1857 (12-23-1857)
Leeper, William H. to Mary L. S. Davidson 4-1-1852 (4-8-1852)
Leftwich, John S. to Amanda E. Davis 12-11-1856
Lehanan, John to Lucy P. Thompson 2-10-1858
Leigh, James H. to Mary A. Dartch 10-13-1853
Leigh, James to Mary P. Sellers 1-5-1852 (1-8-1852)
Leonhard, Frank A. to Sarah P. Voss 9-12-1860
Lester, Napoleon B. to Louisa Nicholson 11-16-1859 (11-23-1859)
Lewis, James H. to Victoria J. Sims 7-29-1861 (7-30-1861)
Lewis, John W. to Julia Ann Nolen 11-23-1864
Lewis, Wm. H. to Rebecca Patterson 11-7-1857
Liggett, Sherrod to Elizabeth Hardison 10-3-1853
Liggitt, John C. to Sarah E. Hardison 12-22-1852 (12-23-1852)
Liles, Lucius to Jane Lee 2-3-1853
Limenstall, Samuel to Sarah McClure 7-3-1865 (7-6-1865)
Linch, Michael to Emeline Hamilton 5-26-1866 (5-27-1866)
Lindsay, Wm. D. to Eliza Jane Weaver 5-23-1856 (5-25-1856)
Lindsey, Amos R. to Sarah S. Nance 9-25-1856? (9-27-1866)
Lindsey, Thomas to Mariah Welles 9-22-1859
Lintz, George W. to Caroline Blocker 6-3-1861 (6-4-1861)
Lipscomb, Arch to Amanda B. Harlan 5-15-1861 (5-16-1861)
Lipscomb, David to Margaret Zellner 7-23-1862
Lipscomb, Theodoric E. to Elvira Walker 9-3-1867
Lisenby, Rufus to Fannie C. Williams 2-11-1861 (2-12-1861)
Little, George W. to Sarah E. Pinkston 8-26-1857 (8-27-1857)
Little, Joseph M. to Rebeca J. Turbeville 8-17-1852 (8-18-1852)
Little, Joseph M. to Rebecka J. Turbeville 8-15-1852 (8-18-1852)
Little, Thomas H. to Nancy W. Russell 8-24-1865
Litton, John Henry to Mary Harbison 9-21-1865
Litton, Wm. C. to Martha A. F. Mullens 1-12-1866 (1-11?-1866)
Lochridge, John H. to Ann T. Blackburn 10-20-1856 (10-21-1856)
Lock, Perry T. to Sarah E. Harbison 2-24-1864 (2-26-1864)
Lockhart, John W. to Mary E. Williams 6-1-1867 (6-2-1867)
Lockridge, John W. to Jennie Davis 10-16-1862
Lockridge, Wesley D. to Olivia P. Lane 4-13-1852 (4-15-1852)
Loftin, John W. to Hariet W. Sowell 1-30-1854
Loftin, Josiah H. to Sarah C. Hines 3-31-1865 (not endrsd)
Lofton, Wm. R. to Allice E. Kinzer 1-3-1866
Logan, George M. to Catharine Williams 1-24-1854 (1-25-1854)
Logue, John B. to Matilda Ann Overstreet 12-12-1866 (12-13-1866)
London, Levi to Caroline Barnett 7-29-1862 (not exec.)
London, Levi to Mary A. Estes 10-5-1863 (10-6-1863)
Long, Johnson to Martha Olivia Harris 12-6-1865 (12-7-1865)
Long, Lemuel to Martha W. Pillow 2-18-1857 (3-2-1857)
Long, Richard T. to Emma Davis 8-26-1865 (8-31-1865)
Long, Willis B. to Elizabeth Dansen (Dawson) 11-15-1852
Long, Willis B. to Elizabeth Dawson 11-15-1852 (no return)
Longhurst, Richard A. to Nannie Johnson 3-4-1856 (3-5-1856)
Lourance, James W. to Agnes E. Fraley 10-17-1860 (10-18-1860)
Lovatt, Charles to Mary J. Ament 11-17-1857
Love, Edom to Mary S. Morrison 2-26-1867 (no return)
Love, John A. to Mary Jane Hines 3-13-1867 (3-14-1867)
Love, John to Mary F. Bailey 12-6-1853 (12-8-1853)
Lovell, James P. to Sarah W. Morris 9-11-1866 (9-18-1866)
Lovett, Moses D. to Sarah E. Roberson 1-13-1864 (1-17-1864)
Lowrance, Wm. J. to Martha Ann Ramsey 10-17-1860 (10-18-1860)
Lowry, John A. to Tina A. Gracy 4-30-1867 (5-2-1867)
Loyd, Zaccheus D. to Mary Lavinia Pratt 9-5-1866 (9-6-1866)
Lucas, George W. to Martha Goad 11-14-1853 (11-13?-1853)
Luckett, George W. to Eliza J. Carrigan 11-8-1859 (11-9-1859)
Luckett, Michael to Sarah Holmes 5-21-1853 (5-22-1853)
Luckett, Wm. K. to Elizabeth Moore 9-17-1860
Luna, Allen P. to Nancy J. Cummings 3-10-1866 (3-11-1866)
Lunn, Eli to Louisa Frances Ragen 3-29-1866
Lunn, Felix to Rebecca J. Hudgens 12-25-1865 (no return)
Lunn, Richard G. to Elizabeth E. Clark 2-28-1853 (2-29-1853)
Luttrell, James B. to America Bennett 11-1-1864
Lyles, John M. to Sallie Holden 5-19-1864 (5-22-1864)
Lynch, Cornelius to Mary Sullivan 1-16-1860

Lynch, John to Mrs. Honora Shae 8-1-1858
Maben, James P. to Elizabeth Ann Boyd 9-5-1866 (9-6-1866)
Mack, Henry C. to Julia A. Perry 12-19-1866 (12-20-1866)
Mack, William R. C. to Mary E. Matthews 1-28-1867 (1-30-1867)
Mackey, John A. to Molley E. Alley 2-22-1866
Madden, Gardiner to Elizabeth Renfro 11-3-1852
Madden, Gardner to Elizabeth Renfro 11-3-1852 (11-4-1852)
Maddox, George W. to Mary J. Moore 5-1-1852 (5-2-1852)
Maheney, Thomas to Arsenith J. Cochran 11-13-1866 (11-15-1866)
Malone, James to Nancy E. Church 1-24-1854 (1-?-1854)
Mangrum, James N. to Margaret Ann Hewdly 9-12-1857 (9-13-1857)
Mangrum, John J. to Mrs. A. J. Easley 4-15-1867 (4-17-1867)
Mansfield, James to Martha A. McCrary 8-10-1865 (8-12-1865)
Marine, G. D. to Esther E. Davis 7-16-1867 (7-17-1867)
Marks, John H. to Martha A. Griffith 4-18-1866 (4-19-1866)
Martin, William H. to Margaret Elizabeth Potts 4-19-1867 (4-24-1867)
Marr, John W. to Allice R. Lowe 1-2-1867 (1-4-1867)
Marsh, Thomas P. to Sallie P. Taylor 4-4-1864 (4-6-1864)
Marshall, William to Mary E. Givens 5-28-1867 (5-25?-1867)
Martin, Andrew J. to Flora O. Smith 7-30-1857
Martin, Caswell C. to Elizabeth J. Johnson (Smith) 4-27-1852
Martin, Caswell C. to Elizabeth J. Smith 4-27-1852 (4-28-1852)
Martin, E. B. to Mary R. Wilkes 3-10-1856 (3-11-1856)
Martin, George M. to Mary H. Porter 5-10-1852 (5-11-1852)
Martin, George M. to Unita Julia Wright 12-28-1854
Martin, George S. to Mary G. Nicholson 11-12-1862 (11-13-1862)
Martin, George W. to Martha J. Wood 11-22-1864 (11-24-1864)
Martin, George to Ruth S. Pickard 11-17-1859
Martin, Hugh to Susan A. Pillow 9-6-1853 (9-7-1853)
Martin, James S. to Sarah C. Cherry 1-16-1855
Martin, John T. to Elizabeth Jackson 2-27-1867 (2-28-1867)
Martin, Marcus L. to Louisa Jane Hodge 10-1-1862 (10-2-1862)
Martin, Thomas G. to Larissa A. Kittrell 11-21-1860 (11-22-1860)
Martin, Thomas G. to Mary M. Wingfield 12-21-1854
Mascko, James D. to Jency Anglen 4-27-1865
Mash, James B. to Eliza Ann Westmoreland 6-3-1864 (6-5-1864)
Masker, Lewis to Margaret Grisham 12-4-1852
Masker, Lewis to Margaret Grisham 12-4-1852 (no return)
Mason, George to Mary Jane Polk 3-2-1858
Massey, Andrew J. to Sallie A. M. Tillmon 7-6-1867 (7-7-1867)
Massey, William R. to Elizabeth Gray 10-4-1866 (10-7-1866)
Mathews, James W. to Mary E. McKenzie 2-11-1867 (2-13-1867)
Mathews, William J. to Susan Ann Garey 10-23-1867 (10-27-1867)
Mathews, William R. to Frances J. Garrett 11-12-1858 (11-16-1858)
Matthews, Felix C. to Mary A. Davis 8-30-1860
Matthews, George H. to M. Isabella Matthews 7-11-1866 (7-12-1866)
Matthews, Gilbert D. to Luina? A. Ramsey 12-12-1866
Matthews, James C. to Margaret A. Sims 11-13-1861 (11-14-1861)
Matthews, Newton J. to Ruth Stockard 1-10-1867
Matthews, Robert R. to Mary J. Galbraith 3-13-1866 (3-14-1866)
Matthews, William to Ann Matthews 12-9-1858
Maury, Abram P. to Mary H. Perkins 6-18-1865
Maxey, Isaiah T. to Eliza Warden 4-23-1855 (4-29-1855)
Maxwell, David S. to Derinda A. Amis 9-9-1852
Maxwell, David S. to Derinda A. Anris 9-9-1852
Maxwell, Elijah to Parallee Dycus 6-16-1860 (6-17-1860)
Maxwell, Robert H. to Molly A. Goodrum 9-30-1856
Mayberry, George W. to Evaline Estes 1-17-1856
Mayberry, Georgee to Martha Johnson 3-15-1856 (no return)
Mayberry, Hardin to America P. Blair 10-17-1859 (10-18-1859)
Maybury, George W. to Elizabeth G. Hardin 4-30-1860 (5-1-1860)
Maybury, Peter to Nancy J. P. Church 12-18-1856
Mayes, F. A. to M. H. Hastings 12-6-1865 (12-8-1865)
Mayes, Felix H. to Mary L. Dodson 12-20-1853 (12-22-1853)
Mayes, James A. to Melissa J. Chaffin 12-12-1860 (12-13-1860)
Mayes, James M. to Willie B. Cheairs 11-24-1857
Mays, Fuston to Cintha A. Priest 9-1-1857 (no return)
McBride, Charles W. to Mary B. Haley 3-11-1861 (no return)
McBride, Samuel J. to Alice E. Mayberry 10-13-1853
McCabe, Terrence to Mrs. Martha J. Pigg 7-17-1865 (7-20-1865)
McCain, John E. to Caledonia C. Carter 4-6-1866 (4-12-1866)
McCandless, James H. to Josephene T. Matthews 3-4-1861
McCarroll, James to Harriet V. Drake 12-17-1866 (12-18-1866)
McCaul, James J. to Mary E. Moody 11-28-1859 (12-1-1859)
McClain, Jesse S. to Louisa C. Hatcher 6-23-1858 (no return)
McClain, John to Angeline Thomason 3-10-1862 (3-15-1862)
McClannahan, Benj. F. to Belinda Bridgeforth 4-27-1860 (10-18-1860)
McClure, William F. to Fannie Willis 8-12-1865
McConnell, Calvin L. to Harriet E. Henderson 1-18-1859 (1-19-1859)
McConnico, Mercer Z. to Eliza E. Alexander 11-15-1858 (11-17-1858)
McConnico, Wm. W. to Matilda G. Satterfield 1-5-1858 (1-6-1858)
McCord, Russell F. to Sarah M. Warren 11-5-1866 (11-8-1866)
McCord, Russell F. to Sarah M. Warren 11-5-1866 (no return)
McCord, William C. to Tennessee Bryan 7-11-1857 (7-12-1857)
McCormack, Charles to Bridgett Raney 12-22-1860 (no return)
McCormack, Robert B. to Anna J. Adkerson 1-5-1867 (1-7-1867)
McCormick, Wm. W. to Martba A. Chappel 7-4-1861 (7-9-1861)

McCoy, Daniel A. to Elizabeth Mantle 5-25-1855 (no return)
McCoy, Edward to Sarah L. Ragsdale 7-6-1853 (no return)
McCrady, Wm. J. to Elizabeth Loftin 1-27-1858
McCrory, Charles to Amanda Gamblin 3-1-1854
McCrory, Thomas M. to Rebecca Lee 8-23-1862 (9-12-1862)
McDaniel, Alexander W. to Sarah D. Gracy 8-18-1865 (8-21-1865)
McDaniel, Riley to Elizabeth Harris 9-7-1859 (9-11-1859)
McDaniel, Robert Jr. to Terecia Cunningham 10-2-1858
McDonald, John R. to Martha E.    ? 9-8-1855 (no return)
McDonald, John R. to Martha E. Rankin 11-3-1855 (11-4-1855)
McDonald, Joseph A. to Sarah A. Pilkenton 2-14-1856
McDonald, Marion to Mary V. Kirks 3-21-1859 (3-23-1859)
McFadden, John C. to Frances Rumage 3-19-1864
McFadden, John Humphrey to Eliza Ann Chunn 9-4-1865 (9-7-1865)
McFall, David D. to Ann T. Dickerson 1-13-1864 (1-14-1864)
McFall, Wm. H. to Emma F. Lipscomb 12-24-1861
McFerrin, John P. to Julia Patten 6-22-1867 (6-23-1867)
McGan?, David to Alzira J. Butler 10-26-1859 (10-27-1859)
McGavock, James H. to Bitta W. Pointer 7-18-1867 (7-22-1867)
McGaw, James C. to Amanda Murphey 2-1-1860 (2-2-1860)
McGee, McCoy C. to Nancy J. Richardson 10-3-1865 (10-4-1865)
McGoldrick, Orean to Tennessee Priest 11-6-1858 (11-7-1858)
McIntosh, Wm. H. to Eliza Jane Duke 11-18-1854 (11-19-1854)
McIntosh, Wm. H. to Louisa Notgrass 8-16-1865 (8-17-1865)
McKannon, Johh H. to Nancy O. Linn 12-22-1857
McKannon, Wm. D. to Martha McBride 1-13-1855 (1-14-1855)
McKechan, James to Martha McDolton 8-8-1857 (8-9-1857)
McKee, Thomas V. to Sarah Ann Morgan 3-29-1860
McKee, Young to Cilia Pigg 8-23-1865 (9-17-1865)
McKennon, A. F. to Alexy J. Linn 1-3-1866
McKennon, Daniel to Caledonia Currey 1-2-1860 (1-8-1860)
McKennon, Edward B. to Elizabeth H. Seargent 2-27-1854 (2-28-1854)
McKennon, G. B. to Georgia Ann Hill 9-17-1866 (9-19-1866)
McKennon, George B. to Mary E. Kinzer 7-1-1864 (not exec.)
McKennon, George W. to Mary L. Kinzer 12-9-1858
McKennon, James H. to Nancy M. Beard 12-11-1865 (12-21-1865)
McKennon, John H. to Elizabeth J. Owen 3-15-1856 (no return)
McKennon, Wm. J. to Nancy Garton 11-27-1856
McKennon, Wm. M. to Louisa F. Donaldson 2-8-1864 (no return)
McKenzie, James N. to Virginia C. Alderson 12-17-1855 (1-4-1856)
McKibbin, John V. to Elizabeth P. Hill 11-29-1854 (11-30-1854)
McKinney, Thomas H. to Emma A. Thomas 4-20-1867 (4-23-1867)
McKissack, George M. to L. Hannah Gibson 10-9-1865 (10-12-1865)
McKissack, James to Martha K. Maneer 2-24-1865 (2-28-1865)
McKissack, John W. to Musdora Barlow 1-26-1865 (2-6-1865)
McKissack, Wm. M. to Fannie O. Mathews 9-29-1857
McKnight, Samuel J. to Delphina Tyler 10-9-1866 (9?-4-1866)
McLain, Martin to Elizabeth Clanahan 11-23-1865
McLean, Ephraim H. to Frances Porter 3-1-1852 (3-3-1852)
McLean, Frank Jay to Sue A. Pillow 8-22-1860
McManis, Nathan to Frances E. Howell 10-23-1861
McMann, John L. to Mary E. Kennedy 1-25-1861 (1-27-1861)
McMannus, Wm. M. to Margaret Ann Garner 9-20-1854
McManus, Aaron to Mynan McClain 1-17-1852 (1-18-1852)
McMeen, David N. to Jane C. McCormick 1-21-1857
McMeen, James O. to Rause Cook 12-1-1866 (12-4-1866)
McMeen, John A. to Harriet D. Cooke 11-14-1859 (11-15-1859)
McMeen, Joseph B. to Margaret E. Dodson 12-2-1852
McMeen, Thomas F. to Caroline Hadley 6-30-1852 (7-1-1852)
McMillian, J. A. to Mary J. Mayfield 8-17-1852
McMillian, J. A. to Mary J. Mayfield 8-17-1852
McMinnis, Neal to Martha E. Huckaby 12-29-1866 (1-3-1866)
McMurry, Wm. to Matildy D. McMurry 4-22-1854 (no return)
McNamara, John to Bridget Brennon 8-16-1857
McNeely, John J. to Harriet E. Bain 5-13-1856
McNight, John S. to Mary C. Fox 1-25-1853 (1-26-1853)
McReadey, Joe to Meece Kerr 11-5-1857 (11-7-1857)
Mckee, A. J. to Elizabeth C. Dodson 3-5-1867 (3-6-1867)
Meacham, J. M. to Lucy K. Cameron 7-19-1866
Meadoncraft, John E. to Kate C. Hart 2-13-1861 (2-14-1861)
Meadows, Noah to Mary Langston 7-27-1853 (no return)
Meece, Abraham to Eliza Phillips 9-16-1863 (9-18-1863)
Melugin, W. G. to E. M. Shaw 12-22-1866 (no return)
Merritt, Columbus to M. L. Lockridge 7-23-1862 (7-31-1862)
Miliken, John C. to Esther Pryor 5-16-1860 (5-17-1860)
Miller, Alfred C. to Manerva J. Akin 2-27-1854 (2-28-1854)
Miller, James N. to Permelia C. Kinzer 12-8-1853 (no return)
Miller, Jeremiah T. to Ruth L. Caughron 12-15-1852 (12-16-1852)
Miller, Jeremiah T. to Ruth L. Coughran 12-15-1852 (12-16-1852)
Miller, John A. to Mary M. Wells 11-28-1866 (11-29-1866)
Miller, John D. to Eliza F. Green 10-19-1859
Miller, Joseph T. to Frances A. Johnson 8-14-1860 (8-16-1860)
Miller, Wm. P. to Sallie A. E. Witherspoon 2-20-1865 (no return)
Miller, Wm. to Narcissa Calwell 10-18-1855
Mills, James C. to Mary E. Underwood 8-27-1859 (8-28-1859)
Mills, Joel J. to Nancy A. Powell 8-10-1860 (8-16-1860)
Mills, Robert H. to Elizabeth P. Caldwell 2-3-1853

Mills, Samuel to Elizabeth Johnson 10-31-1863 (11-1-1863)
Mitchell, James M. to Cynthia J. Hogan 12-27-1865 (12-28-1865)
Mitchell, John D. to Narcissa C. Pillow 10-23-1866 (10-28-1866)
Mitchell, Joseph S. to Lucy A. E. Chennault 3-16-1866 (3-21-1866)
Mitchell, Josiah D. to Mary C. Westmoreland 12-23-1863 (12-24-1863)
Mitchell, Lyman B. to Margaret Bingam 10-23-1866 (10-24-1866)
Mitchell, Maddison M. to Elizabeth Toumbs 12-10-1853 (12-11-1853)
Mitchell, Thomas to Sarah Peyton 3-31-1866 (4-1-1866)
Mitchell, Wiley P. to Elizabeth Craig 5-11-1859 (5-12-1859)
Mitchell, Wm. B. to Sarah R. Davis 10-30-1865 (10-31-1865)
Mitchell, Wm. F. to Susan A. Dillahay 11-27-1860 (11-28-1860)
Mitchner, Isaac F. to Margaret A. Kelpatrick 1-13-1857 (2-13-1857)
Montgomery, John C. to Minerva W. Hardison 11-20-1865 (11-22-1865)
Moon, Dr. Joseph B. to Emily C. Green 10-31-1855
Mooney, H. H. to Mary E. Davidson 2-18-1867 (2-20-1867)
Mooney, Josua J. to Mary E. Owen 4-29-1867 (4-31?-1867)
Moore, A. B. to Amelia E. Grimes 12-19-1866 (12-20-1866)
Moore, Andrew to Sarah A. Hedge (Hodge) 4-13-1852
Moore, Edward J. to Margaret E. Crosby 7-30-1853 (no return)
Moore, Elijah N. to Nancy V. Cannon 9-12-1867
Moore, Francis J. to Susan E. Fitzpatrick 1-16-1855
Moore, James C. to Margaret E. Walker 11-11-1852
Moore, James F. to Mary J. Ingram 1-17-1853 (1-20-1853)
Moore, Jesse to Sarah E. Polk 8-7-1856
Moore, John B. to Elvira L. Turner 10-24-1860
Moore, John D. to Addie Wiley 2-12-1867
Moore, Joseph J. to Catherine T. Hicks 2-28-1852 (2-29-1852)
Moore, Joseph to Frances J. Hunt 1-19-1858
Moore, Robert H. to Caroline Forgey 12-20-1855 (12-23-1855)
Moore, Robert H. to Lavina L. Bryant 4-16-1866 (4-17-1866)
Moore, Robert Irwin to Lena B. McKissack 4-27-1865 (4-17?-1865)
Moore, Robert N. to Roena Harris 4-28-1858 (4-29-1858)
Moore, Stephen J. to Eliza L. Pinkston 2-28-1860 (3-6-1860)
Moore, William R. to Eliza Crutchfield 3-10-1852
Moore, Wm. C. to Ruth M. Fitzpatrick 10-12-1854
Moore, Wm. E. to Maria Naomi Hayes 12-18-1864
Moreton, James F. to Sarah E. Perkinson 9-16-1857 (9-17-1857)
Morgan, Andrew to Sallie Ann Taylor 9-19-1857 (9-20-1857)
Morgan, James M. to Olivia E. Craig 7-20-1852 (7-21-1852)
Morgan, John B. to Mary O. Matthews 11-16-1865
Morgan, John L. to Elizabeth Bryson 12-21-1853 (12-22-1853)
Morgan, John W. to Sophronia Collins 6-2-1856 (no return)
Morgan, Joseph H. to Elizabeth O. Craig 12-22-1852 (12-23-1852)
Morgan, Judson J. M. to Martha Orman 10-8-1857
Morris, James P. to Elizabeth Maxwell 3-6-1867 (3-8-1867)
Morris, Jefferson D. to Amanda C. Thomas 11-6-1860 (11-8-1860)
Morris, Joseph H. to Elizabeth O. Craig 12-22-1852 (12-23-1852)
Morrow, Andrew A. to Sarah C. E. Murphey 7-26-1861 (8-28-1861)
Morrow, James D. to Mary F. Lazenby 7-19-1860
Morrow, Milton K. to M. E. McKissack 2-13-1865 (2-19-1865)
Morrow, Noah R. to Annie E. Hogan 9-19-1855
Morrow, Thomas F. to Rowena J. Thomason 6-2-1859 (6-3-1859)
Morton, James H. to Margaret E. Hardison 3-21-1864 (3-22-1864)
Morton, Wm. B. to Sarah Jane Garnett 2-18-1867
Moseley, Hillary W. to Sarah F. Moseley 4-16-1866 (not endrsd)
Moseley, Hillary to Martha J. Jenkins 4-28-1866 (4-30-1866)
Moseley, Isham to Sallie Dillahay 12-19-1866 (12-23-1866)
Moseley, Wm. H. to Mary F. Wilson 8-8-1860
Moses, Samuel J. to Sarah E. Martin 12-9-1863 (12-20-1863)
Moses, Wm. S. to Bettie A. Jones 11-24-1866 (11-29-1866)
Mulford, John M. to Indianna S. W. Burnes 5-13-1864 (5-14-1864)
Mullens, James C. to Mary Thompson 11-24-1860 (10-30-1867)
Mullens, John H. to Rebecca J. Voss 1-9-1867 (1-10-1867)
Mullens, Oliver H. P. to Sarah M. E. Baker 4-23-1860 (4-26-1860)
Mullins, John W. to Augustina Davis 2-11-1863
Mullins, John to Malinda McClain 3-31-1865
Mullins, W. P. to Jerusha C. Lovell 12-2-1863 (12-5-1863)
Murphey, E. T. to Sallie E. Hill 10-9-1867 (10-10-1867)
Murphey, Jerry to Ellen Mahar 7-3-1867 (no return)
Murphey, Miles P. to Mary L. Park 7-29-1865 (8-1-1865)
Murphey, Wm. N. to Elizabeth C. Dugger 12-11-1854 (12-12-1854)
Murphey, Wm. to Martha Hammonds 5-27-1862 (5-29-1862)
Murphey, Zebulan A. to Edy A. Hickman 6-8-1861 (6-9-1861)
Murphy, Henry to Harriet M. Wilkes 3-16-1853 (3-17-1853)
Murphy, Isacc J. to Josaphine Alderson 10-2-1856 (10-3-1856)
Murphy, James C. to Mattie E. H. Bostick 4-14-1860 (4-18-1860)
Murphy, Wm. L. to Virginia O. Polk 10-8-1867 (10-8-1867)
Nall, Elisha J. D. to Rosana Wright 4-21-1862 (4-22-1862)
Nance, James H. to Martha Mayberry 10-23-1860 (10-25-1860)
Nance, James W. to Mary L. Amis 12-12-1860 (12-13-1860)
Nance, Joseph W. to Nancy Pugh 11-25-1857 (11-29-1857)
Neal, Leonidas to Elvira Richards 5-26-1859
Neal, Leonidas to Martha Harris 12-20-1853 (12-22-1853)
Neeley, A. C. to Carrie C. Wright 4-1-1867 (4-2-1867)
Neeley, Wm. M. to S. A. Stone 2-1-1866
Neelley, John W. to Lizzie A. Cecil 1-17-1861
Neely, John N. to Sallie E. Thernnot? 3-9-1858 (3-10-1858)

Neely, Oswell Y. to Mary F. Gale 9-7-1861 (9-9-1861)
Neely, Wm. S. L. to Lou B. Bryan 11-15-1860
Nellums, Daniel A. to Martha A. Roan 6-11-1859 (6-15-1859)
Nelson, David W. to Eliza Jane Davis 2-9-1859 (2-10-1859)
Nelson, W. H. to Laura E. Crook 2-14-1866 (2-15-1866)
Nelson, Wm. D. to Louisa V. Moss 10-9-1862 (10-16-1862)
Nevils, George B. to Luceilly Scott 5-20-1852
Nevils, George B. to Lucilly Scott 5-20-1852
Nevils, Wm. T. to Mary J. Hanks 6-21-1865 (6-22-1865)
Newcomb, Asa to Catharine Collins 2-6-1865
Newcome, John Calvin to Martha Clarke 9-5-1866 (9-6-1866)
Nichol, Bennett A. to Harriet Kirby 12-18-1854 (12-20-1854)
Nichol, John A. to Carolina Butler 10-3-1855
Nichol, Joseph to Priscilla E. Lockhart 3-30-1865
Nichols, Caleb G. R. to Frances J. Blakely 2-16-1852 (2-18-1852)
Nichols, Campbell to Mary Taylor 9-21-1853 (9-22-1853)
Nichols, Charles S. to Beatrice Chaffin 1-28-1866
Nichols, George W. to Louisa A. McMeen 3-3-1859
Nichols, Levi A. to Jennie C. Grimes 9-8-1860 (9-4?-1860)
Nichols, Richard W. to Emma Coffey 12-27-1866
Nichols, Richard to Emuly H. Coffey 8-14-1865 (not endrsd)
Nicholson, John M. to Victoria Hardison 6-15-1865 (6-29-1865)
Nicholson, John to Sarah Barker 12-20-1853
Nicholson, Nathaniel to Elizabeth C. Wright 1-23-1865 (1-26-1865)
Nicholson, Osborne P. to Sallie M. Bradshaw 2-11-1858
Nicholson, Wm. A. to Margaret P. Williams 10-15-1855 (10-23-1855)
Nickens, H. H. to Elizabeth E. Humphrey 11-20-1861 (11-21-1861)
Nickens, Reddick S. to Susan F. L. Allen 4-6-1855 (no return)
Nickens, Rily H. to Susan Hill 12-27-1856 (21-28-1856)
Nicks, John A. to Sarah T. Lasserter 7-13-1867 (7-14-1867)
Nicks, Stephen P. to Artemesia Warfield 12-16-1853 (12-20-1853)
Nolen, James J. to Ellen E. T. Lester 11-27-1855
Nolen, James M. to Lucinda Smith 10-11-1853 (10-13-1853)
Noles, Austin R. to Laura L. Walker 6-2-1862 (6-10-1862)
Noles, George W. to Sarah O. Patton 12-12-1857 (no return)
Noles, Lyn to Catherine Payton 9-16-1854 (9-21-1854)
Noles, Tyra to Frances H. Baird 4-8-1862
Noles, Tyra to Helena J. Rains 1-30-1865 (2-1-1865)
Norman, Adolphus to Myra McMinnis 1-2-1867
Norman, Huey to Elizabeth Norman 7-5-1864 (7-26-1864)
Norman, Wm. to Mahala J. Thomason 7-4-1865 (7-6-1865)
Norton, James W. to Martha A. Roberts 4-14-1863
Norvell, George P. to Nancy J. Miller 3-17-1858
Norwood, Nathaniel N. to Ellen Williams 6-2-1857 (6-3-1857)
Notgrass, James H. to Sarah C. Dawson 11-28-1854 (11-29-1854)
Notgrass, Terry C. to Tirza E. Wright 5-23-1861 (5-24-1861)
OConnell, Austin to Bridgett O. Laughlin 5-4-1859 (no return)
OConnor, Patrick to Julia Hargolty 10-4-1858
OLeary, Patrick D. to Mary Kelly 11-3-1866
Oakley, Rufus B. to Martha Ann Rail 9-11-1854 (9-23-1854)
Obrien, Thomas S. to Sarah A. Knowles 10-9-1862
Odell, Chauncey C. to Nancy Adams 4-19-1865
Oden, W. A. to M. J. McCullick 1-16-1867 (1-24-1867)
Odil, Wm. M. to Sarah E. Foxall 8-23-1862 (8-24-1862)
Offutt, Wm. to Mary Jackson Speed 11-16-1855 (11-18-1855)
Olds, James to Mazee V. Powell 12-29-1858 (no return)
Oliphant, Eli to Matilda J. Cathy 5-21-1853 (5-22-1853)
Oliver, James C. to Sarah S. Cavender 5-6-1863 (no return)
Oliver, John A. to Edney Passmore 8-6-1853 (8-11-1853)
Olver, Benjamin P. to Virginia C. Estes 12-21-1861 (12-24-1861)
Oneal, Thomas to Mary Dolan 12-5-1866 (no return)
Oneel, Edmond A. to Virginia E. Hodge 12-23-1862
Oneill, Edward A. to Virginia E. Hodge 2-16-1861 (3-20-1861)
Orman, Wm. L. to Sarah S. Childress 1-12-1853 (1-13-1853)
Orr, Robert to Ophelia Mayes 5-7-1866 (5-8-1866)
Orton, John A. to Lou Colburn 11-23-1866 (12-13-1866)
Osborne, Henry T. to Tennessee P. Porter 1-30-1862
Overbey, Wilson to Elizabeth Poyner 8-29-1865 (8-31-1865)
Owen, Jesse M. to Eliza Daniel 10-13-1862 (10-26-1862)
Owen, Littleberry R. to Martha E. Vaughan 12-7-1864 (12-8-1864)
Owen, Noah B. to Kizziah Adams 3-30-1864 (4-5-1864)
Owen, Phillip A. to Barberry A. Rawsey 1-12-1852 (1-13-1852)
Owen, Wm. T. to Martha T. Sowell 8-20-1866 (8-25-1866)
Owens, David S. to Elizabeth Moseley 4-2-1855
Owens, John A. to Rachel A. Morrow 3-31-1852 (4-1-1852)
Owens, John M. to Eliza C. Booker 12-23-1865 (12-24-1865)
Owens, Noah B. to Mary Ann Robertson 6-2-1855 (6-7-1855)
Owings, Benjamin F. to Cordelia Carrigan 10-11-1865
Padgett, James W. to Sarah E. Bingham 6-3-1857 (6-4-1857)
Padgett, John B. to Rebecca O. Phillips 6-22-1853
Page, Wm. F. to Elizabeth M. Crockett 12-20-1865 (12-21-1865)
Parham, Wm. P. to Lucie McKissack 2-4-1853 (no return)
Parish, Levan to Margaret Allen 4-9-1858 (4-11-1858)
Park, G. W. to A. C. Lancaster 8-27-1866
Parker, John W. to Ophelia C. Blanton 10-30-1865 (11-1-1865)
Parker, Willard to Calista Wood 10-30-1866
Parker, Wm. T. to Mary Francis Davis 2-6-1858 (2-7-1858)

Parker, Wm. T. to Polly Jones 9-21-1855 (no return)
Parker, Wm. to Susan C. Kerr 9-18-1861 (9-19-1861)
Parkes, Wm. J. to Annie M. Brown 4-25-1861
Parks, James A. to Sinia E. Stanfield 4-11-1856 (4-13-1856)
Parks, John W. to Emily E. Jamison 5-12-1858
Parks, Josephus C. to Margaret V. Lockridge 12-9-1857 (12-10-1857)
Parner, Archibald to Sarah Walls 3-17-1857 3-18-1857
Parr, Furman C. S. to Sallie E. Johnson 9-19-1861
Parrish, James H. to Lavina W. Green 4-9-1860
Parrish, James K. P. to Martha J. Freeland 5-16-1865 (5-17-1865)
Parsons, Elijah P. to Sarah C. Kinzer 5-15-1856
Parten, James P. to Robecca E. Roberts 1-6-1853
Parten, Wm. J. to Mary E. Dever 1-11-1855
Patrick, Hiram to Margaret Stamps 8-7-1863
Patrick, Thomas to Rachel Rachdael 4-21-1864 (4-22-1864)
Patten, George W. C. to Mary F. James 10-23-1866 (10-24-1866)
Patterson, James B. to Margaret W. Thompson 5-11-1857 (5-12-1857)
Patterson, James M. to Margaret S. Hardison 6-4-1859 (6-5-1859)
Patterson, Jarad E. to Martha E. Maxwell 1-10-1859
Patterson, John R. to A. P. Moss 10-18-1860
Patterson, John R. to Matt A. Estes 10-7-1867 (10-8-1867)
Patterson, Thomas J. to Louisa H. Hardin 10-10-1856 (10-15-1856)
Patton, Alexander E. to Elizabeth Farriss 10-13-1853 (no return)
Patton, J. J. to C. E. Noles 2-19-1859 (2-20-1859)
Patton, James to Elizabeth Byrum 1-5-1860
Patton, Thomas B. to Almed Kish 10-29-1857
Patton, Thomas K. to Mary E. Payne 4-27-1859 (4-28-1859)
Paul, James M. to Martha Kinsey 4-9-1867 (no return)
Paul, Layfayette to Sarah King 11-5-1859 (11-7-1859)
Paul, William F. to Sarah McKinser 12-1-1855 (12-2-1855)
Paul, William to Callie Brown 9-23-1867 (12-10-1867)
Payne, Henry to Darcus L. Evans 8-14-1865 (9-3-1865)
Pearson, George W. to Lucy Thomas 1-18-1864
Pearson, George W. to Tennessee E. Grimes 8-25-1857 (8-26-1857)
Pearson, Wayman to Nancy Jane Morton 12-21-1857 (12-23-1857)
Peavyhouse, James to Arena Bullock 11-26-1860 (11-28-1860)
Peden, J. A. to Kate E. Walker 8-27-1867
Peery, Charles B. to Mary A. Lusk 12-2-1852 (no return)
Pence, John W. to Eliz. A. Alexander 11-22-1864 (11-24-1864)
Pennington, Leroy to Mary A. Garton 6-18-1852 (6-20-1852)
Pennington, William T. to Mary E. Duke 2-4-1865 (2-7-1865)
Perkins, Samuel V. to Mary A. Cox 1-11-1864 (1-13-1864)
Perry, Charles B. to Mary A. Lusk 12-2-1852
Perry, James S. to Ann Smoot 1-6-1859
Perry, James S. to Susan F. Pilkinton 12-29-1865 (12-31-1865)
Perry, James S. to Susan S. Hamilton 1-25-1853 (10-26-1853)
Perry, John S. to Sarah D. Nicholsonn 9-8-1864 (9-14-1864)
Perry, Marquis L. to Alice C. Perry 9-20-1867 (9-22-1867)
Perry, Wiley T. to Martha V. Goodrum 3-14-1862 (3-16-1862)
Perry, William Jr. to Jane W. Kemp 8-29-1853 (no return)
Peters, George B. to Jessie H. McKissack 5-31-1858 (6-1-1858)
Petty, George C. to Sarah C. Coleman 12-22-1866 (12-23-1866)
Petty, Joseph A. to Martha R. Fox 3-23-1867 (3-24-1867)
Pewett, Alexander C. to Martha J. Coleman 10-21-1865 (10-26-1865)
Pewett, James H. to Sarah E. Goad 7-18-1866
Pewett, Joel B. to Mary Jane Coleman 8-27-1860 (9-2-1860)
Pewett, William C. to Jane Lunn 10-10-1857 (10-15-1857)
Peyton, Henry M. to Sarah Jane Murphey 11-22-1860
Peyton, Joseph Sr. to Sarah Caldwell 7-19-1855 (7-23-1855)
Peyton, Rufus H. to Elizabeth Huff 11-3-1859
Phelps, Robert R. to Caledonia Mathews 12-20-1865 (12-21-1865)
Philip, Lemuel H. to Annie M. Walker 12-26-1854
Phillips, Baxter to Emma Lainey 9-16-1865 (9-18-1865)
Pickard, David B. to Avarilla M. Stanfield 2-14-1855
Pickard, William S. to Malissa E. Dickson 8-27-1856 (8-28-1856)
Pickard, Young S. to Mrs. Eliza King 1-9-1867 (1-20-1867)
Pickett, Thomas J. to Mary E. Hodge 9-19-1865 (9-20-1865)
Pigg, James M. to Elizabeth C. Fitzgerald 1-31-1859 (2-3-1859)
Pigg, Wm. H. to Sarah C. Gray 2-19-1866 (2-25-1866)
Pigg, Wm. M. to Sarah F. Thurmond 1-19-1859 (1-20-1859)
Pigge, George W. to Elizabeth Owen 8-31-1854 (no return)
Pilkinton, John M. to Nancy A. Adkins 9-18-1855 (9-20-1855)
Pilkinton, L. L. to E. J. Dickson 1-19-1867 (1-20-1867)
Pilkinton, W. H. to A. E. Hull 12-3-1864 (12-4-1864)
Pillow, E. N. to Eliza L. Pillow 11-1-1856 (11-2-1856)
Pillow, James W. to Cordelia P. Moore 3-23-1853
Pillow, John W. to Harriet A. Chaney 11-11-1856 (no return)
Pillow, Samuel C. to Elizabeth A. McKennon 5-14-1853 (5-15-1853)
Pimon, Younger to Frances Mantle 8-16-1855 (9-12-1855)
Pinion, Lewis to Martha Ann Parish 10-9-1856
Pinkston, Jasper N. to Eliza J. Agnew 11-25-1857 (11-26-1857)
Pinneo, S. M. to Sarah L. Orton 5-7-1858 (5-9-1858)
Piper, Ira A. to Ann A. McCloud 9-22-1852
Pogue, James M. to Sarah C. Graham 9-3-1852 (9-5-1852)
Pogue, John W. to Martha Hines 7-3-1858 (7-4-1858)
Pogue, Samuel H. to C. A. Brickle 7-22-1867
Poiner, David to Mary C. Dockery 8-21-1861 (8-22-1861)

Pointer, Henry P. to Martha J. Caldwell 7-19-1852
Pointer, Henry P. to Martha Jane Caldwell 7-19-1852 (no return)
Polk, James K. to Fannie E. Foster 4-8-1861 (4-9-1861)
Polk, Joseph to Essabella Smith 12-31-1856 (1-1-1856?)
Polk, Thomas M. to Mary A. Braden 1-20-1853
Poore, Frank M. to Sarah Ann Hubble 10-27-1865 (10-28-1865)
Pope, James to Mary F. Runnion 4-26-1866
Pope, McCajah to Rachel Clendenin 1-22-1852 (1-25-1852)
Porter, Isaac R. to Lucinda A. Cabler 9-28-1853
Porter, Sterling R. to Margaret Roberts 11-12-1856
Porter, Thomas L. to Fannie P. Webster 4-18-1860
Porter, William to Martha J. Farriss 2-9-1854
Porter, Wm. T. to Margaret F. O'reilley 10-10-1853 (10-11-1853)
Porter, Wm. T. to Mary J. Russell 9-15-1866 (9-18-1866)
Porter, Wm. T. to Mary Pillow 2-16-1857 (2-17-1857)
Potelo, Thomas to Emily Taylor 9-12-1862
Potts, Calvin to Lucy Lavender 11-24-1852 (11-25-1852)
Potts, Frank O. to Tennessee Hines 12-21-1866 (12-23-1866)
Potts, James to Martha Oakly 4-17-1856 (4-18-1856)
Potts, Milas to Missouri Lavender 3-26-1864 (3-27-1864)
Potts, Robert to Jinsy Hines 6-20-1866 (6-24-1866)
Potts, Stephen J. to Ann E. Clymer 10-3-1865 (10-6-1865)
Potts, Wm. W. to Nancy E. Orton 10-23-1860
Powell, Eli A. to Lucinda Tucker 7-20-1852
Powell, Eli A. to Lucinda Tucker 7-20-1852 (exec. no date)
Poyner, Wm. to Melinda Dockery 8-30-1859 (9-17-1859)
Preston, Thomas W. to Susan B. Maguire 9-21-1852
Prewett, Austin L. to Rebecca J. Fitzpatrick 6-13-1854 (6-14-1854)
Prewett, John P. to Martha Ralston 8-30-1864 (9-1-1864)
Prewett, Joseph to Nancy Emeline Fuller 7-4-1859 (7-5-1859)
Price, Wm. M. to Nannie J. Henderson 9-8-1865 (9-12-1865)
Priest, John M. to Selina Dodson 10-12-1859 (10-13-1859)
Priest, John W. to Sarah C. Thomas 11-11-1859
Priest, Thomas J. to Mary A. E. Harbison 11-13-1861 (11-14-1861)
Primm, Wm. to Mary F. Jackson 7-23-1867
Prowell, Andrew M. to Sarah e. Mayes 2-9-1860 (2-10-1860)
Puckett, John L. C. to Martha J. Oakley 11-7-1859 (11-10-1859)
Puckett, Rufus to Eudora Gault 12-30-1857 (no return)
Puckett, Wiley F. to Saphrona G. Moore 5-27-1852 (no return)
Puckett, Wiley F. to Sophrona G. Moore 5-27-1852
Pugh, Henderson to Elizabeth Lindsey 2-26-1853
Pugh, James W. to Martha Ann Long 5-14-1855 (5-15-1855)
Pugh, James W. to Mary C. Patton 10-29-1866 (10-30-1866)
Pullen, George W. to Jane Coffee 8-26-1867
Purcell, Frances H. to Martha E. Rankin 8-18-1855 (no return)
Purcell, Frank H. to Mary Ellen Whitehead 9-11-1857 (9-14-1857)
Purdue, Pleasant to Greskey Bishop 5-11-1852 (5-12-1852)
Purdue, Pleasant to Grishen Bishop 5-11-1852 (5-12-1852)
Purett, Robert C. to Nancy T. Sellars 9-6-1855 (9-7-1855)
Putman, John R. to Rachael R. James 2-1-1867 (2-3-1867)
Putnam, Charles A. to Susan E. Jones 12-18-1866 (12-20-1866)
Quaits?, Elihu? C. to Cathrine Ford 6-27-1866 (6-28-1866)
Quarterman, Wm. A. to E. S. Johnson 6-20-1865
Quinn, John to Sallie Marine 4-22-1863
Ragan, H. D. to Elizabeth Guarnell 8-5-1865 (8-10-1865)
Ragan, James to Martha Ann Brown 10-7-1857 (10-8-1857)
Ragen, Francis M. to Sarah Jane Matthews 8-24-1865
Ragin, Charles S. to Nancy Eliz. Moore 7-31-1866
Ragsdale, Samuel to Mary A. Woollard 5-31-1853 (6-2-1853)
Rail, Thomas J. to Linda E. Rail 10-1-1861 (10-2-1861)
Raines, Hewlet W. to Emily Harriet Crews 10-14-1865 (10-16-1865)
Rains, Andrew J. to Amanda Wright 4-6-1863 (4-16-1863)
Rains, Felix R. to Mary E. Keeble 8-18-1858
Rains, John W. to Millie J. Cavender 8-5-1861 (no return)
Ramsey, Jame T. to Araminta Chapman 9-4-1858 (9-5-1858)
Ramsey, James T. to Priscilla M. Warden 12-31-1866 (1-1-1867)
Ramsey, Wm. H. to Margaret J. Scott 6-19-1860 (6-20-1860)
Ramsy, Rufus C. to Mary A. Thompson 12-24-1855
Ray, H. M. to Francy C. Hussey 12-26-1865
Ray, John H. to Jane Brown 6-8-1864
Reading, Samuel R. to Laura C. Long 5-8-1852 (5-12-1852)
Reames, Joshua H. to Mary E. Crafton 1-12-1853 (1-13-1853)
Reams, Joshua M. to Harriet L. Haly 8-28-1856
Reaves, Noble to Martha Rickman 7-29-1865 (7-30-1865)
Reaves, Wm. R. to Margaret Johnson 6-4-1855 (no return)
Reddin, Wm. H. to Mary A. Vaughan 7-11-1860
Redding, Joseph T. to Susan Ann Sands 10-25-1864 (10-26-1864)
Redwood, Robert H. to Matte Hamner 3-27-1855
Reed, James M. to Lauretta Doxey 10-4-1854 (10-5-1854)
Reed, Robert J. to C. Jane Biggers 1-2-1857
Reed, Robert to Hannah A. Edgin 7-3-1852 (7-4-1852)
Reese, Wm. A. to Harriet J. Dooley 11-13-1865 (11-14-1865)
Reeves, Nathaniel G. to Susan A. Crawford 1-11-1866
Reeves, Thomas J. to Louisa A. H. Crawford 4-6-1859
Reeves, Wm. J. to Elizabeth S. Pinkleton 2-12-1861 (2-13-1861)
Regan, Andrew to Elizabeth J. Winchester 3-26-1867 (3-28-1867)
Renfro, Bertin A. to Lucy W. Perry 4-19-1867 (4-21-1867)

Renfro, Green to Nancy Ann Bennett 10-18-1864 (10-20-1864)
Renfro, Rufus R. to Mary E. Johnson 10-2-1852 (10-3-1852)
Renfro, Tarleton A. to Elizabeth M. McDonald 3-7-1864 (3-15-1864)
Renfro, Taswell A. to Ann Tidwell 12-9-1857 (12-10-1857)
Renfro, Wilkerson B. to Susan Estis 6-10-1856
Renfro, Willis H. to Lucy Ann Wells 1-27-1858 (1-28-1858)
Renfro, Wm. J. to Susan Hall 9-16-1856 (9-17-1856)
Rently, L. Mino to Isadora O. Spencer 12-28-1857 (12-31-1857)
Reynolds, Charles L. to Abbie E. Hackney 4-16-1863
Reynolds, Isom to Mary A. Grigg 2-21-1852 (2-22-1852)
Reynolds, James H. to Maey Horsford 1-18-1858 (12-19-1858)
Reynolds, Wm. C. to Mary V. Leftwick 5-22-1854 (5-24-1854)
Rhea, Francis A. to Eliza Ann Andrews 1-12-1867 (1-15-1867)
Rhoades, Henry W. to Rachael R. W. Rhoades 3-26-1866 (no return)
Rhoades, Wm. to Barbara Lainey 9-19-1865
Rhodes, James T. to Fannie J. Crockett 8-27-1860 (9-2-1860)
Rich, James D. to Sarah M. Hopper 10-18-1865 (10-19-1865)
Richardson, William C. to Mary A. Hunt 3-10-1852 (3-11-1852)
Richardson, Wilson E. to A. G. Hodge 1-6-1863 (1-7-1863)
Ricketts, Andrew M. to Nancy J. Donaldson 9-9-1858
Ricketts, John to Sarah J. Pugh 10-16-1854 (10-17-1854)
Ricketts, Milton to Susan Kilpatrick 10-12-1857 (10-15-1857)
Rickman, James C. to Sarah J. Hackney 7-13-1867 (7-14-1867)
Ridley, J. W. S. to Ann L. Pillow 11-13-1854 (no return)
Rieves, Wily J. to Amanda F. Johnson 12-23-1856
Rine, Charles R. to America P. Cheek 12-24-1863 (12-27-1863)
Ring, Lewis J. to Sarah Adeline Orr 1-4-1859 (1-11-1859)
Ritchie, Henry to Sarah Ann Love 10-10-1867
Ritter, Peter to Elizabeth Furguson 11-29-1856 (exec. no date)
Rives, Wm. to Rebecca E. Powell 12-1-1855 (12-2-1855)
Roach, Anderson J. to Mary C. Duke 5-26-1864 (no return)
Roach, John H. to Rachel Fleming 12-3-1860 (12-28-1860)
Roach, John L. to Sarah Foster 11-13-1852
Roach, John L. to Sarah Foster 11-13-1852 (no return)
Roan, Evan S. to Amanda C. Mills 9-23-1857 (no return)
Roan, John F. to Martha V. Roan 3-9-1860
Roan, Thomas J. to Sarah J. Chandler 1-16-1867 (1-17-1867)
Roan, Wm. R. to Alsenia Shading 4-5-1864
Roan, Wm. to Eliza M. McClain 8-3-1859
Roan, Wm. to Margaret McDaniel 8-13-1857
Roane, John J. to Priscilla Underwood 12-10-1855 (12-13-1855)
Roberson, Harmon to Malinda Wilson 12-13-1866
Roberson, Jaems M. to Mary P. Wood 9-16-1863
Roberts, Cannon H. to Jane F. Caughran 12-14-1860 (12-16-1860)
Roberts, John A. to Malvina Wallis 9-10-1852 (9-12-1852)
Roberts, M. C. to Mary A. Roberts 3-3-1854 (3-5-1854)
Roberts, Maury O. to Fidelia Brooks 3-19-1857
Roberts, Samuel J. to Angeline B. Wisener 10-14-1852 (10-15-1852)
Roberts, Wm. J. to Sallie D. Smith 2-21-1866 (2-22-1866)
Roberts, Wm. O. to Malinda R. Kinzer 7-19-1860 (7-22-1860)
Robertson, G. W. to Margaret J. Andrews 6-10-1854 (6-13-1854)
Robertson, Jack to Angeline Byrd 11-24-1865
Robertson, W. B. to Tennessee O. Younger 5-27-1865 (5-28-1865)
Robertson, Zadock R. to Mollie J. Thomas 12-14-1865
Robinson, A. S. to Cordilia N. Wood 2-15-1865 (no return)
Robinson, B. F. to Nettie F. Grantt 11-5-1866 (11-6-1866)
Robinson, John L. to Elizabeth J. McCalpin 4-16-1855 (no return)
Robinson, Samuel D. to Elizabeth Crawford 2-9-1857 (exec. no date)
Robison, David H. to Elizabeth A. M. Jordan 6-21-1859 (6-23-1859)
Robison, John W. to Josephine Troster 8-17-1857 (exec. no date)
Robison, Soverign G. to Martha J. Riggins 12-21-1857 (12-22-1857)
Rodgers, Jackson to Sarah J. Bryant 1-17-1857
Rogers, Benjamin A. to Figure A. McLemore 12-31-1866 (1-1-1867)
Rogers, Pheril V. to Margaret E. Wells 6-1-1853 (6-2-1853)
Rolen, Michail C. to Nancy C. Coffey 2-12-1852
Rolen, Wiley to Sarah M. Partin 9-1-1852
Roler, Wiley to Sarah M. Parten 9-1-1852
Roth, Emanuel to Annie Lou Kennedy 6-25-1866 (7-4-1866)
Rountree, Charles W. to Louisa J. Nicholls 1-21-1867 (2-7-1867)
Rountree, George W. to Margaret J. Riggs 6-22-1853
Rountree, John to Mary McKee 10-25-1852 (10-28-1852)
Rountree, John to Mary McKee 10-26-1852 (10-28-1852)
Rountree, Richard A. to Rebecca Trimble 1-15-1866
Rowe, Johnson to Emerine H. McMillan 9-4-1856 (9-23-1856)
Rowekeeble, Walter to Millicent B. Westmoreland 2-2-1860
Ruage, Joseph to Susan Hargrove 2-13-1854 (2-14-1854)
Rucker, James H. to Helen A. Sowell 7-18-1853 (8-16-1853)
Rucker, James W. to Permelia c. Stanfield 8-13-1853 (8-16-1853)
Rumage, Joseph A. to Sarah Hargrove 11-22-1855
Rumba, Elias to Martha J. Alexander 1-7-1857 (no return)
Rumbo, Thomas J. to Mary Jiggers 12-17-1866 (12-18-1866)
Rumbo, William L. to Mary Mitchell 1-18-1866
Rummage, James K. P. to Caroline H. Bigger 10-29-1860 (10-30-1860)
Runions, Joseph D. to Helen W. Hogwood 8-29-1861
Rushton, George W. to Sarah H. S. Fitzgerald 1-1-1852 (1-2-1852)
Rushton, James R. to Margaret E. Thomas 8-14-1861 (8-15-1861)
Russell, Edward E. to Martha Ann Owen 9-17-1857 (no date)

Russell, Ferdinand B. to Sarah E. Garey 1-12-1866 (1-15-1866)
Russell, Peyton T. to Eliza Jane Nicks 7-7-1860 (7-10-1860)
Rustin, Henry T. to Elizabeth Alderman 5-28-1853 (5-29-1853)
Ruston, William W. to Mary M. Wrenn 8-28-1852 (8-29-1852)
Ruston, Wm. W. to Mary M. Winn? 8-28-1852 (8-29-1852)
Rutledge, Gabriel T. to Frances Holly 4-13-1857 (4-16-1857)
Sandefer, John L. to Mary V. Strange 12-27-1862 (12-28-1862)
Sanders, George S. to Nancy P. Brown 1-24-1860 (1-25-1860)
Sanders, Hugh W. to Fannie C. Witherspoon 1-25-1866
Sanders, James D. to Ann Lessley 3-22-1853
Sanders, Lucius A. to Louisa Geasley 4-5-1867
Sanders, Pinkney C. to Mary C. Latta 9-19-1857 (10-20-1857)
Sandifer, Preston to Adie Stanfield 8-11-1862
Sands, Simeon F. to Susan A. Pullin 2-10-1858 (2-11-1858)
Sarver, Isaac to Nancy Holloway 8-16-1865 (8-17-1865)
Satterfield, Addison to Sarah P. Leetch 9-1-1852
Satterfield, Benjamin F. to Amanda Rutledge 8-7-1864
Saunder, George to Susan F. Fogleman 2-25-1853 (3-1-1853)
Saunders, Overton to Mary T. McBride 6-29-1855 (7-3-1855)
Saunders, Robert to Annie Cheatham 10-25-1861 (10-27-1861)
Saunders, Robert to Eliza A. Cheatham 5-22-1854 (5-23-1854)
Saunders, Rolf S. to Eliza Anderson 3-1-1854
Saunders, William J. to Allice B. Knowles 12-27-1860
Savage, James J. to Elizabeth Region 2-11-1857 (no return)
Savage, Jesse J. to Frances C. Wiley 6-15-1863 (no return)
Scales, Samuel W. to Mary E. Hughes 11-21-1857 (12-1-1857)
Schlimmer, Nicholas to Matilda E. Hoffman 12-20-1855
Scott, Andrew J. to Ellen W. McCain 2-23-1854
Scott, Charles S. to Calbernia S. Ralston 7-21-1859
Scott, David C. to Sarah E. Amis 9-6-1858 (9-7-1858)
Scott, Fountain to Leoticy Griffin 8-25-1852 (8-26-1852)
Scott, Henry B. to Anna Mack 9-3-1866 (9-4-1866)
Scott, Henry S. to Louisa Jane Farris 1-12-1857 (no return)
Scott, James B. to Annie Henderson 11-21-1866 (11-22-1866)
Scott, Thomas A. to Nancy L. Moore 9-1-1854 (9-6-1854)
Scott, William D. to Sallie J. Nevils 6-28-1865
Scott, William J. to Mahala T. Martin 4-29-1856 (5-1-1856)
Scott, William M. B. to Margaret Malinda Farriss 2-20-1856 (2-28-1856)
Scribner, James N. to Louisa Dillahy 2-22-1856 (2-23-1856)
Scribner, Lewis S. to Fannie Cheatham 8-15-1866
Scroggin, Charles G. to Eliza H. Campbell 8-9-1854 (8-10-1854)
Seagraves, M. L. to Martha Jane Pullin 2-16-1865 (2-17-1865)
Sealey, J. W. to Tennie Huckaby 5-1-1866
Sealey, Samuel D. to J. A. Floyd 1-18-1865 (1-19-1865)
Sealey, Thos. G. to Mary A. Pillow 3-25-1853
Sealy, Amos C. to Susan A. M. Russell 9-25-1856 (9-26-1856)
Sealy, Samuel D. to Delia Hood 3-2-1863 (3-3-1863)
Sealy, Samuel D. to Virginia Strange 12-23-1862 (no endorsement
Searnase, John H. to Martha A. Roberts 9-23-1865 (9-24-1865)
Seaton, William R. to Mary E. Johnson 1-18-1860 (1-26-1860)
Sedberry, James A. to Mary A. Kinger 2-8-1854 (2-9-1854)
Sedberry, William G. to Eliza J. Timmons 10-5-1859 (10-6-1859)
Seekers, T. J. to Mary J. Pinston 7-5-1866
Seeley, Samuel D. to Malinda J. Wright 10-24-1860 (10-25-1860)
Selders, Thomas B. to Amanda Chchaffin? 9-1-1865 (9-3-1865)
Sellars, James L. to Eliza Garner 5-3-1852 (5-5-1852)
Sellars, James Y. to Mary J. Hill 5-2-1853
Sellars, James to Manerva A. Curry 8-1-1856 (no return)
Sellars, John J. to Mary A. Neely 4-23-1867 (4-25-1867)
Sellars, William C. to Ellenor Harris 1-2-1856
Sellars, William to Anna Brown 3-12-1867
Sellars, William to Mary D. Sanders 7-12-1864 (7-14-1864)
Sellers, James L. to Eliza Garner 5-3-1852 (5-5-1852)
Sewall, Joseph W. to Leanna A. Jackson 1-10-1866 (1-16-1866)
Shadden, William to Rebecca Fain 1-27-1863
Shae, Daniel to Bercia Ann Ragsdale 12-26-1862 (12-28-1862)
Shake, William to Jane Hashbarker 5-16-1867
Shan, Calvin J. to M. J. E. Stephenon 1-19-1858 (1-24-1858)
Sharber, J. H. to Annie L. Huey 12-28-1858
Sharp, Jacob to Susan Jane Voss 2-27-1856 (2-28-1856)
Sharp, William A. to Sallie E. Jones 8-22-1864 (9-4-1864)
Sharpe, Thomas A. to Nancy J. Jones 1-7-1865 (1-10-1865)
Shaw, Ebenezer to L. J. A. McMillan 2-26-1855 (2-27-1855)
Shaw, Joseph B. to Martha E. Wilkes 1-17-1855
Shaw, William F. A. to Mary A. E. Renfro 11-13-1865 (11-15-1865)
Shelton, Collin A. to Elizabeth McMannon 10-5-1853 (no return)
Shephard, Alfred to Mary Stamps 2-24-1864 (2-25-1864)
Shires, Ira to Caroline B. Smith 3-5-1861 (3-6-1861)
Shires, Joseph to Martha Jane Smith 7-22-1854 (7-30-1854)
Shires, William H. to Mary A. Clark 2-21-1853 (2-27-1853)
Shires, Wm. to Martha W. Orr 9-2-1867 (9-5-1867)
Shirley, T. C. to Helen M. McKormack 2-17-1866 (2-20-1866)
Short, Thomas M. to Mary J. Akin 11-26-1857
Shulsky, Robert P. to Mary E. Lauhorn 2-7-1860 (2-8-1860)
Simmons, John to Mary J. A. Smith 3-12-1866 (3-20-1866)
Simmons, William to Margaret Graham 8-14-1861
Sims, Augustus to Rachael E. Irwin 3-17-1864 (no return)

Sims, Benjamin A. to Rachel L. Counaster? 4-5-1865
Sims, Thomas H. to Harriet A. Lee 11-12-1856
Skelley, John B. to Louisa Jane Alderson 11-4-1865 (11-5-1865)
Skelley, Samuel to Martha E. Dotson 1-12-1859
Skelley, Sparkman to Darcas Baker 11-19-1866 (11-22-1866)
Skelly, William D. to Mary M. Robison 2-19-1856
Skillington, Joseph J. to Caroline Askew 10-31-1857 (11-1-1857)
Skipworth, Edward E. to Martha E. Ross 3-24-1853 (3-29-1853)
Skipworth, P. H. to Frances D. Polk 11-12-1866 (11-13-1866)
Slate, Wm. Lee to Matilda Caroline Hutcherson 12-26-1866 (1-2-1867)
Slaughter, Stanton to Louisa F. Noles 12-13-1858 (12-14-1858)
Slaydon, Joseph E. to Elizabeth Latta 10-16-1858 (10-19-1858)
Sleight, Edmond B. to Elizabeth Hood 4-10-1867 (4-12-1867)
Small, Thomas J. to Rebecca E. Gibson 5-3-1859 (5-4-1859)
Smalley, George W. to Mary Jane West 8-5-1859 (8-7-1859)
Smally, George to Mary Duke 4-18-1862
Smiser, Joseph W. to Martha P. Frierson 12-22-1856 (12-23-1856)
Smith, Andrew D. to Mary E. Moore 7-15-1852
Smith, C. M. to M. A. Easley 4-10-1867
Smith, Charles N. to Nancy A. Hicks 9-3-1860 (9-4-1860)
Smith, Edward E. to Rebecca A. Shull 4-27-1852 (4-28-1852)
Smith, Elisha D. to Margaret Dickson 2-23-1860 (2-26-1860)
Smith, G. W. to Elizabeth A. Cofer 7-4-1865 (7-6-1865)
Smith, G. W. to Martha C. Walzon 4-17-1854 (4-19-1854)
Smith, J. H. to Elizabeth Wiley 3-19-1853 (3-20-1853)
Smith, James C. to Mary E. Ashton 12-18-1865 (no return)
Smith, James H. to Sarah E. Coleburn 4-20-1864 (4-21-1864)
Smith, James M. to Mary E. Paul 1-7-1867 (1-8-1867)
Smith, John B. to Nancy Maywood 10-25-1853 (10-26-1853)
Smith, John R. to L. W. H. Hobson 12-19-1857 (12-20-1857)
Smith, John to Lucy Erwina 12-5-1859 (12-7-1859)
Smith, Lemuel M. to Martha Ann McFadden 12-2-1866 (12-12-1866)
Smith, Robert Davis to Margaret J. Thomas 4-20-1867 (4-23-1867)
Smith, Terry to Martha J. Roundtree 9-22-1859 (9-23-1859)
Smith, Thomas M. to Sallie J. Moore 1-18-1866
Smith, Thomas P. to Sarelda M. Hicks 12-14-1858 (12-15-1858)
Smith, William J. to Mary E. Pope 12-14-1858 (12-16-1858)
Smith, William M. to Nancy Ann Howard 12-30-1857 (12-31-1857)
Smith, William R. to Eliza L. Mangrum 2-24-1859
Smotherman, James A. to Emily Roan 4-24-1863
Sneed, James to Mary A. Stone 5-3-1862 (5-5-1861?)
Sneed, John to Lovinia Lindsley 11-1-1858 (11-2-1858)
Snell, Anber H. to Elizabeth S. Mitchell 9-2-1854
Snider, Michael to Mary Worgum 4-2-1860
Southall, Patrick H. to Cynthia A. Kinnard 9-4-1861 (9-5-1861)
Sowell, Augustus T. to Margie T. Martin 10-22-1867 (10-24-1867)
Sowell, James H. to Laura J. Miller 1-9-1865 (1-10-1865)
Sowell, James K. P. to Eudora D. Hardison 9-11-1861
Sowell, James W. to Anna J. Patterson 10-23-1865 (10-261-1865)
Sowell, Thomas M. to Mary E. Caldwell 11-14-1859 (11-15-1859)
Sowell, Thomas to Sarah (Susan?) Ann Tatum 6-5-1852 (6-6-1852)
Sowell, Thomas to Sarah A. Tatum 6-5-1852 (6-6-1852)
Spain, Addison H. to Sarah J. G. Henderson 3-13-1854
Spain, Alexander S. to Elizabeth J. McMenis 3-9-1853 (3-10-1853)
Spain, Alexander T. to Mary Ann Barnett 10-30-1855 (10-31-1855)
Spain, Howell T. to Mrs. Jos. T. McCandless 2-1-1866 (2-5-1866)
Spain, John N. to Mary E. Nichols 5-12-1864 (no return)
Spain, Robert M. to Margaret E. Benderman 11-4-1856 (11-6-1856)
Sparkman, Francis B. to Sarah C. Keirsey 6-15-1854
Sparkman, Jacob G. to Selina T. Church 9-6-1865 (9-7-1865)
Sparkman, James A. to Manerva A. Hill 10-19-1854
Sparkman, John M. to Rachael E. Alexander 1-12-1866 (1-14-1866)
Sparkman, Samuel T. to Eliza A. Oakley 11-12-1859 (11-13-1859)
Sparks, John to Sarah T. Gantt 6-6-1863 (6-9-1863)
Speed, Francis to Eliza Tucker 2-29-1853
Speed, Robert M. to Cordelia Hale 10-27-1855 (10-28-1855)
Speed, Theodore S. to Elizabeth Griffin 10-17-1867
Speer, William S. to Martha P. Fielder 6-21-1853
Spencer, Handel C. to Sarah A. Milliken 2-14-1866 (5-15-1866)
Spencer, James K. P. to Margaret E. Jones 4-3-1866 (4-4-1866)
Spencer, Samuel to Minerva Bell 9-11-1856 (no return)
Sprinkle, William to Susan Sprinkle 7-8-1852
Sprinkles, Richard Thomas to Narcissa Everett 7-18-1864 (7-25-1864)
Sprott, William H. to Hary S. Foster 9-22-1860 (10-3-1860)
Squires, Uriah E. to Sarah Jane Cundiff 9-15-1856 (no return)
Stacy, George L. to Sarah Murphy 8-24-1853 (8-25-1853)
Stacy, Thomas G. to Mary A. McKnight 2-6-1865 (2-8-1865)
Stallings, Joseph T. to Mary A. Oliphant 10-1-1858 (no return)
Stallings, Thomas S. to Sarah M. Sowell 1-19-1857 (no return)
Stamps, George to Mary Mills 10-15-1854
Stamps, James C. to Nancy A. S. Reed 3-31-1866 (4-1-1866)
Stamps, James W. to Maria D. Gunnell 8-4-1854 (8-5-1854)
Standemann, John H. to Mary Jane Whitehead 8-15-1857 (no return)
Standrige, A. K. to Eliza A. Latta 9-9-1867 (no return)
Stanfield, George W. to Alice E. Cathey 3-11-1862 (3-12-1862)
Stanfill, Andrew J. to Frances A. Isom 8-30-1864 (8-31-1864)
Stanfill, G. W. to J. Fannie McConick 10-24-1866

Starkey, A. J. to Priscilla M. Dix 3-2-1859
Stauderman, John H. to Rebecca P. James 6-12-1858 (6-13-1858)
Steel, John T. to Josephine C. Wilkes 12-1-1853 (no return)
Steepleton, Thomas B. to Jossie A. Sheppard 12-18-1865
Stephens, Alexander to Matilda E. Brooks 2-23-1857
Stephens, Henry to Frances C. Norman 7-12-1864 (7-14-1864)
Stephens, Robert to Mary M. Thomas 6-29-1860 (7-1-1860)
Stephens, Scott to Alice A. Evans 11-22-1866
Stephenson, Jonathan B. to Margaret M. Childress 12-17-1860 (12-18-1860)
Stephenson, Thomas J. to Mary E. McClanahan 12-23-1862 (no return)
Stephenson, Wm. W. to Letha K. Duke 4-6-1865
Stewart, Alexander to Fannie Collins 3-3-1858
Stewart, Calvin B. to Sarah J. Covey 1-18-1864 (1-19-1864)
Stewart, Mount Levanus to Lucy C. Wood 11-22-1855
Stewart, Thomas J. to Martha Latta 12-19-1866 (12-20-1866)
Stewart, William A. to Mahala Powell 6-12-1852
Stockard, John J. to Susan L. Warden 12-31-1866 (1-1-1867)
Stockard, John to Mary T. West 11-1-1864 (11-2-1864)
Stockard, Martin L. to Ann E. Caldwell 1-11-1855
Stockerd, George W. to Sallie C. Walker 4-7-1862 (4-8-1862)
Stone, Benjamin F. to Elizabeth H. Dobbin 11-7-1865 (11-8-1865)
Stone, George T. to Sarah Jane Wisener 6-22-1867 (6-23-1867)
Stone, John W. S. to Jane A. Snipe 12-22-1860 (12-24-1860)
Stone, Thomas J. to Mary E. Cook 9-12-1860
Strange, James W. to Harriet T. Bunch 4-7-1859
Strange, Thomas A. to Elizabeth Snell 10-17-1865 (10-19-1865)
Stratton, James F. to Permelia E. Leftwick 9-11-1854 (9-13-1854)
Straughan, Robert N. to Mary E. Pilkinton 12-26-1859 (12-27-1859)
Street, Wm. M. to Lizzie C. Johnson 6-12-1855 (6-14-1855)
Stricklin, James to Sarah Barbee 1-1-1867
Strother, George W. to Virginia C. Goodloe 6-15-1858 (exec. no date)
Stubblefield, Lawson W. to Elizabeth S. Bradshaw 9-2-1856 (9-3-1856)
Stultz, Lorenzo to Catharine Childress 5-3-1865
Sughruo?, John to Lucinda Ragsdale 4-7-1865
Sullivan, Dennis to Catharine Shea 5-18-1860 (5-19-1860)
Sullivan, James to Ellen Sullivan 2-7-1861
Sullivan, L. A. to Mary M. Philips 10-17-1867
Sullivan, Patrick to Mary Hand 1-1-1859 (1-2-1859)
Sutton, George E. to Serena A. Williams 8-20-1861 (8-22-1861)
Swan, John N. to Sarah A. Hill 3-15-1858 (3-17-1858)
Swan, John N. to Sarah J. Spencer 2-6-1865 (2-7-1865)
Sykes, A. M. P. to Nancy A. Powell 10-27-1866 (10-29-1866)
Sykes, George A. to Mary E. Rivers 10-27-1856 (10-28-1856)
Sykes, L. L. to Susan Hall 6-30-1862 (7-1-1862)
Talley, Benjamin F. to Margaret Duke 10-12-1853
Tanner, Moses to Mary Wylie 8-11-1858 (8-12-1858)
Tarpley, Benjamin M. to Manerva E. Gilbreath 2-5-1855 (2-8-1855)
Tate, John E. to Dorcas E. Harbison 10-3-1860 (10-11-1860)
Tatum, Allen V. to Mary A. Sowell 8-4-1858 (no return)
Tatum, Jesse to Sarah Russell 2-8-1855 (no return)
Taylor, James M. to Margaret J. Barker 7-30-1857
Taylor, James M. to Rebecca Frances Roane 11-28-1866
Taylor, John P. to Emeline Hedpeth 10-8-1864 (10-9-1864)
Taylor, Perry P. to Mary M. S. Caldwell 10-16-1858 (10-17-1858)
Teas, Robert to Amanda M. Bryan 3-2-1853 (4-3-1853)
Temple, Jeremiah to Julia Ann Pillow 2-19-1865
Terass, John W. to Mary E. Hoge 11-1-1852 (no return)
Terass, John W. to Mary E. Hoge 11-15-1852
Terry, John M. to S. A. Caldwell 5-9-1867 (5-10-1867)
Thomas, A. G. W. to Mary E. Johnson 9-18-1865
Thomas, Albert G. to Mary A. Haynes 2-17-1853
Thomas, Archibald E. L. to Mary R. Alexander 9-17-1863 (9-18-1863)
Thomas, Burrell M. to Emerine Rowe 1-27-1859 (1-29-1859)
Thomas, David to Sarah A. Witham 10-19-1852 (10-20-1852)
Thomas, Ellis to Nancy Cooper 8-12-1854
Thomas, John D. to W. A. Nicholson 12-21-1858
Thomas, Joshua J. T. to Mary E. Walker 4-10-1855 (4-11-1855)
Thomas, Nathaniel A. H. to Catharine Alderson 7-11-1853 (7-12-1853)
Thomas, Rufus to Mary Jane Henderson 10-30-1856
Thomas, S. H. to Z. Conkey 5-24-1852 (5-25-1852)
Thomas, Tennessee to Oly Robertson 8-15-1857 (8-16-1857)
Thomason, Alexander to Elizabeth Chumbly 8-22-1864
Thomason, F. M. to Margaret A. Smith 8-26-1862 (8-28-1862)
Thomason, Israel to Ann Eliza Chumler 3-27-1866 (4-1-1866)
Thomason, J. E. to Nancy E. Hale 7-6-1863 (9-28-1865)
Thomason, Jackson to Margaret Sneed 6-5-1865 (6-11-1865)
Thomason, James R. to Malinda Thomason 7-22-1855
Thomason, Jones to Mary Davidson 6-2-1863 (6-4-1863)
Thomasson, Porter L. to Mary M. J. Spencer 8-5-1867 (8-27-1867)
Thompson, Alexander to Sarah Rainey 9-11-1854 (9-14-1854)
Thompson, George W. to Margaret E. Fitzgerald 4-13-1854
Thompson, Hiram Vance to Mary F. Stephenson 11-5-1857
Thompson, James F. to Mary Jane Cavender 12-29-1855 (1-3-1856)
Thompson, John A. to Mary Ann Wiem 8-7-1852 (8-10-1852)
Thompson, John A. to Mary Ann Wiern (Wiser?) 8-7-1852 (8-10-1852)
Thompson, John A. to Mary Ann Winn 8-7-1852
Thompson, John R. to Martha L. Goodrich 10-16-1861 (10-17-1861)

Thompson, Moses S. to Manerva A. Hadley 11-12-1853 (11-13-1853)
Thompson, Newton A. to Martha E. Hobbs 11-21-1866
Thompson, Pleasant to Harriet E. Brown 11-1-1860
Thompson, Thomas A. to Sarah E. Cross 11-23-1859
Thompson, V. N. to Mary A. Erwin 10-19-1854
Thompson, Wm. H. to Eliza A. Jenkins 2-12-1867 (2-19-1867)
Thompson, Wm. O. to Martha E. Wilson 10-17-1853 (no return)
Thoms, Erwin to Emeline Thomas 8-9-1860
Thurmond, Addison S. to Elizabeth J. Stevens 6-20-1855 (no return)
Tidwell, Henry to Mary R. Stallings 10-15-1859 (10-16-1859)
Tidwell, Joseph to Nancy Tidwell 11-29-1852
Tidwell, Joseph to Nancy Tidwell 11-29-1852 (no return)
Tilford, John A. to Louceana B. Smith 12-13-1860 (12-16-1860)
Timmons, James K. P. to Mary B. Evans 7-13-1865
Timmons, Squire H. to Martha J. Evans 4-8-1864 (4-12-1864)
Tindel, Robert W. to Lamyra Vincent 11-25-1858 (11-26-1858)
Tindle, Robert W. to Eliza A. Hardison 11-3-1866 (11-4-1866)
Tindle, Wm. H. H. to Hannah E. Keltner 4-29-1861
Titcomb, Hiram B. to Mattie E. Ordon 5-29-1860
Tizner, Wm. to Mary Jane Neeley 9-25-1860
Toad, Wm. B. to Martha a. Mangrum 10-29-1857
Todd, Joh to Amanda M. Flanegan 9-15-1852
Todd, John to Amanda M. Flanegan 9-15-1852
Tomlinson, M. B. to M. F. Dillard 9-8-1866
Toombs, Anthony M. to Nancy A. Bradley 11-22-1853 (no return)
Toombs, James L. to Nancy America Reaves 11-29-1859
Townson, Robert W. to Martha F. Reynolds 3-28-1859 (3-30-1859)
Travis, Jacob to Nancy A. Daniels 3-22-1865
Treppard, Thomas J. to Mollie Long 2-12-1859 (2-14-1859)
Trewitt, Wm. L. to Mary Robertson 12-18-1862
Trimble, Alexander to Mary M. Sparkman 9-2-1854 (no return)
Trimble, Alexander to Rebecca S. Boaz 11-3-1860 (11-4-1860)
Trotter, Eli T. to Alabama Roberson 10-9-1856
Trotter, John to Maria A. Anderson 11-27-1856
Trousdale, David to Henrietta Brandon 9-30-1867 (10-1-1867)
Trousdale, Johnston to Eliza P. Goff 6-2-1856
Tucker, James M. to France C. Crawford 10-13-1855 (10-14-1855)
Tucker, James to Arriet Robinson 10-23-1862 (10-26-1862)
Tucker, Jeremiah F. to Lucy Ann Robison 2-15-1858 (2-17-1858)
Tucker, Junius F. to Fannie W. Anderson 9-5-1866 (9-6-1866)
Tucker, Stephen P. to Martha C. Carpenter 4-22-1864 (4-28-1864)
Tucker, Wilson M. to Fannie E. Denton 12-17-1858 (12-22-1858)
Tuley, Charles A. to Mary Wright 12-28-1855
Turnbow, John L. to E. J. Green 8-20-1861 (8-22-1861)
Turner, Benjamin F. to Margaret F. Hill 12-11-1865 (12-13-1865)
Turner, Jessee to Susan E. Garner 10-24-1853 (10-25-1853)
Tye, W. H. to Rebecca M. Smith 1-14-1867 (1-15-1867)
Tylor, William C. to Martha E. Binham 1-12-1861 (1-16-1861)
Underwood, William to Mary L. Williams 1-1-1866 (1-4-1866)
Vaughan, James to Susan C. Pillow 3-18-1859 (no return)
Vaughan, Thomas to Lila Cooper 10-7-1865
Vaughn, Newton J. to Fancy E. Warren 1-12-1858 (1-13-1858)
Vaught, Charles N. to Robina Voorhies 11-27-1866
Veatch, Silas L. to Mary Beasly 12-6-1856 (12-9-1856)
Veetch, Silas L. to Jane Barnett 12-7-1861 (12-10-1861)
Vestal, Aaron T. to Rebecca Sedburry 1-6-1857 (1-8-1857)
Vestal, Anon T. to Anna E. Erwin 9-6-1853 (9-8-1853)
Vestal, James M. to Rachel E. Younger 11-10-1852 (11-11-1852)
Vestal, James M. to Sarah F. Fox 5-27-1865 (5-28-1865)
Vestal, Joseph A. to Margaret E. Hill 1-5-1853 (1-6-1853)
Vestal, William J. to Lamira? Vestal 10-23-1865 (10-24-1865)
Vestel, William to Harriet J. Judd 3-29-1856 (3-30-1856)
Vincent, Nenniah to Lucinda E. Pugh 7-15-1858
Vincent, Robert Wm. to Pricilla Ann Pugh 7-15-1858
Vond, Henry to Mary Ann Huggins 11-3-1858 (11-4-1858)
Vorhies, Robert A. to Nannie E. Burkett 10-23-1860 (no return)
Voss, Leroy to Josie E. Williams 11-27-1866 (11-29-1866)
Voss, Lucius P. to Mary F. Kennedy 12-21-1858 (12-22-1858)
Voucher, Caleb T. to Margaret Grean 12-31-1863
Waddell, James to Mary Jane Denton 2-9-1860
Wakfield, William L. to Martha L. Fly 4-3-1865 (4-6-1865)
Walker, Griffith C. to Louisa P. Reveer 3-22-1853 (3-24-1853)
Walker, John P. to Rebeca Ann Puckett 3-24-1857 (no return)
Walker, Joseph N. to Emily Jamison 5-30-1855 (5-31-1855)
Walker, Richard C. to Louisa G. Kerr 12-22-1853
Walker, Thomas A. to C. P. Fitzgerald 8-23-1855 (8-30-1855)
Walker, Thomas J. to Mary A. Sowell 2-20-1860 (2-21-1860)
Walker, Washington P. to Frances Taylor 1-26-1852
Walker, William R. to Ann Jane Gilmer 7-26-1859 (7-27-1859)
Walrup, David to Mary J. Garrett 2-9-1857 (2-10-1857)
Walters, Charles A. to Nancy A. Fitzgerald 12-18-1860 (12-20-1860)
Walters, Henry H. to Mary E. J. Denny 4-4-1861
Walters, Robert L. to Mrs. Sarah J. Younger 8-21-1865
Walters, William B. to Naomi J. Hight 1-23-1864 (1-24-1864)
Wantland, R. B. to Mary Murphey 9-16-1854 (9-17-1854)
Ward, Hezekiah to Josephine E. Craig 7-22-1852
Warden, Calvin K. to Jane E. McCain 11-8-1864

Warden, John to Paralee Higdon 8-17-1860 (8-19-1860)
Wardin, James to Mary A. Ramsy 5-8-1856
Warfield, Amos W. to Cornelia A. Francis 4-11-1854
Warfield, Burton to Nancy Ann Worley 2-10-1858
Warning, William L. to Octavia O. Smith 12-8-1866 (12-12-1866)
Warr, James M. to Martha E. F. Perry 8-9-1866
Warren, Robert to Hannah M. McFarland 7-2-1854 (7-27-1854)
Warren, Walter M. to Ellen Bratton 12-5-1866
Watel, Andrew to Elizabeth F. C. Trainum 10-2-1865
Waterhouse, James T. to Almira B. Long 2-24-1852 (2-25-1852)
Waters, Z. J. C. to Lau W. Foster 10-12-1858
Watkins, Saml. R. to Virginia Mayes 9-5-1865
Watkins, William A. to Harriet A. Tomlinson 9-18-1865 (9-10-1865)
Watkins, William H. to Mary E. Bird 8-8-1864 (8-10-1864)
Watkins, Wm. W. to Harriet Ann Green 11-1-1859
Watkins, Wm. to Martha Dawson 1-16-1864 (date unclear)
Watson, Gustavus to Sarah Ann Alederson 6-23-1855
Watson, James C. to Mary Bennett 1-2-1860 (1-5-1860)
Watson, James T. to Martha J. Johnson 9-10-1859 (9-11-1859)
Watson, James to Naomi T. Dortch 9-4-1856 (9-5-1856)
Watson, John B. to Martha S. Chaffin 1-26-1865
Watson, John to Louisa Turner 1-11-1858 (1-14-1858)
Watson, Robert to Martha Heralson 12-20-1866 (12-23-1866)
Watson, William W. to Talitha K. Barnett 1-10-1853 (no return)
Wear, William D. to Mary Jane Moody 9-25-1854 (9-26-1854)
Weatherly, Joseph to Susan E. Trigg 10-26-1863 (no return)
Weaver, John C. to Mary E. Lindsey 12-31-1856 (1-1-1857)
Weaver, Leeander to Margaret Weaver 10-19-1860 (10-21-1860)
Webb, Charles S. to Nannie Baldridge 2-12-1867 (2-13-1867)
Webb, Gray P. to Emily Phillipps 4-18-1867 (4-19-1867)
Webb, James A. to Martha J. Bolton 9-24-1857 (9-27-1857)
Webster, Albert G. to Mary Fisher 10-20-1853
Welch, James H. to Mary E. Grant 2-6-1867 (2-7-1867)
Welch, William G. to Louisa P. Calvert 5-24-1855
Wells, David to Priscilla Kerr 8-10-1863 (8-13-1863)
Wells, George W. to Dovey A. Ausban 7-21-1866 (7-26-1866)
Wells, James P. to Ellen Powell 1-7-1861 (1-8-1861)
Wells, John F. to M. L. Williams 7-17-1865 (7-19-1865)
Wells, Joseph N. to Mary Jane Thurmond 2-2-1867 (2-13-1867)
Wells, Mark L. to Lucy E. Collier 9-13-1865 (9-14-1865)
Wells, Thomas J. to Mary J. Kerr 12-18-1866
Wells, William F. to Henrietta C. Cannon 1-5-1858 (1-7-1858)
West, Benjamin F. to Martha Fisher 5-22-1856
West, Homer R. to Mary E. Gilmer 9-10-1860 (9-11-1860)
West, James J. to Mary F. Moore 1-11-1859 (1-13-1859)
West, John S. to Mary M. Orsborn 7-31-1856
West, Martin V. to Martha S. Coffee 6-4-1866 (6-14-1866)
West, P. T. to L. T. Mangrem 8-4-1862 (8-7-1862)
West, Zachariah Y. to Nancy T. Prewett 11-20-1860 (11-29-1860)
Westmoreland, Robert W. to Penie E. Scribner 3-11-1867 (3-12-1867)
Westmoreland, William R. to Martha A. Eves 4-18-1853 (4-19-1853)
Wheatley, A. C. C. to Sarah F. Nicholson 1-15-1853 (1-18-1853)
Wheatley, Pearce to Mary E. Wright 8-21-1865
Wheatly, Drury to Sarah E. Madden 11-27-1855
Wheatly, James to Mary R. Campbell 1-8-1856
Wheeler, William H. to Alice A. Patton 11-27-1852 (11-29-1852)
Wheeler, William H. to Susan M. Wilcox 6-29-1858 (6-30-1858)
Whitaker, George P. to Susan P. Nicholson 9-11-1865
Whitaker, James M. to Margaret M. Lockhart 4-20-1858 (no return)
Whitaker, James M. to Martha M. McKnight 10-10-1862 (no return)
White, Albert A. to Mary J. Brum 12-9-1854 (12-10-1854)
White, B. L. to Mary White 5-13-1865 (5-14-1865)
White, Daniel to Alabama Fitzgerald 8-22-1864 (8-25-1864)
White, Ed to Ida Brayman 5-14-1866 (5-16-1866)
White, Erastus D. to Ellen Norman 12-5-1854
White, George W. to Mary E. Pipkin 7-15-1856 (7-17-1856)
White, Gray to Caledonia Blucher 11-14-1857 (11-15-1857)
White, Henry R. to Sarah Ann Alderson 1-21-1860
White, Hugh L. to Helen E. O. Brien 3-24-1863 (3-25-1863)
White, James B. to Rebecca Denton 2-28-1866
White, James L. to Ophelia Davidson 9-3-1866 (9-6-1866)
White, James P. to Sarah L. Tankersly 10-10-1866
White, John J. to Abigail Wood 7-19-1866 (7-25-1866)
White, John W. to Mary W. Blair 10-13-1866 (10-16-1866)
White, Joseph W. to Susan Smith 5-17-1862 (5-18-1862)
White, Luke S. to Nancy J. Sparkman 12-25-1852 (12-27-1852)
White, Luke to Polly Askew 3-2-1857 (3-5-1857)
White, Mathias to Sarah E. Smithson 1-19-1863 (2-6-1863)
White, Peter to Ava E. Haley 5-23-1866
White, Samuel D. to Martha A. Hall 7-15-1863
White, Thomas J. to Martha F. Bond 4-22-1858
Whiteside, Alexander A. to Mary J. Anderson 8-4-1859 (8-7-1859)
Whitesides, Milton to Nancy E. Rhodes 6-19-1862
Whitley, Flemming W. to Naoma Nellums 1-30-1866 (2-1-1866)
Whittaker, William A. to Rebecca Brooks 10-31-1865
Whitthurst?, William H. to Mrs. Eliza Jane Elmore 3-18-1856
Whitworth, James to Rutha Lambert 9-23-1865 (9-29-1865)

Whitworth, John W. to Martha F. Mitchell 11-7-1855
Wiem, Franklin L. P. to Nancy P. Cheatham 2-1-1854 (3-22-1854)
Wigginton, John K. G. to Martha A. Burns 9-6-1867 (9-8-1867)
Wilbanks, William N. to Cintha E. Jones 10-20-1857 (10-23-1857)
Wilber, John F. to Henrietta E. Powell 7-3-1865 (7-6-1865)
Wilborn, Nathaniel P. to Emma J. Harris 12-9-1856 (12-10-1856)
Wilcoxen, G. P. to Charlotte Coffee 4-27-1854
Wileford, Willis to Jane Willett 6-29-1860 (6-30-1860)
Wiles, James A. to Nancy C. Andrews 10-16-1852 (10-17-1852)
Wiley, John to Susan Fariss 6-1-1853 (6-2-1853)
Wiley, Samuel to Rhoda K. Jamison 2-5-1866 (2-6-1866)
Wiley, Wm. Young to Caledonia Chaffin 7-25-1866
Wilis, James A. to Nancy C. Andrews 10-16-1852 (10-17-1852)
Wilkerson, Alonzo A. to Lucy Ann Brown 12-26-1856
Wilkerson, William P. to Rachael V. Hughes 9-29-1859 (10-4-1859)
Wilkes, Benjamin L. to Sarah E. Moore 1-15-1855 (1-16-1855)
Wilkes, E. H. to Sarah L. Parish 9-6-1862 (9-16-1862)
Wilkes, Milton A. to Louisa J. Wright 7-31-1856
Wilkes, Nathaniel R. to Jennie C. Thompson 10-20-1858 (10-21-1858)
Wilkes, Rev. Wm. H. to Zurilda Amis 12-30-1856 (1-1-1857)
Wilkes, Richard S. to Elvira O. Moore 10-25-1852 (no return)
Wilkes, Richard to Elvira O. Moore 10-25-1852
Wilkes, William A. to Sina Ann White 1-16-1860 (1-19-1860)
Wilkes, Wm. H. to Eliz. J. Martin 1-4-1861 (1-8-1861)
Wilkins, John to Jane Thurman 8-27-1853 (8-28-1853)
Wilkins, Uriah to Martha Mantle 1-22-1866
Wilks, William L. to Sarah E. Foster 6-9-1852 (6-10-1852)
Willard, Hosea E. to Mrs. Margaret A. Kirby 2-27-1866
Willett, Robert to Sarah A. Maxwell 1-11-1860 (1-15-1860)
Williams, Alexander to Lizzie E. Rains 11-29-1865 (11-30-1865)
Williams, Alfred F. to Eveline Howard 2-15-1867 (2-17-1867)
Williams, Allis to Nancy Bucker 12-17-1856 (12-1856)
Williams, Alvis to Caroline M. Cox 1-4-1864 (1-5-1864)
Williams, Benjamin F. to Mary P. Vestal 4-19-1854 (no return)
Williams, C. F. to Bettie Armstrong 4-19-1854 (no return)
Williams, Carson to Mary Jane Wills 4-28-1857 (4-29-1857)
Williams, J. R. D. to M. J. Walker 11-6-1865 (11-9-1865)
Williams, James A. to Jeannie Stewart 11-27-1863
Williams, James M. to Mary E. Roan 3-1-1863 (3-11-1863)
Williams, James N. to Elizabeth Nicholson 12-26-1855
Williams, Joseph M. to Emily D. Polk 11-12-1860 (11-13-1860)
Williams, Nathaniel G. B. to Mary Lee E. A. Wortham 2-26-1855 (2-27-1855)
Williams, Oliver W. to Nancy F. Kennedy 11-20-1865 (11-21-1865)
Williams, Peter to Nancy P. Boaz 12-26-1853 (12-27-1853)
Williams, Robert C. to Hattie A. Kercheval 1-28-1852 (1-29-1852)
Williams, Thomas B. to Irene Hammond 11-27-1865 (11-28-1865)
Williams, Thomas H. to Anna C. White 2-4-1867 (2-5-1867)
Williams, Thomas J. to Elizabeth Smith 1-26-1854 (1-27-1854)
Williams, William D. to Mary Garrett 1-27-1854 (1-29-1854)
Williamson, George R. to Martha J. Hewett 11-13-1854 (11-14-1854)
Williamson, Joseph M. to Cynthia E. Hale 1-12-1855 (1-13-1855)
Williamson, Thomas D. to Susan C. Cannon 12-22-1857
Willis, Benjamin F. to Elizabeth C. Coleman 1-28-1853 (2-3-1853)
Willis, Benjamin F. to Martha S. Thomason 12-27-1858 (12-28-1858)
Willis, F. W. to Ednie A. Cook 6-2-1864
Willis, Richard T. to Julia A. Sealey 1-24-1865 (2-25-1865)
Willis, Thomas to Inda Stephenson 6-2-1866 (6-3-1866)
Willis, William J. to Mary Ann Massey 2-21-1866 (2-22-1866)
Willis, William M. to Mrs. Margaret E. Rusten 11-1-1866 (11-4-1866)
Wilsoin, John to Fannie K. Pinkston 6-13-1867 (6-16-1867)
Wilson, George D. to Mary R. Ward 7-26-1865 (7-30-1865)
Wilson, Henry C. to Nancy Jane Fitzgerald 11-22-1864
Wilson, Henry L. to Amanda J. Williams 11-29-1856 (no endorsement
Wilson, James M. to Lizzie Derryberry 10-2-1861 (10-3-1861)
Wilson, John A. to Ophelia L. Turner 3-21-1865 (3-22-1865)
Wilson, Junius A. to Maria J. Hales 2-19-1865
Wilson, Moreen to Rosanna D. Braden 10-1-1855 (10-14-1855)
Wilson, Uriah J. to Caroline A. Burnett 1-1-1866 (1-2-1866)
Wilson, William A. to Kate M. Odell 12-19-1865
Wilson, William B. to Louisa B. Wilkins 5-8-1861
Wilson, Zacheus D. to Frances J. Walker 1-14-1860 (no return)
Winchester, James L. to Ophelia J. Killingsworth 12-18-1866 (12-20-1866)
Wisener, Samuel to Adaline Brooks 10-1-1853 (10-3-1853)
Witerspoon, Samuel to Jeanette K. B. Oakley 1-27-1855 (1-30-1855)
Witherspoon, Joshua T. to Louisa P. Mullins 4-3-1858 (4-4-1858)
Witt, Carter H. to Talitha C. Amis 1-6-1853
Wolf, Charley B. to Matilda Greener 10-28-1857 (10-29-1857)
Wood, Freaylenhuyson to Nancy E. Nance 4-3-1866 (4-5-1866)
Wood, William H. to Mary L. Bynum 2-6-1866 (2-7-1866)
Wood, William H. to Sarah J. Stewart 8-15-1860
Wood, Willis H. to Caledonia Phillips 1-14-1861
Woods, Butler to Liddy Ray 2-20-1867 (2-25-1867)
Woodside, Joseph B. to Nancy E. Witham 1-31-1853
Woodward, Albert G. to Nannie T. Gell 12-27-1866
Woodward, John J. to Susannah Pingleton 3-29-1866
Woody, James H. to Milly O. E. Fitzgerald 8-29-1865 (8-31-1865)
Woody, Jasper to Elizabeth J. Johnson 6-30-1855 (7-1-1855)

Woody, John N. to Martha J. Caldwell 12-17-1856 (no return)
Woody, Rufus to Sarah E. Wells 9-14-1857 (9-17-1857)
Woody, Samuel S. to Susan Catharine Harbison 8-27-1864 (8-31-1864)
Woody, William J. to Frances M. Caldwell 2-28-1859 (3-1-1859)
Woolverton, John T. to Evaline F. Ray 8-14-1867 (no return)
Workman, C. to Mary J. Stamps 5-10-1864 (no return)
Workman, Isaaiah E. to Mrs. Ellen Norwood 11-20-1865
Worley, Samuel A. to Martha M. Strong 12-13-1865 (12-15-1865)
Worsham, Thomas to Sarah Hendricks 4-15-1864 (4-16-1864)
Worster, John W. to Mary E. Foster 10-30-1865 (12-1-1865)
Wrenn, Thomas W. to Mildred B. Poyner 7-22-1865 (7-27-1865)
Wright, Archibald L. to Martha A. Burkett 1-11-1854 (1-12-1854)
Wright, Daniel to Milly Sloan 8-9-1852
Wright, Egbert G. to Martha P. Terry 2-22-1864 (2-24-1864)
Wright, Frederick to Martha Smithson 11-3-1853
Wright, Hillary to Mary Jane Crawford 12-1-1855 (12-2-1855)
Wright, James E. to Amanda Seagraves 6-1-1865
Wright, John F. to Margaret J. Mitchell 12-18-1854 (12-19-1854)
Wright, John S. to E. J. Denton 2-11-1865 (2-15-1865)
Wright, Joseph B. to Martha J. Turbeville 12-28-1865
Wright, Reuben to Matilda Forehand 5-19-1858 (5-20-1858)
Wright, Robert M. to Nancy J. Blackwood 12-18-1852 (12-19-1852)
Wright, Robert to Sarah Bennett 5-30-1867
Wright, Thompson to Susan R. Keltner 1-5-1853
Wright, Washington to Harriet Lawrence 2-18-1852 (2-19-1852)
Wright, Washington to Sarah Ann Curry 3-20-1856 (3-23-1856)
Wright, William to Eliza Brown 12-31-1864 (1-1-1865)
Wylie, Robert to Frances C. Delk 1-2-1860 (1-10-1860)
Yancy, Samuel L. to Frances J. Fleming 10-21-1861 (10-24-1861)
Yankey, Michael to Martha Lambert 4-18-1864
Yarborough, James P. to Mary L. Holmes 7-11-1867 (7-14-1867)
Yarbrough, William to Sarah E. Steele 8-20-1860 (8-21-1860)
Yeatman, Henry C. to Mary Brown Polk 9-1-1858 (9-2-1858)
Yokeam, Thomas to Malinda Hardin 2-17-1865 (2-21-1865)
Yokely, Thomas to Amanda Workman 9-8-1864 (9-19-1864)
York, Coleman W. to Rutha E. McPherson 8-23-1865
Young, Alexander H. to Fannie T. Compton 6-20-1860 (6-21-1860)
Young, Franklin to Senia Craig 9-19-1865
Young, George W. to Mary J. Haley 11-3-1853 (10?-4-1853)
Young, John A. to Melissa Fitzgerald 11-23-1865 (no return)
Young, Joseph T. to Sophia E. Vestal 12-15-1852
Young, Joseph T. to Sophia E. Vestal 12-15-1852 (no return)
Young, William L. to Mary White 5-1-1865 (5-11-1865)
Young, William N. to Sarah L. Gibson 10-1-1863 (no return)
Young, William P. to Mary E. McMeen 6-8-1857 (6-11-1857)
Younger, James C. to Sarah J. Adkinson 1-14-1856 (no return)
Younger, William to Lucinda M. Dodson 10-25-1852
Younger, Wm. to Lucinda M. Dodson 10-25-1852 (no return)
Zeiner, William J. to Sallie R. Alexander 1-17-1866 (1-18-1866)

?, Martha E. to John R. McDonald 9-8-1855 (no return)
Adams, Kizziah to Noah B. Owen 3-30-1864 (4-5-1864)
Adams, Nancy to Chauncey C. Odell 4-19-1865
Adams, Polly to Soloman Edgin 5-22-1856
Adams, Sarah L. to Aaron B. Frank 7-28-1865 (7-29-1865)
Adcock, Joanna to George W. Huntt 10-4-1866
Adkerson, Anna J. to Robert B. McCormack 1-5-1867 (1-7-1867)
Adkins, Amanda J. to William J. Childress 12-29-1853
Adkins, Malinda to David B. Aldridge 10-8-1856
Adkins, Nancy A. to John M. Pilkinton 9-18-1855 (9-20-1855)
Adkins, Sarah D. to Swinford B. Forgy 10-8-1857 (10-11-1857)
Adkinson, Sarah J. to James C. Younger 1-14-1856 (no return)
Adkison, Rachael E. to John M. Sparkman 1-12-1866 (1-14-1866)
Adkisson, Julia A. to John M. Hobbs 12-19-1866 (no return)
Adkisson, Margaret M. to John P. Gilmer 11-6-1854 (11-8-1854)
Adkisson, Mollie E. to William J. Allen 7-29-1861 (7-30-1861)
Agent, Caladonia to Peter Hoosford 9-19-1866 (9-21-1866)
Agnew, Eliza J. to Jasper N. Pinkston 11-25-1857 (11-26-1857)
Akin, Manerva J. to Alfred C. Miller 2-27-1854 (2-28-1854)
Akin, Martha F. E. to William G. Cates 9-22-1857 (9-24-1857)
Akin, Mary J. to Flavius J. Ewing 7-5-1859
Akin, Mary J. to Thomas M. Short 11-26-1857
Alderman, Elizabeth to Henry T. Rustin 5-28-1853 (5-29-1853)
Alderson, Amarintha to James M. Dockery 2-12-1861 (2-21-1861)
Alderson, Catharine to Nathaniel A. H. Thomas 7-11-1853 (7-12-1853)
Alderson, Cynthia A. to Wm. H. Fitzgerald 12-20-1858 (12-24-1858)
Alderson, Josephine to Isacc J. Murphy 10-2-1856 (10-3-1856)
Alderson, Louisa Jane to John B. Skelley 11-4-1865 (11-5-1865)
Alderson, Margaret J. to Michael G. Connelly 12-29-1865
Alderson, Mary J. to William F. Cooper 5-28-1853 (5-29-1853)
Alderson, Mary to William M. Collier 12-28-1853 (1-3-1854)
Alderson, Nancy Jane to William S. Alderson 7-3-1855 (7-4-1855)
Alderson, Sallie E. to James W. Jennings 11-26-1860 (11-27-1860)
Alderson, Sarah Ann to Henry R. White 1-21-1860
Alderson, Virginia C. to James N. McKenzie 12-17-1855 (1-4-1856)
Aldridge, Emely P. to Robert S. Crawford 7-22-1854 (10-29-1854)
Alederson, Sarah Ann to Gustavus Watson 6-23-1855
Alexander, Eliz. A. to John W. Pence 11-22-1864 (11-24-1864)
Alexander, Eliza E. to Mercer Z. McConnico 11-15-1858 (11-17-1858)
Alexander, Golden to James W. Cook 8-12-1865 (8-17-1865)
Alexander, Malinda A. to Andrew H. Buchanan 7-9-1855 (7-10-1855)
Alexander, Martha J. to Elias Rumba 1-7-1857 (no return)
Alexander, Mary R. to Archibald E. L. Thomas 9-17-1863 (9-18-1863)
Alexander, Molly J. to John Milton Burney 12-6-1859 (12-8-1859)
Alexander, Sallie R. to William J. Zelner 1-17-1866 (1-18-1866)
Allen, Elizabeth R. to C. A. Farriss 2-20-1867
Allen, Frances Jane to John T. Holland 7-15-1861
Allen, Henrietta to John T. Hood 8-11-1863 (8-16-1863)
Allen, Margaret to Levan Parish 4-9-1858 (4-11-1858)
Allen, Martha L. to Thompson H. King 10-28-1853 (10-30-1853)
Allen, Susan F. L. to Reddick S. Nickens 4-6-1855 (no return)
Alley, Molley E. to John A. Mackey 2-22-1866
Altmyer, Elizabeth to Peter Bakenbach 10-13-1859 (10-16-1859)
Ament, Mary J. to Charles Lovatt 11-17-1857
Amich, Leemy to George W. Brown 4-7-1864
Amick, Paralee to John A. Brown 2-15-1864 (no return)
Amis, Derinda A. to David S. Maxwell 9-9-1852
Amis, Mary L. to James W. Nance 12-12-1860 (12-13-1860)
Amis, Sarah E. to David C. Scott 9-6-1858 (9-7-1858)
Amis, Talitha C. to Carter H. Witt 1-6-1853
Amis, Zurilda to Rev. Wm. H. Wilkes 12-30-1856 (1-1-1857)
Anderson, Arzilia to Alexander C. Blocker 9-1-1866 (9-6-1866)
Anderson, Eliza to Rolf S. Saunders 3-1-1854
Anderson, Ellen to Thomas Coleman 11-5-1866 (11-8-1866)
Anderson, Fannie W. to Junius F. Tucker 9-5-1866 (9-6-1866)
Anderson, Maria A. to John Trotter 11-27-1856
Anderson, Martha to James Hood 4-12-1861 (4-13-1861)
Anderson, Mary J. to Alexander A. Whiteside 8-4-1859 (8-7-1859)
Anderson, Sallie to George Hunter 10-6-1866 (10-7-1866)
Anderson, Tabitha J. to Josephus F. Hudspeth 1-13-1860 (1-15-1860)
Andrews, Ann to Titus Holmes 3-22-1853 (3-24-1853)
Andrews, Eliza Ann to Francis A. Rhea 1-12-1867 (1-15-1867)
Andrews, Margaret J. to G. W. Robertson 6-10-1854 (6-13-1854)
Andrews, Nancy C. to James A. Wiles 10-16-1852 (10-17-1852)
Andrews, Nancy C. to James A. Wilis 10-16-1852 (10-17-1852)
Andrews, Rutha A. to David F. Bryant 10-16-1862 (no return)
Andrews, Sallie E. to Wm. R. Elam 8-14-1865 (8-16-1865)
Andrews, Sarintha H. to Wm. A. Dobbin 7-22-1857 (7-23-1857)
Andrews, Unis P. to W. J. T. Bills 12-14-1853
Anglen, Jency to James D. Mascko 4-27-1865
Anglin, Susan to James W. Hill 11-1-1855 (no return)
Anris, Derinda A. to David S. Maxwell 9-9-1852
Armstrong, Bettie to C. F. Williams 4-19-1854 (no return)
Armstrong, Mary E. to John Sloan Beecher 2-13-1862
Ashton, M. E. J. to William P. Crews 3-10-1863 (3-11-1866)
Ashton, Mary E. to James C. Smith 12-18-1865 (no return)
Askew, Caroline to Joseph J. Skillington 10-31-1857 (11-1-1857)

Askew, Polly to Luke White 3-2-1857 (3-5-1857)
Ausban, Dovey A. to George W. Wells 7-21-1866 (7-26-1866)
Aydelotte, Levina to Thomas B. Cournell 2-18-1867
Ayres, Helen M. to Robert M. Blackburn 7-26-1861
Babbett, Angeline to J. J. Lantham 3-20-1860 (3-25-1860)
Bailey, Felicia E. to Samuel M. Craig 2-10-1866 (2-11-1866)
Bailey, Marg. Jane to Cornelius P. W. Fitzgerald 5-17-1855 (no return)
Bailey, Mary A. to Wm. G. Duke 1-28-1865 (no return)
Bailey, Mary F. to John Love 12-6-1853 (12-8-1853)
Bailey, Susan H. to Thomas Alexander 10-25-1865 (10-26-1865)
Baily, Mrs. Louisa A. to Dr. Charles C. Crump 6-17-1858
Bain, Harriet E. to John J. McNeely 5-13-1856
Bain, Kissirah J. to John Boman 3-14-1853
Baird, Frances H. to Tyra Noles 4-8-1862
Baker, Darcas to Sparkman Skelley 11-19-1866 (11-22-1866)
Baker, Ellen to John Anderson 10-17-1866 (10-24-1866)
Baker, Lucinda to James H. Cavender 10-10-1859
Baker, Nancy E. to Joseph Cox 12-9-1856
Baker, Sarah M. E. to Oliver H. P. Mullens 4-23-1860 (4-26-1860)
Baldridge, Judtina to J. T. Farney 11-1-1853
Baldridge, Mary to David A. Dugger 12-1-1853 (12-3-1853)
Baldridge, Nannie to Charles S. Webb 2-12-1867 (2-13-1867)
Ballard, Julia to Wm. J. Elam 9-4-1865 (9-5-1865)
Barbee, Sarah to James Stricklin 1-1-1867
Bargain, Catarine to Thomas Donahar 7-31-1858
Barker, Margaret J. to James M. Taylor 7-30-1857
Barker, S. E. to William Brazier 8-5-1852 (8-7-1852)
Barker, Sarah to John Nicholson 12-20-1853
Barlow, Musdora to John W. McKissack 1-26-1865 (2-6-1865)
Barnes, Maria to James Johnson 8-30-1854 (8-20?-1854)
Barnett, Caroline to Levi London 7-29-1862 (not exec.)
Barnett, Jane to Silas L. Veetch 12-7-1861 (12-10-1861)
Barnett, Mariah to George D. Johnston 8-30-1865 (8-31-1865)
Barnett, Mary Ann to Alexander T. Spain 10-30-1855 (10-31-1855)
Barnett, Nancy J. to Robert Dial 7-24-1852 (7-25-1852)
Barnett, Talitha K. to William W. Watson 1-10-1853 (no return)
Barr, Eliza K. to Charles D. Cranford 3-8-1855
Barrett, Mary Jane to Wm. E. Horton 3-13-1859 (no return)
Barrett, Nancy J. to Robert Dial 7-24-1852 (7-25-1852)
Barrick, Ellen to Wm. Henry 1-2-1854
Batin, Sarah to William Hommel 8-3-1852 (8-5-1852)
Baton, Sarah to Wm. Hommel 8-3-1852 (8-5-1852)
Batt, Palatira to Wiley Harris 7-19-1852 (7-22-1852)
Baughan, Lucy A. to Lambert M. Alford 4-23-1859 (4-24-1859)
Bauguss, Alice L. to McCoy C. Campbell 2-7-1866
Bauguss, Sarah L. to A. G. Gill 12-24-1856
Beard, Frances H. to William J. Briggs 6-2-1862 (no return)
Beard, Martha A. to James L. Curry 10-5-1853 (10-6-1853)
Beard, Mary Jane to Jerome Lavender 2-11-1865 (2-16-1865)
Beard, Nancy M. to James H. McKennon 12-11-1865 (12-21-1865)
Beasly, Mary to Silas L. Veatch 12-6-1856 (12-9-1856)
Bell, Ann to Henry Forguson 8-30-1866 (8-31-1866)
Bell, Frances to Andrew J. Boshear 1-23-1867 (1-26-1867)
Bell, Mary Jane to Samuel H. Hines 2-22-1865
Bell, Minerva to Samuel Spencer 9-11-1856 (no return)
Benderman, Margaret A. to Robert P. Lanier 1-12-1858 (1-13-1858)
Benderman, Margaret E. to Robert M. Spain 11-4-1856 (11-6-1856)
Benner, Roxie J. to Wm. E. Dillin 6-10-1864 (6-12-1864)
Bennett, America to James B. Luttrell 11-1-1864
Bennett, Mary to James C. Watson 1-2-1860 (1-5-1860)
Bennett, Nancy Ann to Green Renfro 10-18-1864 (10-20-1864)
Bennett, Sarah to Robert Wright 5-30-1867
Berry, Salley to Monroe Allford 10-10-1867
Bess, Betty to George Hartman 8-23-1859
Bibb, Desdemoa A. to William M. Harbison 12-23-1865 (12-31-1865)
Bigger, Caroline H. to James K. P. Rummage 10-29-1860 (10-30-1860)
Biggers, C. Jane to Robert J. Reed 1-2-1857
Biggers, Margaret L. to David Furlow 11-21-1864 (11-22-1864)
Bingam, Margaret to Lyman B. Mitchell 10-23-1866 (10-24-1866)
Bingham, Laura to William A. Gale 9-15-1856 (9-16-1856)
Bingham, Margaret C. to George W. Blackburn 8-2-1856 (no return)
Bingham, Sarah E. to James W. Padgett 6-3-1857 (6-4-1857)
Binham, Martha E. to William C. Tylor 1-12-1861 (1-16-1861)
Bird, Martha E. to Samuel B. Gardner 9-16-1865 (9-17-1865)
Bird, Mary E. to William H. Watkins 8-8-1864 (8-10-1864)
Birney, Sarah A. to Archabald Glenn 1-5-1853 (1-6-1853)
Bishop, Greskey to Pleasant Purdue 5-11-1852 (5-12-1852)
Bishop, Grishen to Pleasant Purdue 5-11-1852 (5-12-1852)
Bishop, Melissa to Joseph Johnson 9-16-1865 (9-20-1865)
Bishop, Talitha to Levi G. Ballard 3-21-1866 (3-22-1866)
Blackburn, Ann T. to John H. Lochridge 10-20-1856 (10-21-1856)
Blackman, Laura to Martin P. Erwin< 5-6-1852
Blackman, Louisa to Martin P. Erwin 5-6-1852
Blackwood, Nancy A. to Robert M. Wright 12-18-1852 (12-19-1852)
Blagg, Charlotte S. to William H. Harden 7-12-1860
Blair, America P. to Hardin Mayberry 10-17-1859 (10-18-1859)
Blair, Julia E. to James L. Jones 2-15-1860

Blair, Kitty C. to Frederick C. Harmon 2-11-1867 (2-13-1867)
Blair, Mary W. to John W. White 10-13-1866 (10-16-1866)
Blakely, Elizabeth A. to Nathaniel B. Akin 8-18-1852
Blakely, Elizabeth A. to Nathaniel B. Akin 8-18-1852 (no return)
Blakely, Frances J. to Caleb G. R. Nichols 2-16-1852 (2-18-1852)
Blakely, Rachel A. to William L. Harris 12-12-1855 (12-13-1855)
Blanton, Ophelia C. to John W. Parker 10-30-1865 (11-1-1865)
Blanton, Susan J. to Thomas W. Blair 5-8-1866 (5-13-1866)
Bledsoe, Annie E. to Willis C. Jones 9-30-1867 (10-1-1867)
Bledsoe, Medora E. to Samuel T. Brown 1-15-1866 (1-17-1866)
Blocker, Caroline to George W. Lintz 6-3-1861 (6-4-1861)
Blocker, Clarissa J. to Joseph S. Jaggers 1-16-1860 (1-18-1860)
Blocker, Martha to William R. Conner 6-14-1852
Blucher, Caledonia to Gray White 11-14-1857 (11-15-1857)
Boaz, Nancy P. to Peter Williams 12-26-1853 (12-27-1853)
Boaz, Parthena C. to Willis A. Baily 12-1-1855 (12-3-1855)
Boaz, Rebecca S. to Alexander Trimble 11-3-1860 (11-4-1860)
Bobbitt, M. H. to John D. Harbison 9-2-1867 (9-6-1867)
Boles, Jemimal H. to Edmund P. Haywood 3-17-1853
Bolton, Martha J. to James A. Webb 9-24-1857 (9-27-1857)
Bond, Elizabeth M. to R. S. Cook 2-6-1857
Bond, Martha F. to Thomas J. White 4-22-1858
Bond, Martha to Archibald D. Frith 9-17-1856 (9-18-1856)
Bonharner, Nancy to Ferdinand Gabriel 8-4-1864 (8-6-1864)
Booker, Caroline to Nimrod Johnson 12-16-1854 (12-17-1854)
Booker, Eliza C. to John M. Owens 12-23-1865 (12-24-1865)
Booker, Mary T. to B. Drake Clopton 11-25-1858
Booker, Mary to Thomas Jr. Douglass 2-13-1867 (2-14-1867)
Booker, Mrs. Ruth A. to William S. Flemming 2-8-1860
Bordus, Sue H. to Leonidas P.? Kirby 3-21-1866
Boshears, Honor to Jason Boshears 8-31-1861 (9-1-1861)
Bostick, Mary A. B. to A. W. Collier 9-14-1859
Bostick, Mattie E. H. to James C. Murphy 4-14-1860 (4-18-1860)
Bowes, Elvira to James Gunning 9-17-1863
Box, Harriet E. to Samuel P. Kirk 10-11-1859 (10-12-1859)
Box, Mary M. to N. G. Cockrell 3-9-1853
Boyd, Elizabeth Ann to James P. Maben 9-5-1866 (9-6-1866)
Braden, Mary A. to Thomas M. Polk 1-20-1853
Braden, Rosanna D. to Moreen Wilson 10-1-1855 (10-14-1855)
Braden, Sarah to J. D. Hansell 1-11-1858 (1-12-1858)
Bradley, M. A. to Henry H. Fuller 9-6-1865
Bradley, Nancy A. to Anthony M. Toombs 11-22-1853 (no return)
Bradshaw, Elizabeth S. to Lawson W. Stubblefield 9-2-1856 (9-3-1856)
Bradshaw, Martha H. to John G. Horseley 6-12-1861 (6-13-1861)
Bradshaw, Mary Margaret to Curtis Coe Bean 10-16-1864
Bradshaw, Sacha to Edward D. Baker 3-15-1865 (3-16-1865)
Bradshaw, Sallie M. to Osborne P. Nicholson 2-11-1858
Bradshaw, Sarah A. to Thomas Faulkner 7-4-1859 (7-10-1859)
Bradshaw, Sarah to Thomas Faulkner 2-3-1858 (not solemnized
Branch, Frances C. to Lucius C. Garrett 2-17-1865 (2-19-1865)
Branch, Martha E. to Lucius R. Bryant 11-15-1865 (11-16-1865)
Brandon, Henrietta to David Trousdale 9-30-1867 (10-1-1867)
Bratton, Ellen to Walter M. Warren 12-5-1866
Brayman, Ida to Ed White 5-14-1866 (5-16-1866)
Brayman, Mary to Laban Hartly 6-29-1855
Brazier, Corintha A. to Elisha Barker 10-28-1858
Brazier, Fannie A. to Wm. McKinney Dooley 7-24-1866 (7-25-1866)
Bregester, Annie to Marvin L. Eddy 11-13-1865 (11-15-1865)
Brennon, Bridget to John McNamara 8-16-1857
Brickle, C. A. to Samuel H. Pogue 7-22-1867
Brickle, Sidney A. to James T. Brooks 7-23-1866 (7-26-1866)
Bridgeforth, Belinda to Benj. F. McClannahan 4-27-1860 (10-18-1860)
Bridgeforth, S. E. F. to William B. Andrews 12-2-1856
Brien, Helen E. O. to Hugh L. White 3-24-1863 (3-25-1863)
Briggs, Laura C. to Thos. L. Baird 1-7-1861 (ret,not exec.)
Briggs, Maria E. to Henry Carter 9-29-1865 (10-1-1865)
Briggsa, Laura C. to Thomas L. Beard 7-31-1861 (8-4-1861)
Brinn, Rachael J. to James Herring 12-20-1865 (12-21-1865)
Brooks, Adaline to Samuel Wisener 10-1-1853 (10-3-1853)
Brooks, Callie J. to James T. Johnson 9-23-1858
Brooks, Fidelia to Maury O. Roberts 3-19-1857
Brooks, Mary E. to Hugh F. Fariss 4-14-1866 (4-15-1866)
Brooks, Matilda E. to Alexander Stephens 2-23-1857
Brooks, Rebecca to William A. Whittaker 10-31-1865
Brown, Agness to Towns? Christopher 1-1-1855 (1-2-1855)
Brown, Anna to William Sellars 3-12-1867
Brown, Annie M. to Wm. J. Parkes 4-25-1861
Brown, Callie to William Paul 9-23-1867 (12-10-1867)
Brown, Eliza to Joseph M. Bailey 7-2-1866 (7-4-1866)
Brown, Eliza to William Wright 12-31-1864 (1-1-1865)
Brown, Elizabeth to John B. Hendricks 8-29-1866 (9-16-1866)
Brown, Gustavus D. to George W. Fitzgerald 6-23-1852 (6-24-1852)
Brown, Gustavus D.? to George W. Fitzgerald 6-12-1852 (6-24-1852)
Brown, Harriet E. to Pleasant Thompson 11-1-1860
Brown, Jane to John H. Ray 6-8-1864
Brown, Judith E. to John R. Evans 7-20-1865
Brown, Laura A. to John Haddox 3-6-1854 (3-7-1854)

Brown, Louisa A. to John H. Hoy 2-28-1864
Brown, Lucy Ann to Alonzo A. Wilkerson 12-26-1856
Brown, Marian to Thomas J. Dillaha 12-26-1866 (12-27-1866)
Brown, Martha Ann to James Ragan 10-7-1857 (10-8-1857)
Brown, Mary Frances to Lucretus Green 9-17-1859
Brown, Mary Jane to John Gilbreath 3-8-1861 (3-10-1861)
Brown, Mary M. to J. J. Beaty 12-10-1866 (12-25-1866)
Brown, Nancy P. to George S. Sanders 1-24-1860 (1-25-1860)
Brown, Paralee to H. D. Chagle 12-27-1864 (12-28-1864)
Brown, Sue A. to Joseph J. Granberry 11-29-1860
Bruce, Dicey K. to J. R. Birdsong 9-22-1866 (no return)
Brum, Mary J. to Albert A. White 12-9-1854 (12-10-1854)
Bryan, Amanda M. to Robert Teas 3-2-1853 (4-3-1853)
Bryan, Lou B. to Wm. S. L. Neely 11-15-1860
Bryan, Tennessee to William C. McCord 7-11-1857 (7-12-1857)
Bryan, Virginia to James H. Hughes 7-12-1858 (7-28-1858)
Bryant, Lavina L. to Robert H. Moore 4-16-1866 (4-17-1866)
Bryant, Nancy J. to Thomas S. Bryant 3-15-1852 (3-18-1852)
Bryant, Sarah J. to Jackson Rodgers 1-17-1857
Bryant, Sarah to Charles M. Hughes 1-9-1867 (no return)
Bryson, Elizabeth to John L. Morgan 12-21-1853 (12-22-1853)
Bucker, Nancy to Allis Williams 12-17-1856 (12-1856)
Bucker, Yurildia B. to John M. Bright 6-3-1857 (6-4-1857)
Buckner, Henrietta J. to Greenberry Cates 11-30-1857 (12-1-1857)
Buckner, Martha to Joseph Blair 12-22-1852 (12-30-1852)
Buie, Evaline to Samuel Hodge 7-17-1856
Bullock, Arena to James Peavyhouse 11-26-1860 (11-28-1860)
Bullock, Effee to James Cathey 12-3-1861
Bullock, Maggie to Sandy Chappell 12-8-1857 (12-10-1857)
Bunch, Harriet T. to James W. Strange 4-7-1859
Bunch, Mary P. to A. B. Hughs 12-4-1854 (12-7-1854)
Burass, Celia to Ephram Brown 5-22-1852 (5-23-1852)
Burkett, Martha A. to Archibald L. Wright 1-11-1854 (1-12-1854)
Burkett, Nannie E. to Robert A. Vorhies 10-23-1860 (no return)
Burkett, Ruth H. to John G. Atkinson 12-14-1864 (12-15-1864)
Burkett, Sallie to Wm. Kernell 2-4-1867 (2-7-1867)
Burnes, Indianna S. W. to John M. Mulford 5-13-1864 (5-14-1864)
Burnes, Martha J. to Wm. R. Johnson 2-18-1853
Burnett, Caroline A. to Uriah J. Wilson 1-1-1866 (1-2-1866)
Burns, Martha A. to John K. G. Wigginton 9-6-1867 (9-8-1867)
Burrass, Celia to Ephraim Brown 5-22-1852 (5-23-1852)
Burton, Annie E. to Samuel W. Damewood 1-7-1867 (1-9-1867)
Butler, Alzira J. to David McGan? 10-26-1859 (10-27-1859)
Butler, Carolina to John A. Nichol 10-3-1855
Butler, Elizabeth to Thomas P. Hill 3-8-1860
Butts, Amanda to Edmond A. Frazier 10-10-1855
Butts, Amantha to John A. Fraser 3-25-1852
Butts, Paladira to Wiley Harris 7-19-1852 (7-22-1852)
Bynum, Frances J. to Eli Harris 7-13-1853
Bynum, Jessie A. to Wm. F. Holman 2-14-1866 (2-15-1866)
Bynum, Mary A. to Hugh C. Kirf 11-2-1857 (no return)
Bynum, Mary L. to William H. Wood 2-6-1866 (2-7-1866)
Bynum, Polly to John Cooper 4-24-1866
Byrd, Angeline to Jack Robertson 11-24-1865
Byrd, Sarah J. to Renfro Garner 11-3-1852 (11-5-1852)
Byrd, Sarah Y. to Renfro Garner 11-3-1852 (11-5-1852)
Byrum, Elizabeth to James Patton 1-5-1860
Cabler, Lucinda A. to Isaac R. Porter 9-28-1853
Caker, Nancy S. to James A. Gregory 4-18-1857 (4-22-1857)
Calahan, Maria to John J. Baty 8-16-1852 (8-26-1852)
Caldwell, Ann E. to Martin L. Stockard 1-11-1855
Caldwell, Bettie E. to James O. Blanton 4-20-1867 (4-24-1867)
Caldwell, Elizabeth P. to Robert H. Mills 2-3-1853
Caldwell, Frances M. to William J. Woody 2-28-1859 (3-1-1859)
Caldwell, Louisa M. to James H? W. Gibson 9-20-1861 (9-22-1861)
Caldwell, Martha J. to Henry P. Pointer 7-19-1852
Caldwell, Martha J. to John N. Woody 12-17-1856 (no return)
Caldwell, Martha Jane to Henry P. Pointer 7-19-1852 (no return)
Caldwell, Mary E. to Alexander J. Caldwell 8-5-1853 (8-?-1853)
Caldwell, Mary E. to James R. Harris 9-27-1866 (10-2-1866)
Caldwell, Mary E. to Thomas M. Sowell 11-14-1859 (11-15-1859)
Caldwell, Mary M. S. to Perry P. Taylor 10-16-1858 (10-17-1858)
Caldwell, Robina C. to Robert A. Daniel 5-16-1865 (5-18-1865)
Caldwell, S. A. to John M. Terry 5-9-1867 (5-10-1867)
Caldwell, Sarah to Joseph Sr. Peyton 7-19-1855 (7-23-1855)
Callins?, Mary A. to Narman? Baker 12-7-1857
Calvert, Louisa P. to William G. Welch 5-24-1855
Calwell, Narcissa to Wm. Miller 10-18-1855
Cameron, Lucy K. to J. M. Meacham 7-19-1866
Campbell, Cordelia A. to Samuel R. Journey 4-29-1867 (6-20-1867)
Campbell, Eliza H. to Charles G. Scroggin 8-9-1854 (8-10-1854)
Campbell, Frances L. to Asa A. Gresham 3-9-1854
Campbell, Jane E. to James M. Alexander 3-12-1855 (3-15-1855)
Campbell, Martha A. to James A. Jameson 10-30-1865 (11-30-1865)
Campbell, Mary R. to James Wheatly 1-8-1856
Campbell, Naoma A. to T. E. Jameson 1-15-1859 (1-16-1859)
Cannon, Henrietta C. to William F. Wells 1-5-1858 (1-7-1858)

Cannon, M. E. to W. H. Davis 3-25-1857 (3-27-1857)
Cannon, Nancy V. to Elijah N. Moore 9-12-1867
Cannon, Sophia to William T. Autry 1-17-1860 (1-18-1860)
Cannon, Susan C. to Thomas D. Williamson 12-22-1857
Caperton, Mary E. to Wm. T. Edwards 10-1-1866 (10-2-1866)
Carigan, Adaline to Squire H. Duke 10-16-1854
Carigan, Louisa B. to Aaron Aldridge 3-21-1864 (3-22-1864)
Carpenter, Martha C. to Stephen P. Tucker 4-22-1864 (4-28-1864)
Carr, Sue A. to Alexander Johnson 10-30-1866
Carrigan, Cordelia to Benjamin F. Owings 10-11-1865
Carrigan, Eliza J. to George W. Luckett 11-8-1859 (11-9-1859)
Carrigan, Fanney A. to Wiley T. Goad 6-13-1857 (1?-14-1857)
Carrigan, Frances O. to Berry H. Baker 3-2-1866 (3-11-1866)
Carrigan, Lucinda to John H. Dodson 4-27-1861 (4-29-1861)
Carrigan, Martha to George H. Currey 1-9-1867 (1-10-1867)
Carrigan, Mary J. to J. C. Baugh 9-5-1866 (9-7-1866)
Carrigan, Patsey A. to James E. Fitzgerald 1-13-1859
Carter, Caledonia C. to John E. McCain 4-6-1866 (4-12-1866)
Carter, Louisa to George Brown 9-1-1865
Cartright?, Ann to Humphrey C. Hackney 11-15-1866
Casey, Mary J. to James B. F. Dowell 12-26-1866 (12-27-1866)
Caskey, Susan B. to Frederick W. Bain 4-3-1859 (4-12-1859)
Cathey, Alice E. to George W. Stanfield 3-11-1862 (3-12-1862)
Cathey, Josephine to Richard Anderson 7-19-1859 (7-24-1859)
Cathey, Sarah J. to B. M. Dickey 10-4-1866 (10-17-1866)
Cathy, Matilda J. to Eli Oliphant 5-21-1853 (5-22-1853)
Caugham, Sarah J. to James H. Huey 1-12-1853 (1-13-1853)
Caughran, Jane F. to Cannon H. Roberts 12-14-1860 (12-16-1860)
Caughran, Lizzie T. to Thomas C. Adams 2-17-1866 (2-18-1866)
Caughron, Rachel to Wm. Latta 11-18-1854 (11-21-1854)
Caughron, Ruth L. to Jeremiah T. Miller 12-15-1852 (12-16-1852)
Cavender, Mary Jane to James F. Thompson 12-29-1855 (1-3-1856)
Cavender, Millie J. to John W. Rains 8-5-1861 (no return)
Cavender, Sarah S. to James C. Oliver 5-6-1863 (no return)
Cecil, Lizzie A. to John W. Neelley 1-17-1861
Cecil, Marinda W. to James H. Akin 10-31-1859 (11-2-1859)
Cecil, Mary E. to Henry G. Goodloe 10-25-1852
Cecil, Mary E. to John W. Howard 7-19-1865 (7-20-1865)
Chaffin, Beatrice to Charles S. Nichols 1-28-1866
Chaffin, Caledonia to Wm. Young Wiley 7-25-1866
Chaffin, Eliza J. to D. R. Hickman 9-19-1867 (9-20-1867)
Chaffin, Fanney to Marcus L. Barnett 10-26-1863 (10-28-1863)
Chaffin, Martha S. to John B. Watson 1-26-1865
Chaffin, Melissa J. to James A. Mayes 12-12-1860 (12-13-1860)
Chaffin, Nancy C. to Joseph H. Hickman 1-3-1855 (1-4-1855)
Chandler, Caroline to Francis M. Fitzgerald 10-1-1857 (10-2-1857)
Chandler, Mary C. to Gabriel Hammonds 1-20-1864 (1-21-1864)
Chandler, Sarah J. to Thomas J. Roan 1-16-1867 (1-17-1867)
Chaney, Harriet A. to John W. Pillow 11-11-1856 (no return)
Chaney, Henrietta to Andrew R. Gracy 9-25-1867 (9-29-1867)
Chapman, Araminta to Jame T. Ramsey 9-4-1858 (9-5-1858)
Chapman, Mary to Henry Ham 3-4-1861
Chappel, Martha A. to Wm. W. McCormick 7-4-1861 (7-9-1861)
Chchaffin?, Amanda to Thomas B. Selders 9-1-1865 (9-3-1865)
Cheairs, Jennie to A. C. Hickey 10-24-1866 (11-24-1866)
Cheairs, Mary F. to A. M. Bailey 9-3-1866 (9-5-1866)
Cheairs, Nannie R. to Eugene Greenlaw 10-30-1865 (11-1-1865)
Cheairs, Willie B. to James M. Mayes 11-24-1857
Cheatham, Amanda to Isaac A. Holt 9-16-1862 (9-25-1862)
Cheatham, Annie to Robert Saunders 10-25-1861 (10-27-1861)
Cheatham, Eliza A. to Robert Saunders 5-22-1854 (5-23-1854)
Cheatham, Fannie to Lewis S. Scribner 1-15-1866
Cheatham, Judith C. to James E. Bryant 10-14-1856 (10-15-1856)
Cheatham, Nancy P. to Franklin L. P. Wiem 2-1-1854 (3-22-1854)
Cheatham, Nannie P. to J. F. Exum 6-13-1863 (6-16-1863)
Cheek, America P. to Charles R. Rine 12-24-1863 (12-27-1863)
Cheek, Martha E. to Hampton J. Hardison 8-7-1865 (8-10-1865)
Chennault, Lucy A. E. to Joseph S. Mitchell 3-16-1866 (3-21-1866)
Cherry, Josephine to Blackburn W. Gillespie 6-30-1857 (7-1-1857)
Cherry, Sarah C. to James S. Martin 1-16-1855
Childress, Catharine to Lorenzo Stultz 5-3-1865
Childress, Margaret M. to Jonathan B. Stephenson 12-17-1860 (12-18-1860)
Childress, Mary J. to Samuel B. Caperton 8-7-1854 (8-8-1854)
Childress, Sarah S. to Wm. L. Orman 1-12-1853 (1-13-1853)
Chumbly, Elizabeth to Alexander Thomason 8-22-1864
Chumbly, Martha to Calvin Kincaid 4-17-1852 (4-18-1852)
Chumler, Ann Eliza to Israel Thomason 3-27-1866 (4-1-1866)
Chunn, Eliza Ann to John Humphrey McFadden 9-4-1865 (9-7-1865)
Church, Fannie E. to John S. Irwin 9-4-1860
Church, Martha J. to William M. Adkison 11-29-1860
Church, Nancy E. to James Malone 1-24-1854 (1-?-1854)
Church, Nancy J. P. to Peter Maybury 12-18-1856
Church, Paralee E. to S. K. P. Godwin? 7-18-1866 (7-26-1866)
Church, Rachael L. B. to John J. L. Godwin 11-23-1852 (11-25-1852)
Church, Rachel L. B. to John J. S. Godwin 11-23-1852 (11-25-1852)
Church, Selina T. to Jacob G. Sparkman 9-6-1865 (9-7-1865)
Clanahan, Elizabeth to Martin McLain 11-23-1865

Clark, Elizabeth E. to Richard G. Lunn 2-28-1853 (2-29-1853)
Clark, Mariah C. to Daniel J. Isbell 3-9-1864 (3-10-1864)
Clark, Mary A. to William H. Shires 2-21-1853 (2-27-1853)
Clark, Nancy to Vivaldy Bradley 7-19-1856 (7-20-1856)
Clarke, Martha to John Calvin Newcome 9-5-1866 (9-6-1866)
Clendenan, Sarah L. to Robert B. Dodson 4-3-1858 (4-4-1858)
Clendenin, Rachel to McCajah Pope 1-22-1852 (1-25-1852)
Clendennin, Emely to Tristam B. Alfrod 2-20-1856 (2-21-1856)
Clinch, Frances to Beverly R. Dotson 11-16-1858
Clymer, Ann E. to Stephen J. Potts 10-3-1865 (10-6-1865)
Cochran, Arsenith J. to Thomas Maheney 11-13-1866 (11-15-1866)
Cochran, Mary D. to Wm. R. Gresham 12-3-1866 (12-6-1866)
Cockrell, Eliza to Joseph Lee 8-1-1866 (8-2-1866)
Cofer, Elizabeth A. to G. W. Smith 7-4-1865 (7-6-1865)
Coffee, Charlotte to G. P. Wilcoxen 4-27-1854
Coffee, Jane to George W. Pullen 8-26-1867
Coffee, Martha S. to Martin V. West 6-4-1866 (6-14-1866)
Coffee, Sarah Ann to Robert W. Calvert 4-18-1867
Coffey, Elizabeth A. to Alexnader Copeland 9-27-1866 (9-29-1866)
Coffey, Emma to Richard W. Nichols 12-27-1866
Coffey, Emuly H. to Richard Nichols 8-14-1865 (not endrsd)
Coffey, Jane C. to Thomas J. Hobbs 10-30-1852
Coffey, Jane C. to Thomas J. Hobbs 10-30-1852 (11-3-1852)
Coffey, Martha E. to John Hess 10-13-1852 (10-14-1852)
Coffey, Mary L. to Isaiah R. Gilbreath 8-12-1862 (8-19-1862)
Coffey, Mary Luncinda to John S. Green 9-4-1855
Coffey, Nancy C. to Michail C. Rolen 2-12-1852
Coffey, Nancy L. to John H. Douglass 8-29-1853 (8-30-1853)
Coffman, Susan S. K. to Isaac G. Barr 2-9-1852 (2-27-1852)
Colburn, Lou to John A. Orton 11-23-1866 (12-13-1866)
Coleburn, Sarah E. to James H. Smith 4-20-1864 (4-21-1864)
Coleman, Elizabeth C. to Benjamin F. Willis 1-28-1853 (2-3-1853)
Coleman, Indiana V. to Thomas Jones 4-22-1856 (no return)
Coleman, Martha J. to Alexander C. Pewett 10-21-1865 (10-26-1865)
Coleman, Mary Jane to Joel B. Pewett 8-27-1860 (9-2-1860)
Coleman, Mrs. Nancy to T. P. Carter 10-30-1858 (10-31-1858)
Coleman, Sarah C. to George C. Petty 12-22-1866 (12-23-1866)
Colier, Alice to Wm. C. Joyce 12-7-1865
Collier, Lucy E. to Mark L. Wells 9-13-1865 (9-14-1865)
Collins, Catharine to Asa Newcomb 2-6-1865
Collins, Elizabeth to Robert Brown 6-4-1852 (6-6-1852)
Collins, Fannie to Alexander Stewart 3-3-1858
Collins, Malinda to Augustus Bumpass 7-31-1852
Collins, Sarah J. to Joseph H. Derryberry 10-8-1866 (10-15-1866)
Collins, Sophronia to John W. Morgan 6-2-1856 (no return)
Collins, Victoria to Robert M. Johnson 3-3-1858
Compton, Fannie T. to Alexander H. Young 6-20-1860 (6-21-1860)
Compton, Mattie A. to Samuel M. Coffey 12-18-1865 (12-19-1865)
Conkey, Z. to S. H. Thomas 5-24-1852 (5-25-1852)
Conner, Mary W. to S. H. Bratton 2-17-1866 (2-20-1866)
Cook, Ednie A. to F. W. Willis 6-2-1864
Cook, Elizabeth to Jerome Alexander 8-30-1865 (9-3-1865)
Cook, Lizie G. to Henry Clay Brooks 10-26-1864 (10-27-1864)
Cook, Malvina to Andrew J. Haley 11-17-1853
Cook, Mary A. to Pinkney C. Gray 1-14-1852 (1-15-1852)
Cook, Mary E. to Thomas J. Stone 9-12-1860
Cook, Mrs. Sarah to William Hatcher 8-4-1864 (8-5-1864)
Cook, Rause to James O. McMeen 12-1-1866 (12-4-1866)
Cook, Rebecca A. to George W. Haley 11-16-1854
Cooke, Harriet D. to John A. McMeen 11-14-1859 (11-15-1859)
Cooper, Ann Eliza to William R. Cawsey 5-30-1864 (5-31-1864)
Cooper, Lila to Thomas Vaughan 10-7-1865
Cooper, Louisa to Flower George 12-13-1856 (12-14-1856)
Cooper, Martha F. to Isaac Gresham 8-1-1857 (8-2-1857)
Cooper, Mary P. to Fountian D. Hunt 9-2-1855
Cooper, Nancy to Ellis Thomas 8-12-1854
Cooper, Sarah E. to Martin V. Brown 2-2-1865 (3-2-1865)
Coughran, Ruth L. to Jeremiah T. Miller 12-15-1852 (12-16-1852)
Counaster?, Rachel L. to Benjamin A. Sims 4-5-1865
Covey, Sarah J. to Calvin B. Stewart 1-18-1864 (1-19-1864)
Covington, Elizabeth to Charles Holden 9-20-1865
Cox, Caroline M. to Alvis Williams 1-4-1864 (1-5-1864)
Cox, Ellen E. to Henry E. Graham 1-29-1858 (1-31-1858)
Cox, Frances to J. W. Dicus 3-24-1852
Cox, Margaret E. to Wm. B. Howell 4-9-1866 (4-10-1866)
Cox, Mary A. to Samuel V. Perkins 1-11-1864 (1-13-1864)
Cox, Sarah E. to James A. Gibson 10-29-1864 (10-30-1864)
Cox, Sarah F. to Charles W. Harman 5-4-1867 (5-8-1867)
Cox, Sophronia C. to Barclay M. Derryberry 2-2-1864 (2-11-1864)
Crafton, Mary E. to Joshua H. Reames 1-12-1853 (1-13-1853)
Craig, Elizabeth O. to Joseph H. Morgan 12-22-1852 (12-23-1852)
Craig, Elizabeth O. to Joseph H. Morris 12-22-1852 (12-23-1852)
Craig, Elizabeth to Wiley P. Mitchell 5-11-1859 (5-12-1859)
Craig, Josephine E. to Hezekiah Ward 7-22-1852
Craig, Martha J. to Nathaniel W. Grimes 1-24-1852 (1-29-1852)
Craig, Nancy J. to Robert L. Cheek 6-9-1865 (6-20-1865)
Craig, Olivia E. to James M. Morgan 7-20-1852 (7-21-1852)

Craig, Prisc. E. to Reuben E. J. Branch 12-25-1865 (12-26-1865)
Craig, Senia to Franklin Young 9-19-1865
Craig, Volucia B. to Simpson Irvine 1-13-1857 (1-16-1857)
Cranford, Lucinda P. to Wm. D. Jackson 8-27-1859 (8-30-1859)
Crawford, Angeline to Hardin Crawford 5-25-1854
Crawford, Elizabeth to Samuel D. Robinson 2-9-1857 (exec. no date)
Crawford, France C. to James M. Tucker 10-13-1855 (10-14-1855)
Crawford, Isabella C. to Thomas J. Allen 4-8-1861 (not executed)
Crawford, Louisa A. H. to Thomas J. Reeves 4-6-1859
Crawford, Mary Jane to Hillary Wright 12-1-1855 (12-2-1855)
Crawford, Mary to James M. Hiett 8-10-1863 (8-12-1863)
Crawford, Nancy to J. V. Bohananan? 2-14-1863 (2-15-1863)
Crawford, Susan A. to Nathaniel G. Reeves 1-11-1866
Crews, Ann to Wm. N. Demastew 1-19-1867 (1-22-1867)
Crews, Elizabeth L. to Isaac Holt 12-29-1857 (12-30-1857)
Crews, Emily Harriet to Hewlet W. Raines 10-14-1865 (10-16-1865)
Crews, Mary to Nathaniel T. Childrey 11-27-1865 (12-7-1865)
Crews, Nancy C. to Stephen S. Cross 7-19-1860
Crockett, Elizabeth M. to Wm. F. Page 12-20-1865 (12-21-1865)
Crockett, Fannie J. to James T. Rhodes 8-27-1860 (9-2-1860)
Crook, Laura E. to W. H. Nelson 2-14-1866 (2-15-1866)
Crosby, Margaret E. to Edward J. Moore 7-30-1853 (no return)
Cross, Lizzie to Charles A. Douglas 12-20-1865
Cross, Sarah E. to Thomas A. Thompson 11-23-1859
Crowell, Martha E. to Marshall A. Goodman 1-5-1867
Crowell, Sarah to Henry L. Edwards 11-3-1866 (11-4-1866)
Cruise, Julie A. to Albert Childery 12-27-1858 (12-29-1858)
Crunk, Fannie T. to James C. Davidson 4-12-1867 (4-17-1867)
Crunk, Margaret J. to William A. Davidson 9-9-1867 (9-12-1867)
Crutchfield, Eliza to William R. Moore 3-10-1852
Culberson, Mary P. to George W. Jenkins 11-12-1853 (11-13-1853)
Cummings, Nancy J. to Allen P. Luna 3-10-1866 (3-11-1866)
Cundiff, Sarah Jane to Uriah E. Squires 9-15-1856 (no return)
Cunningham, Frances to Sam Booth 7-1-1858
Cunningham, Terecia to Robert Jr. McDaniel 10-2-1858
Currey, Caledonia to Daniel McKennon 1-2-1860 (1-8-1860)
Curry, Jane to John Chambers 8-22-1853
Curry, Manerva A. to James Sellars 8-1-1856 (no return)
Curry, Nancy E. to Robert B. Crowder 7-18-1867
Curry, Sarah Ann to Washington Wright 3-20-1856 (3-23-1856)
Cyrus, Virginia V. to John T. Bingham 11-17-1860 (11-20-1860)
Dale, Frances P. to Lionel Hawkins 5-22-1855
Daniel, Eliza to Jesse M. Owen 10-13-1862 (10-26-1862)
Daniel, Margaret H. to John D. Amis 6-8-1852 (6-10-1852)
Daniel, Margaret H. to John D. Amis 6-8-1852 (6-10-1865)
Daniels, Nancy A. to Jacob Travis 3-22-1865
Dansen (Dawson), Elizabeth to Willis B. Long 11-15-1852
Dark, Rebecca C. to Elijah F. Journey 3-20-1865 (3-21-1865)
Dartch, Mary A. to James H. Leigh 10-13-1853
Davidson, Jane C. to James T. Henderson 6-10-1852 (6-11-1852)
Davidson, Mary E. to H. H. Mooney 2-18-1867 (2-20-1867)
Davidson, Mary L. S. to William H. Leeper 4-1-1852 (4-8-1852)
Davidson, Mary to Jones Thomason 6-2-1863 (4-17-1863)
Davidson, Ophelia to James L. White 9-3-1866 (9-6-1866)
Davidson, Sarah E. to John T. Caskey 9-28-1867 (10-2-1867)
Davis, Alfreda to James Chapman 6-22-1852
Davis, Alzada to James Chapman 6-22-1852
Davis, Amanda E. to John S. Leftwich 12-11-1856
Davis, Augustina to John W. Mullins 2-11-1863
Davis, E. A. to Wm. J. Kinsey 7-31-1861 (8-1-1861)
Davis, Eliza Jane to David W. Nelson 2-9-1859 (2-10-1859)
Davis, Elizabeth R. to George W. Howell 3-25-1852
Davis, Emma to Richard T. Long 8-26-1865 (8-31-1865)
Davis, Esther E. to G. D. Marine 7-16-1867 (7-17-1867)
Davis, Grizilla A. to Newton C. Derryberry 8-3-1866 (8-5-1866)
Davis, Jennie to John W. Lockridge 10-16-1862
Davis, Lucindy to James Brock 6-7-1852
Davis, Martha A. to John H. Grimes 11-14-1853
Davis, Martha H. to James K. Haggard 2-24-1863
Davis, Martha M. to Alfred M. Burney 1-6-1858 (1-8-1858)
Davis, Mary A. to Felix C. Matthews 8-30-1860
Davis, Mary D. to Joseph A. Irvine 9-25-1856
Davis, Mary F. to Wm. J. Johnson 2-28-1862 (3-4-1862)
Davis, Mary Francis to Wm. T. Parker 2-6-1858 (2-7-1858)
Davis, Mary J. to Felix G. Coffey 11-30-1863 (no return)
Davis, Mary J. to Felix Jones 11-30-1859
Davis, Mary S. to Francis M. Crawford 12-3-1856
Davis, Sallie to John M. Ingram 4-21-1863
Davis, Sarah A. to Wm. H. Easom 1-18-1859 (no return)
Davis, Sarah R. to Wm. B. Mitchell 10-30-1865 (10-31-1865)
Davis, Sarah T. to Robert W. Kirkpatrick 1-22-1856 (1-24-1856)
Davis, Susan J. to James W. Cox 1-18-1859
Dawson, Charity A. to John M. Kitrell 5-31-1859 (6-1-1859)
Dawson, Elizabeth to Willis B. Long 11-15-1852 (no return)
Dawson, Martha to Wm. Watkins 1-16-1864 (date unclear)
Dawson, Sarah C. to James H. Notgrass 11-28-1854 (11-29-1854)
Deal, Elizabeth to James Barnett 4-29-1857

Dean, Elizabeth to Samuel W. Grimes 3-9-1867 (3-14-1867)
Dean, Emma to Isaac Daws 4-7-1863 (4-8-1863)
Dean, Nancy to Columbus Hudson 4-15-1867
Delk, Elitha to N. D. Garner 12-8-1866 (not solemnized
Delk, Frances C. to Robert Wylie 1-2-1860 (1-10-1860)
Delk, Talitha to John F. T. Jones 12-29-1866 (12-30-1866)
Denham, Caraline M. to John Cox 10-26-1857 (10-27-1857)
Denham, Lydia M. to Edmund Cooper 8-27-1856 (8-28-1856)
Denham, Mary M. to John A. J. Howard 11-23-1853 (11-24-1853)
Denham, Mary M. to Newton G. Cockrill 12-20-1865
Denham, Nancy Jane to James M. Gilliam 2-19-1866 (3-7-1866)
Denny, Mary E. J. to Henry H. Walters 4-4-1861
Denton, E. J. to John S. Wright 2-11-1865 (2-15-1865)
Denton, Elizabeth A. to Robert C. Jones 12-9-1857 (12-10-1857)
Denton, Fannie E. to Wilson M. Tucker 12-17-1858 (12-22-1858)
Denton, Mary Jane to James Waddell 2-9-1860
Denton, Mary to Joseph Gibson 8-31-1867 (9-22-1867)
Denton, Rebecca to James B. White 2-28-1866
Denton, Sue to Wm. D. Dodson 3-10-1864
Derryberry, Emily O. to John C. Davis 8-8-1865 (9-7-1865)
Derryberry, Lizzie to James M. Wilson 10-2-1861 (10-3-1861)
Derryberry, Permelia J. to James M. Andrews 4-27-1852
Dever, Mary E. to Wm. J. Parten 1-11-1855
Dew, Margaret to Jonas H. Erwin 10-16-1861
Dial, Eliza A. to James P. Dillahay 12-14-1857
Dickerson, Ann T. to David D. McFall 1-13-1864 (1-14-1864)
Dickey, Catharine F. to Moses G. Armstrong 9-13-1854 (9-14-1854)
Dickey, Sarah to James H. Atkisson 8-24-1865
Dickson, E. J. to L. L. Pilkinton 1-19-1867 (1-20-1867)
Dickson, Emma P. to A. F. Johnston 5-27-1865 (6-1-1865)
Dickson, M. E. to James M. Anderson 11-14-1859 (11-15-1859)
Dickson, Malissa E. to William S. Pickard 8-27-1856 (8-28-1856)
Dickson, Margaret to Elisha D. Smith 2-23-1860 (2-26-1860)
Dickson, Sarah to James King 11-16-1857 (11-17-1857)
Dillahay, Sallie to Isham Moseley 12-19-1866 (12-23-1866)
Dillahay, Susan A. to Wm. F. Mitchell 11-27-1860 (11-28-1860)
Dillahy, Louisa to James N. Scribner 2-22-1856 (2-23-1856)
Dillard, M. F. to M. B. Tomlinson 9-8-1852
Dix, Priscilla M. to A. J. Starkey 3-2-1859
Dixon, Nancy M. to Thomas Hanna 9-6-1853
Dobbin, Elizabeth H. to Benjamin F. Stone 11-7-1865 (11-8-1865)
Dobbin, Louisa M. to Wm. N. Hill 10-8-1855 (no return)
Dobbin, Sarah A. to John H. Kittrell 12-14-1854 (no return)
Dobbins, Eve M. to J. B. Borum 1-22-1867
Dobbins, Jessee S. to Daniel A. Davidson 1-15-1861 (1-16-1861)
Dockery, Beckey Ann to Benjamin F. Adkerson 3-5-1866 (3-6-1866)
Dockery, Elizabeth A. to Wm. W. Latta 10-21-1867 (10-24-1867)
Dockery, Mary C. to David Poiner 8-21-1861 (8-22-1861)
Dockery, Melinda to Wm. Poyner 8-30-1859 (9-17-1859)
Dockery, Nancy Ann to Jas. Cinc. Adkisson 12-22-1866 (12-31-1866) *
Dodson, Ann to William Grimes 10-4-1860 (10-5-1860)
Dodson, Elizabeth C. to A. J. Mckee 3-5-1867 (3-6-1867)
Dodson, Elizabeth to Robert R. Dortch 2-8-1854 (2-9-1854)
Dodson, Lucinda M. to William Younger 10-25-1852
Dodson, Lucinda M. to Wm. Younger 10-25-1852 (no return)
Dodson, Margaret E. to Joseph B. McMeen 12-2-1852
Dodson, Margaret to James M. Harbison 10-30-1866 (11-1-1866)
Dodson, Martha K. to Granville Hunter 9-10-1855
Dodson, Mary L. to Felix H. Mayes 12-20-1853 (12-22-1853)
Dodson, Myra to Wm. T. Kincaid 2-9-1867 (2-17-1867)
Dodson, Nancy Jane to Thomas J. Blankenship 10-9-1863 (10-28-1863)
Dodson, Selina to John M. Priest 10-12-1859 (10-13-1859)
Dolan, Mary to Thomas Oneal 12-5-1866 (no return)
Donaldson, Elizabeth to Lewis G. Grimes 11-1-1865
Donaldson, Louisa F. to Wm. M. McKennon 2-8-1864 (no return)
Donaldson, Mary to James P. Hines 12-30-1865 (12-31-1865)
Donaldson, Nancy J. to Andrew M. Ricketts 9-9-1858
Donelson, Martha to William A. Crews 10-25-1858 (10-28-1858)
Dooley, Belle to Sandie Chappell 11-14-1865 (11-16-1865)
Dooley, Cornelia T. to Barrett M. Evans 12-31-1866
Dooley, Harriet J. to Wm. A. Reese 11-13-1865 (11-14-1865)
Dooly, Mary J. to James A. Frierson 12-16-1856 (12-16-1856)
Dortch, Eliz. Jane to Abraham H. Cooper 11-21-1855
Dortch, Nancy V. to Charles C. Irvine 2-7-1865 (no return)
Dortch, Naomi T. to James Watson 9-4-1856 (9-5-1856)
Dorton, Elizabeth to Thomas Clendenan 2-11-1857 (no return)
Dotson, Martha E. to Samuel Skelley 1-12-1859
Douell, Amanda to Allen Adcock 1-20-1855 (1-21-1855)
Douglass, Ellen J. to Ephraim F. Everett 11-17-1857
Douglass, Frances J. E. to John Bendamin 1-2-1860 (1-5-1860)
Dowell, Pheba Ann to Beverly A. Dodson 1-2-1856 (1-24-1856)
Dowell, Sarah J. to Carter J. Booker 9-8-1859 (9-11-1859)
Doxey, Lauretta to James M. Reed 10-4-1854 (10-5-1854)
Doxey, Melissa to John Hall 7-11-1854
Drake, Harriet V. to James McCarroll 12-17-1866 (12-18-1866)
Dugger, Elizabeth C. to Wm. N. Murphey 12-11-1854 (12-12-1854)
Dugger, Mary A. F. to Alonzo Hill 1-25-1865 (1-27-1865)

Dugger, Sarah M. to James H. Hopper 12-18-1862 (12-23-1862)
Duke, Eliza Jane to Wm. H. McIntosh 11-18-1854 (11-19-1854)
Duke, Letha K, to Wm. W. Stephenson 4-6-1865
Duke, Margaret to Benjamin F. Talley 10-12-1853
Duke, Mary Ann to Robert M. Hubbard 9-29-1862 (9-30-1862)
Duke, Mary C. to Anderson J. Roach 5-26-1864 (no return)
Duke, Mary E. to William T. Pennington 2-4-1865 (2-7-1865)
Duke, Mary H. to Thomas Foster 9-30-1856
Duke, Mary to Anderson N. Gibson 6-27-1864 (6-28-1864)
Duke, Mary to George Smally 4-18-1862
Duke, Nancy M. to David W. Johnson 8-1-1854
Dunham, Isabella to Frederick Altmeyer 2-27-1865 (3-2-1865)
Durham, Nancy to John Durham 1-18-1865 (1-26-1865)
Durham, Sarah Jane to Jesse A. Cheek 9-17-1862 (no return)
Dycus, Matilda J. to James W. Denton 11-24-1866 (11-26-1866)
Dycus, Parallee to Elijah Maxwell 6-16-1860 (6-17-1860)
Easley, Elizabeth A. to Rufus L. Garner 9-1-1860 (9-2-1860)
Easley, M. A. to C. M. Smith 4-10-1867
Easley, Mrs. A. J. to John J. Mangrum 4-15-1867 (4-17-1867)
Edgin, Hannah A. to Robert Reed 7-3-1852 (7-4-1852)
Edgins, Celia to Cornelius N. Foster 2-9-1854 (2-12-1854)
Edmondson, Fannie G. to Alphonso J. Armstrong 4-27-1859
Edwards, Martha J. to Thomas H. Edwards 12-6-1865 (no return)
Edwards, Sarah Jane to William R. Cawsey 9-15-1855 (9-16-1855)
Edwards, Silla S. to Henry D. Goodman 1-26-1858 (1-27-1858)
Egnew, Margaret A. to Wm. R. H. Benton 2-23-1853 (3-1-1853)
Ellis, Margaret Ann to John Foster 4-12-1867
Ellis, Sarah Jane to Jesse C. Lassiter 2-8-1865
Ellis, Susannah to John F. Henshaw 3-4-1867
Elmore, Mrs. Eliza Jane to William H. Whitthurst? 3-18-1856
Emerson, Sallie J. to John E. Fox 10-19-1864 (10-27-1864)
Emler, Betsy to Hugh Dicken 11-23-1855 (11-25-1855)
Emmerson, Catharine R. to Wm. B. Lamar 10-11-1859 (10-13-1859)
English, Martha Jane to Samuel W. Akin 11-21-1859 (11-23-1859)
English, Virginia A. to John W. Akin 11-29-1865 (11-30-1865)
Epps, Martha A. to Thomas E. Epperson 4-8-1856
Erwin, Anna E. to Anon T. Vestal 9-6-1853 (9-8-1853)
Erwin, Lucy to John Smith 12-5-1859 (12-7-1859)
Erwin, Margaret E. to John B. Due 11-19-1857
Erwin, Margaret H. C. to George B. Flanigan 9-6-1852
Erwin, Margaret H. to George B. Flanigan 9-6-1852
Erwin, Mary A. to V. N. Thompson 10-19-1854
Erwin, Mrs. Mary B. to John M. Frierson 10-15-1859 (10-18-1859)
Estes, Dillie E. to Ira T. Harris 4-10-1867 (4-11-1867)
Estes, Evaline to George W. Mayberry 1-17-1856
Estes, Hester Ann to Neuton Goad 6-27-1857 (6-29-1857)
Estes, Mary A. to Levi London 10-5-1863 (10-6-1863)
Estes, Mary Ann H. to Benjamin F. Fielder 10-5-1855 (10-7-1855)
Estes, Matt A. to John R. Patterson 10-7-1867 (10-8-1867)
Estes, Mollie to J. W. T. Hilliard 6-22-1863 (no return)
Estes, Viana to Samuel H. Burkett 7-15-1862 (7-16-1862)
Estes, Virginia C. to Benjamin P. Olver 12-21-1861 (12-24-1861)
Estis, Susan to Wilkerson B. Renfro 6-10-1856
Evans, Alice A. to Scott Stephens 11-22-1866
Evans, Darcus L. to Henry Payne 8-14-1865 (9-3-1865)
Evans, Martha J. to Squire H. Timmons 4-8-1864 (4-12-1864)
Evans, Mary B. to James K. P. Timmons 7-13-1865
Evans, Nancy R. to Silvester Finch 7-24-1856 (no return)
Everett, Fannie to David A. Caldwell 3-8-1856 (3-9-1856)
Everett, Narcissa to Richard Thomas Sprinkles 7-18-1864 (7-25-1864)
Eves, Martha A. to William R. Westmoreland 4-18-1853 (4-19-1853)
Fagan, Bridget to James Haley 11-22-1857
Fain, Rebecca to William Shadden 1-27-1863
Faris, Rebecca E. to Thomas E. Butler 6-5-1867
Fariss, Susan to John Wiley 6-1-1853 (6-2-1853)
Farless, Elizabeth to Ira E. Burnham 4-12-1858 (4-15-1858)
Farley, Catharine to Jonathan Amis 11-28-1863 (12-2-1863)
Farmer, Elizabeth to John Adkins 3-16-1854
Farmer, Maria J. to A. J. Baxter 8-14-1866 (8-16-1866)
Farney, Pauline B. to George Greiz 3-17-1857
Farris, Louisa Jane to Henry S. Scott 1-12-1857 (no return)
Farriss, Elizabeth to Alexander E. Patton 10-13-1853 (no return)
Farriss, Margaret Malinda to William M. B. Scott 2-20-1856 (2-28-1856)
Farriss, Martha J. to William Porter 2-9-1854
Fester, Lucinda to David Fargo 5-25-1864 (5-26-1864)
Fielder, Martha P. to William S. Speer 6-21-1853
Fields, Sarah P. to George M. D. Hutchinson 8-14-1865 (8-15-1865)
Finch, Henrietta to George S. Head 10-11-1855
Finch, Martha Ann to Clincey Browning 1-8-1856
Finch, Sarah to Rob. S. Blackburn 11-29-1856 (no date)
Finch, Susan B. to Jesse B. Holly 6-4-1856 (6-5-1856)
Fisher, Martha to Benjamin F. West 5-22-1856
Fisher, Mary to Albert G. Webster 10-20-1853
Fitzgerald, Alabama to Daniel White 8-22-1864 (8-25-1864)
Fitzgerald, C. P. to Thomas A. Walker 8-23-1855 (8-30-1855)
Fitzgerald, Cynthia to Robert Goad 1-27-1858 (1-28-1858)
Fitzgerald, Elizabeth C. to James M. Pigg 1-31-1859 (2-3-1859)

Fitzgerald, Emily N. to Richard B. Hight 12-1-1857
Fitzgerald, Joanna to John Cutran 12-1-1866 (12-5-1866)
Fitzgerald, Johanna to James Hand 10-24-1865 (10-25-1865)
Fitzgerald, Lydia D. to Wm. T. Dodson 2-1-1858 (2-8-1858)
Fitzgerald, Margaret E. P. to Thomas H. Jacobs 4-12-1867 (4-18-1867)
Fitzgerald, Margaret E. to George W. Thompson 4-13-1854
Fitzgerald, Martha D. J. to Samel E. G. Jack 9-30-1854 (10-1-1854)
Fitzgerald, Martha R. to J. A. J. Chaney 4-27-1864 (5-1-1864)
Fitzgerald, Martha to Marion L. Dodson 9-24-1852 (9-25-1852)
Fitzgerald, Melissa to John A. Young 11-23-1865 (no return)
Fitzgerald, Milly O. E. to James H. Woody 8-29-1865 (8-31-1865)
Fitzgerald, Nancy A. to Charles A. Walters 12-18-1860 (12-20-1860)
Fitzgerald, Nancy Jane to Henry C. Wilson 11-22-1864
Fitzgerald, Nancy S. to Jesse Burns 2-22-1852 (1-29-1852)
Fitzgerald, Rosina S. A. to John R. Dortch 12-20-1858 (12-23-1858)
Fitzgerald, Sarah H. S. to George W. Rushton 1-1-1852 (1-2-1852)
Fitzgerald, Sirena P. to W. D. Dodson 6-21-1852 (6-22-1852)
Fitzgerald, Sirena P. to W. D. Dodson 6-21-1852 (6-24-1852)
Fitzgerald, W. Ann to John Adkisson 2-10-1858
Fitzpatrick, Margaret A. to Wm. J. Abernathy 6-29-1858
Fitzpatrick, Nancy R. to John W. Killingsworth 9-29-1857 (9-30-1857)
Fitzpatrick, Rebecca J. to Austin L. Prewett 6-13-1854 (6-14-1854)
Fitzpatrick, Ruth M. to Wm. C. Moore 10-12-1854
Fitzpatrick, Susan E. to Francis J. Moore 1-16-1855
Flanegan, Amanda M. to Joh Todd 9-15-1852
Flanegan, Amanda M. to John Todd 9-15-1852
Flanigan, M. P. to Samuel W. Currey 7-25-1866 (7-26-1866)
Fleming, Ann W. to George M. Kittrell 10-15-1855 (10-16-1855)
Fleming, Florence to Duncan B. Cooper 10-19-1865
Fleming, Frances J. to Samuel L. Yancy 10-21-1861 (10-24-1861)
Fleming, Maria A. to Obadiah A. Jarrett 12-24-1852
Fleming, Maria A. to Obadiah A. Jarrett 12-24-1852 (no return)
Fleming, Mary White to Albert N. Dobbins 10-18-1865 (10-19-1865)
Fleming, Rachel to John H. Roach 12-27-1860 (12-28-1860)
Flemming, Euphemia P. to Edward F. Henderson 7-24-1867 (7-25-1867)
Flowers, Sarah to John s. Crews 8-2-1858 (8-3-1858)
Floyd, J. A. to Samuel D. Sealey 1-18-1865 (1-19-1865)
Fly, M. M. to Fielding H. Baker 12-27-1853 (12-29-1853)
Fly, Malinda C. to William B. Harris 9-3-1863
Fly, Martha L. to William L. Wakfield 4-3-1865 (4-6-1865)
Fly, Mary C. to John N. Jarrett 1-1-1852
Fly, Mary C. to Joshua T. Harbison 10-10-1853
Fogleman, Mary E. to Wm. S. Hurt 6-22-1857 (6-24-1857)
Fogleman, Susan F. to George Saunder 2-25-1853 (3-1-1853)
Fogleman, Susan F. to William T. Almond 12-9-1861 (12-11-1861)
Fonville, Frances E. to John J. Hazlewood 5-20-1854 (5-25-1854)
Ford, Cathrine to Elihu? C. Quaits? 6-27-1866 (6-28-1866)
Ford, Cynthia C. to Hugh Bradshaw 1-21-1863 (1-23-1863)
Forehand, Matilda to Reuben Wright 5-19-1858 (5-20-1858)
Forgey, Caroline to Robert H. Moore 12-20-1855 (12-23-1855)
Forsyth, Mary E. to John L. Johnson 5-29-1863
Forsyth, Sarah E. to James B. Cabler 2-15-1858
Foster, Eliza A. to Flavius J. Journey 2-11-1852
Foster, Fannie E. to James K. Polk 4-8-1861 (4-9-1861)
Foster, Hary S. to William H. Sprott 9-22-1860 (10-3-1860)
Foster, Lau W. to Z. J. C. Waters 10-12-1858
Foster, Lilli R. to J. M. Fry 12-5-1866 (12-6-1866)
Foster, M. L. to Peter R. H. Joyce 3-14-1854 (3-16-1854)
Foster, Mary E. to John W. Worster 10-30-1865 (12-1-1865)
Foster, Mary to Wm. C. Hood 1-7-1861 (1-10-1861)
Foster, Sarah E. to William L. Wilks 6-9-1852 (6-10-1852)
Foster, Sarah to John L. Roach 11-13-1852
Foster, Sarah to John L. Roach 11-13-1852 (no return)
Fox, Huldy to Samuel L. Hardison 10-12-1853 (10-13-1853)
Fox, Martha Jane to Robert Jackson 8-16-1864 (8-18-1864)
Fox, Martha R. to Joseph A. Petty 3-23-1867 (3-24-1867)
Fox, Mary C. to John S. McNight 1-25-1853 (1-26-1853)
Fox, Mrs. Frances to Kinchen Godwin 6-6-1855 (6-10-1855)
Fox, Narcissa to Joseph H. Clymer 12-13-1865 (12-17-1865)
Fox, Ruth A. to David Jones 11-2-1853 (no return)
Fox, Sarah F. to James M. Vestal 5-27-1865 (5-28-1865)
Foxall, Sarah E. to Wm. M. Odil 8-23-1862 (8-24-1862)
Fraley, Agnes E. to James W. Lourance 10-17-1860 (10-18-1860)
Fraly?, Tabitha to John H. Lawless 4-10-1866 (5-12-1866)
Francis, Cornelia A. to Amos W. Warfield 4-11-1854
Franklin, Martha A. E. to William R. (Dr.) Johnston 10-25-1852 (10-26-1852)
Franklin, Martha A. E. to Wm. R. Johnson 10-25-1852 (10-26-1852)
Freeland, Martha J. to James K. P. Parrish 5-16-1865 (5-17-1865)
Freeland, Mary U. to M. G. Cockrill 4-3-1856
Frierson, Cornelia to Thomas N. Jones 10-9-1860 (10-10-1860)
Frierson, Eliza R. to George C. Dixon 12-18-1860
Frierson, Frances J. to Merrill W. Embry 12-16-1854 (no return)
Frierson, Harriet A. to Theodore Frierson 11-28-1860
Frierson, Margaret E. to John A. Engle 11-10-1852 (11-11-1852)
Frierson, Martha P. to Joseph W. Smiser 12-22-1856 (12-23-1856)
Frierson, Mary J. to Walter Akin 6-18-1867
Frierson, Mary M. to Thomas J. Carthel 7-12-1859 (7-13-1859)

Frierson, Mary S. to Robert D. Blakeley 10-18-1858 (10-20-1858)
Frierson, Mary W. to William S. Fleming 1-12-1854
Frierson, Mrs. Mary J. to Claudius F. Barnes 11-15-1859
Frierson, Rebecca M. to Wm. J. Frierson 11-21-1866 (11-22-1866)
Frowly, Judea to John Lanoon 2-27-1858
Fry, Martha A. to Samuel M. Daniels 1-18-1862 (2-9-1862)
Fulks, Mrs. Susan to William Cummons 3-5-1856 (3-6-1856)
Fuller, Nancy Emeline to Joseph Prewett 7-4-1859 (7-5-1859)
Fuller, Sarah A. to Edward Harris 12-10-1866 (12-16-1866)
Fulp, Sarah to George C. Fuller 12-22-1855 (12-23-1855)
Furguson, Elizabeth to Peter Ritter 11-29-1856 (exec. no date)
Furlow, Esther to Abner T. Burpo 7-13-1855 (7-14-1855)
Fussell, Eliza K. to Baxter C. Chapman 2-13-1862
Fuzzell, Sue C. to A. F. Alexander 2-15-1860
Gaither, Eliza J. to Ebenezer P. Alexander 11-26-1866 (11-27-1866)
Gaither, Susan to Alexander E. Hardin 8-27-1855 (8-29-1855)
Galbraith, Mary J. to Robert R. Matthews 3-13-1866 (3-14-1866)
Gale, Mary F. to Oswell Y. Neely 9-7-1861 (9-9-1861)
Galloway, Nancy A. E. to Chas. H. Bieard? 6-25-1866 (6-27-1866)
Gamblin, Amanda to Charles McCrory 3-1-1854
Gant, Virginia C. to W. T. Erwin 12-20-1854 (12-21-1854)
Gantt, Amanda to Johnson Davis 2-19-1861
Gantt, Jennie L. to Thomas E. Alderson 1-3-1861
Gantt, Jinnie to William P. Fields 12-19-1860 (not endorsed)
Gantt, Sarah T. to John Sparks 6-6-1863 (6-9-1863)
Gardner, J. M. to James M. C. Fox 12-17-1860 (12-20-1860)
Gardner, Mrs. Olley to Joseph A. Fox 10-30-1865 (11-2-1865)
Gardner, Parthenia C. to Wm. B. Gray 2-9-1860
Gardner, Rutha to Calvin Beck 3-17-1865 (no return)
Garey, Sarah E. to Ferdinand B. Russell 1-12-1866 (1-15-1866)
Garey, Susan Ann to William J. Mathews 10-23-1867 (10-27-1867)
Garner, Eliza to James L. Sellars 5-3-1852 (5-5-1852)
Garner, Eliza to James L. Sellers 5-3-1852 (5-5-1852)
Garner, Margaret Ann to Wm. M. McMannus 9-20-1854
Garner, Mary to John Donly 4-7-1862
Garner, Susan E. to Jessee Turner 10-24-1853 (10-25-1853)
Garnett, Sarah Jane to Wm. B. Morton 2-18-1867
Garrett, Frances J. to William R. Mathews 11-12-1858 (11-16-1858)
Garrett, Mary E. to G. W. Daugherty 4-24-1854 (4-25-1854)
Garrett, Mary J. to David Walrup 2-9-1857 (2-10-1857)
Garrett, Mary to William D. Williams 1-27-1854 (1-29-1854)
Garrett, N. J. E. to G. J. House 11-21-1860 (11-22-1860)
Garton, Mary A. to Leroy Pennington 6-18-1852 (6-20-1852)
Garton, Nancy to Wm. J. McKennon 11-27-1856
Gaskill, Drucilla to George C. Dixon 12-1-1853
Gates, Rebecca J. to Wm. C. Gray 3-22-1859
Gault, Eudora to Rufus Puckett 12-30-1857 (no return)
Geasley, Louisa to Lucius A. Sanders 4-5-1867
Gee, Cornelia C. to John J. Fleming 9-27-1855 (no return)
Gell, Nannie T. to Albert G. Woodward 12-27-1866
Gibson, Elizabeth M. to William P. Grines 7-14-1854 (7-16-1854)
Gibson, L. Hannah to George M. McKissack 10-9-1865 (10-12-1865)
Gibson, Margaret Ann to George W. Burpo 8-1-1855 (8-2-1855)
Gibson, Martha Ann to George Denton 4-9-1867
Gibson, Mary Ann to Luke Huggins 8-29-1859
Gibson, Rachal to William P. Grimes 7-30-1853 (7-31-1853)
Gibson, Rebecca E. to Thomas J. Small 5-3-1859 (5-4-1859)
Gibson, Sarah F. to William E. Cox 9-29-1864
Gibson, Sarah F. to Wm. E. Cox 9-27-1864 (no return) *
Gibson, Sarah L. to William N. Young 10-1-1863 (no return)
Gidwin, Martha A. to Wilie Jones 9-25-1861 (9-26-1861)
Gilbreath, Manerva E. to Benjamin M. Tarpley 2-5-1855 (2-8-1855)
Gilbreath, Martha Jane to William Armstrong 3-2-1858
Gilbreath, Mary J. to William D. Bendermand 12-20-1864 (12-27-1864)
Gilbreath, Nancy J. to William M. Cannon 12-9-1854 (11?-10-1854)
Gill, Mrs. Rachel J. to Algernon Barr 12-5-1855
Gill, Sarah E. to George A. Bullard 7-12-1865 (7-13-1865)
Gillespie, Fannie A. to John C. Gordon 10-26-1865
Gillespie, Susan E. to Simpson H. Irwin 5-12-1864 (5-17-1864)
Gillian, Amanda J. to James P. Journey 1-27-1865 (1-29-1865)
Gilmer, Ann Jane to William R. Walker 7-26-1859 (7-27-1859)
Gilmer, Mary E. to Homer R. West 9-10-1860 (9-11-1860)
Gilmore, Louisa to David Holden 7-2-1866 (7-19-1866)
Gist, Margaret to William J. Caldwell 4-10-1860 (4-12-1860)
Gist, Nancy J. to Thomas J. Caldwell 9-27-1859 (9-29-1859)
Givens, Mary E. to William Marshall 5-28-1867 (5-25?-1867)
Glenn, Bettie T. to Robert J. Fleming 6-17-1867 (6-18-1867)
Goad, Louisa J. to Daniel J. Hubble 12-6-1858
Goad, Martha to George W. Lucas 11-14-1853 (11-13?-1853)
Goad, Mary M. to Samuel M. Craig 4-7-1865
Goad, Sarah E. to James H. Pewett 7-18-1866
Goad, Virginia to Francis Journey 7-17-1867 (7-18-1867)
Godwin, Martha Jane to Rufus P. Fitzgerald 2-1-1858 (2-3-1858)
Godwin, Nancy C. to William M. Goad 12-8-1866 (12-9-1866)
Goff, Eliza P. to Johnston Trousdale 6-2-1856
Gooding, Eliza to Nathaniel Holman 11-27-1862
Goodloe, Virginia C. to George W. Strother 6-15-1858 (exec. no date)

Goodrich, Martha L. to John R. Thompson 10-16-1861 (10-17-1861)
Goodrum, Margaret E. to Dewitt C. Hanna 1-17-1854
Goodrum, Martha V. to Wiley T. Perry 3-14-1862 (3-16-1862)
Goodrum, Molly A. to Robert H. Maxwell 9-30-1856
Gordon, Manerva to James H. Green 7-2-1854 (no return)
Gracy, Sarah D. to Alexander W. McDaniel 8-18-1865 (8-21-1865)
Gracy, Tina A. to John A. Lowry 4-30-1867 (5-2-1867)
Graham, Margaret to William Simmons 8-14-1861
Graham, Sarah C. to James M. Pogue 9-3-1852 (9-5-1852)
Granberry, Annie M. to Rufus C. Jackson 12-20-1860
Granberry, Martha L. to Robert A. F. Duncan 7-24-1856 (7-28-1856)
Grant, Emily A. to Joshua Goad 6-15-1853
Grant, Mary E. to James H. Welch 2-6-1867 (2-7-1867)
Grantt, Nettie F. to B. F. Robinson 11-5-1866 (11-6-1866)
Graves, Alesey J. to James N. Cram 10-12-1858
Graves, Elmyra J. to James Aldridge 5-20-1865 (no return)
Graves, Emily C. to Charles L. Bailess 3-21-1866 (3-22-1866)
Graves, Mary A. to Thomas A. Laniere 2-8-1866 (2-9-1866)
Gray, America to Harvey H. Hill 1-30-1865 (2-2-1865)
Gray, Cynthianna to M. M. Harris 1-6-1859 (1-9-1859)
Gray, Eliza K. to Thomas M. Graves 9-1-1854 (9-2-1854)
Gray, Elizabeth to Absalom F. Johnstone 2-22-1853
Gray, Elizabeth to William R. Massey 10-4-1866 (10-7-1866)
Gray, Julia to John L. Johnson 5-22-1856 (5-23-1856)
Gray, Martha J. to James M. Harris 2-21-1852 (2-22-1852)
Gray, Nancy J. to Robert S. Elam 2-5-1866 (2-8-1866)
Gray, Olly L. to Andrew Garnder 4-3-1858 (4-7-1858)
Gray, Sarah C. to Wm. H. Pigg 2-19-1866 (2-25-1866)
Gray, Sarah D. to Alfred Gardner 9-24-1858 (10-31-1858)
Grean, Margaret to Caleb T. Voucher 12-31-1863
Green, Betsey Jane to Henry William Davis 12-23-1865
Green, E. J. to John L. Turnbow 8-20-1861 (8-22-1861)
Green, Eliza F. to John D. Miller 10-19-1859
Green, Elizabeth A. to John Aigius? 2-13-1854 (no return)
Green, Elizabeth to William C. Beard 7-3-1855 (no return)
Green, Emily C. to Dr. Joseph B. Moon 10-31-1855
Green, Harriet Ann to Wm. W. Watkins 11-1-1859
Green, Lavina W. to James H. Parrish 4-9-1860
Green, Lucretia to Henderson Embler 1-15-1857 (no return)
Green, Nancy Ann to William Beales 3-29-1855 (no return)
Greener, Matilda to Charley B. Wolf 10-28-1857 (10-29-1857)
Greenhorn, Catharine to Felix G. Coffey 2-28-1866 (3-1-1866)
Greer, Catharine Mahala to Wm. Hood 3-7-1859 (no return)
Gresham, Jane W. to A. S. Bryant 1-8-1855 (1-11-1855)
Gresham, Mary W. to John A. Coffey 11-21-1865
Gresham, Nannie S. to John A. Coffey 2-3-1862 (2-4-1862)
Griffin, Elizabeth to Theodore S. Speed 10-17-1867
Griffin, Leoticy to Fountain Scott 8-25-1852 (8-26-1852)
Griffith, Martha A. to John H. Marks 4-18-1866 (4-19-1866)
Grigg, Catharine to Thompson Greer 12-19-1856 (no return)
Grigg, Mary A. to Isom Reynolds 2-21-1852 (2-22-1852)
Grimes, Amelia E. to A. B. Moore 12-19-1866 (12-20-1866)
Grimes, Elizabeth to Charles D. Cooper 1-10-1853 (1-11-1853)
Grimes, Ellen J. to Elisha A. Brooks 9-4-1866 (9-6-1866)
Grimes, Jennie C. to Levi A. Nichols 9-8-1860 (9-4?-1860)
Grimes, Mary Ann to John Williamson Akin 8-18-1856 (8-19-1856)
Grimes, Mary E. to John Gibson 8-13-1857 (no date)
Grimes, Tennessee E. to George W. Pearson 8-25-1857 (8-26-1857)
Grimmett, Roxana A. E. to Newton J. Anderson 8-9-1867 (8-14-1867)
Grines, Martha A. to Isaac P. Grines 1-1-1855 (1-2-1855)
Grisham, Margaret to Lewis Masker 12-4-1852
Grisham, Margaret to Lewis Masker 12-4-1852 (no return)
Groves, Mrs. Emily to Peter Crowell 3-22-1866
Guarnell, Elizabeth to H. D. Ragan 8-5-1865 (8-10-1865)
Guest, Addie A. E. to Hiram L. Hendley 1-29-1861
Guin, Jinsey L. to Joseph W. Atkin 1-31-1867
Gullett, Mary G. to Ira Hardison 11-29-1862 (12-4-1862)
Gunnell, Maria D. to James W. Stamps 8-4-1854 (8-5-1854)
Gwinn, Mary E. to John Campbell 12-13-1854 (12-17-1854)
Hackney, Abbie E. to Charles L. Reynolds 4-16-1863
Hackney, Fannie to Jordan M. Hunter 12-25-1865
Hackney, Lucinda E. to William E. Bigger 3-8-1867 (3-10-1867)
Hackney, Mary C. to Sims Latta 11-10-1860 (11-11-1860)
Hackney, Mary E. to William F. Bendamin 8-22-1859 (8-25-1859)
Hackney, Sarah J. to James C. Rickman 7-13-1867 (7-14-1867)
Hadley, Caroline to Thomas F. McMeen 6-30-1852 (7-1-1852)
Hadley, Manerva A. to Moses S. Thompson 11-12-1853 (11-13-1853)
Hain, Eliza to Wm. King 7-8-1865 (7-9-1865)
Hair, Emely to C. D. Aydolette 3-9-1861 (no return)
Hale, Cordelia to Robert M. Speed 10-27-1855 (10-28-1855)
Hale, Cynthia M. to Joseph M. Williamson 1-12-1855 (1-13-1855)
Hale, Nancy E. to J. E. Thomason 7-6-1865 (9-28-1865)
Hales, Maria J. to Junius A. Wilson 2-19-1865
Haley, Ava E. to Peter White 5-23-1866
Haley, Laura B. to James K. P. Davis 8-6-1867 (8-8-1867)
Haley, Mary B. to Charles W. McBride 3-11-1861 (no return)
Haley, Mary J. to George W. Young 11-3-1853 (10?-4-1853)

Haley, Mary to William L. Begly 3-9-1857
Haley, Milley Ann to William L. Bagley 9-13-1854 (9-14-1854)
Hall, Ann to F. S. Hall 10-3-1855 (no return)
Hall, Eliza M. to Wootson D. Davis 8-29-1855
Hall, H. Francis to Abraham Gregory 12-19-1853 (no return)
Hall, Izora to John L. Branden 3-16-1852
Hall, Malinda to Martin Doxey 10-17-1855 (10-18-1855)
Hall, Margaret to David S. Black 5-22-1865 (5-23-1865)
Hall, Martha A. to Samuel D. White 7-15-1863
Hall, Susan to L. L. Sykes 6-30-1862 (7-1-1862)
Hall, Susan to Wm. J. Renfro 9-16-1856 (9-17-1856)
Haly, Harriet L. to Joshua M. Reams 8-28-1856
Ham, Mary E. C. to W. F. Guest 4-18-1854 (4-19-1854)
Hamilton, Emeline to Michael Linch 5-26-1866 (5-27-1866)
Hamilton, Susan S. to James S. Perry 1-25-1853 (10-26-1853)
Hammer, Virginia A. to George W. Hammer 10-5-1858
Hammond, Irene to Thomas B. Williams 11-27-1865 (11-28-1865)
Hammonds, Martha to Wm. Murphey 5-27-1862 (5-29-1862)
Hammox, Sarah to William F. Chapman 4-27-1866 (4-29-1866)
Hamner, Lulie M. to Charles F. Collins 2-10-1857 (2-11-1857)
Hamner, Matte to Robert H. Redwood 3-27-1855
Hand, Mary to Patrick Sullivan 1-1-1859 (1-2-1859)
Handy, Maria L. to Edward M. Crutcher 2-11-1854
Hankins, Parthenia E. to John S. Edwards 12-24-1861 (12-26-1861)
Hanks, Mary J. to Wm. T. Nevils 6-21-1865 (6-22-1865)
Hanna, Margaret Ann to John B. Galloway 12-19-1855 (12-20-1855)
Hanna, Martha E. to James F. Gracey 12-12-1864 (12-13-1864)
Hanna, Mary H. to Wm. L. Henderson 4-25-1861 (4-26-1861)
Hanna, Sarah J. to William C. Hart 10-24-1854 (10-25-1854)
Harbison, Darcus J. to John A. Baker 1-11-1858 (1-17-1858)
Harbison, Dorcas A. to Alexander Harbison 8-16-1854
Harbison, Dorcas E. to John E. Tate 10-3-1860 (10-11-1860)
Harbison, Mary A. E. to Thomas J. Priest 11-13-1861 (11-14-1861)
Harbison, Mary to John Henry Litton 9-21-1865
Harbison, Orena Ann to James Erwin 11-19-1855 (11-22-1855)
Harbison, Sarah E. to Perry T. Lock 2-24-1864 (2-26-1864)
Harbison, Sarah M. to George W. Baker 10-9-1860 (10-14-1860)
Harbison, Susan Catharine to Samuel S. Woody 8-27-1864 (8-31-1864)
Hardeman, Mary H. to Wm. H. Lee 12-7-1858 (12-8-1858)
Hardgraves, Mary E. to Thomas H. Caperton 7-18-1853 (7-22-1853)
Hardin, Allice M. to Isaac B. Hawley 12-24-1858 (12-27-1858)
Hardin, America P. to George H. Blair 4-20-1852 (5-4-1852)
Hardin, Elizabeth A. G. to George W. Maybury 4-30-1860 (5-1-1860)
Hardin, Louisa H. to Thomas J. Patterson 10-10-1856 (10-15-1856)
Hardin, Malinda to Thomas Yokeam 2-17-1865 (2-21-1865)
Hardison, Eliza A. to Robert W. Tindle 11-3-1866 (11-4-1866)
Hardison, Elizabeth to Sherrod Liggett 10-3-1853
Hardison, Eudora D. to James K. P. Sowell 9-11-1861
Hardison, Eugenia F. to Wm. A. Derryberry 12-19-1865 (12-24-1865)
Hardison, Malissa E. to James D. Derryberry 9-1-1856 (9-3-1856)
Hardison, Margaret D. to John D. Amis 10-19-1854
Hardison, Margaret E. to James H. Morton 3-21-1864 (3-22-1864)
Hardison, Margaret S. to James M. Patterson 6-4-1859 (6-5-1859)
Hardison, Mary Ann to Jesse Cheek 5-4-1859 (5-5-1859)
Hardison, Mary C. to Robert H. Hardison 9-25-1855 (no date)
Hardison, Minerva W. to John C. Montgomery 11-20-1865 (11-22-1865)
Hardison, Mrs. Nancy C. to James P. Daniel 1-24-1866 (1-25-1866)
Hardison, Sarah E. to John C. Liggitt 12-22-1852 (12-23-1852)
Hardison, Victoria to John M. Nicholson 6-15-1865 (6-29-1865)
Hardwicke, Frances H. to Richard B. Jones 10-10-1860
Hargolty, Julia to Patrick OConnor 10-4-1858
Hargrove, Lydia to Henry Kingcade 11-25-1854
Hargrove, Nancy to Thomas S. Chumbly 11-1-1855 (11-4-1855)
Hargrove, Sarah J. to Alexander Dooley 10-27-1865 (10-29-1865)
Hargrove, Sarah to John Burditt 1-6-1865 (1-7-1865)
Hargrove, Sarah to Joseph A. Rumage 11-22-1855
Hargrove, Susan to Joseph Ruage 2-13-1854 (2-14-1854)
Harlan, Amanda B. to Arch Lipscomb 5-15-1861 (5-16-1861)
Harmon, Juda A. to James N. Chumbly 2-29-1864 (3-1-1864)
Harris, Elizabeth to Riley McDaniel 9-7-1859 (9-11-1859)
Harris, Ellenor to William C. Sellars 1-2-1856
Harris, Emma J. to Nathaniel P. Wilborn 12-9-1856 (12-10-1856)
Harris, Frances N. to Napoleon King 2-16-1858 (2-17-1858)
Harris, Hannah A. to James K. P. Andrews 4-22-1864 (no return)
Harris, Martha Ann to William D. Frazier 5-6-1859
Harris, Martha Olivia to Johnson Long 12-6-1865 (12-7-1865)
Harris, Martha to Leonidas Neal 12-20-1853 (12-22-1853)
Harris, Mary to John Duram 8-16-1859
Harris, Nannie E. to Michael P. Andrews 6-13-1865 (6-15-1865)
Harris, O. J. to David Harris 5-24-1867 (6-2-1867)
Harris, Paulina L. to Wm. A. Griffin 6-2-1866 (no return)  .
Harris, Rena to J. C. Henderson 7-12-1865
Harris, Roena to Robert N. Moore 4-28-1858 (4-29-1858)
Harris, Salina to Edward Harris 12-30-1852
Harris, Sallie Lee to James H. Gray 10-22-1867 (no return)
Harris, Sarah E. to Richardson Haywood 5-4-1864
Harrison, Margaret M. to James D. Blair 5-3-1861 (5-12-1861)

Harrison, Sallie E. to Andrew H. Kerr 11-9-1858 (exec. no date)
Hart, Elizabeth to James Bigham 10-18-1852 (10-21-1852)
Hart, Elizabeth to James Bigham 10-18-1852 (no return)
Hart, Evaline A. to Alexander Bingham 11-24-1859
Hart, Kate C. to John E. Meadoncraft 2-13-1861 (2-14-1861)
Hart, Rachael to David F. Brown 11-27-1865 (no return)
Hart, Susan M. to Wm. H. Dodson 5-20-1853 (5-22-1853)
Hashbarker, Jane to William Shake 5-16-1867
Hassell, D. M. to J. H. Carothers 8-17-1859
Hastings, M. H. to F. A. Mayes 12-6-1865 (12-8-1865)
Hatcher, Louisa C. to Jesse S. McClain 6-23-1858 (no return)
Hauser, Johanah Amelia to John F. Howser 12-30-1857 (exec. no date)
Hawkins, Rowena to George L. Grimes 10-12-1854 (no return)
Hayes, Eliz. L. to Pervinus Jr. Fox 10-2-1856
Hayes, Eliza A. to John F. Bracheen 9-23-1863
Hayes, Jane Virginia to Edward F. Lee 12-26-1854
Hayes, Maria Naomi to Wm. E. Moore 12-18-1864
Haynes, Mary A. to Albert G. Thomas 2-17-1853
Haynes, Mary Jane to J. A. Andrews 10-22-1853 (10-25-1853)
Hays, Mary L. to William M. Crutcher 3-5-1866 (3-20-1866)
Haywood, Elizabeth to Elis Harris 12-22-1859
Haywood, Jane to William Harris 12-8-1859
Haywood, Lucy C. to Joel Goad 9-4-1865 (9-12-1865)
Haywood, Martha to Edward Harris 4-3-1858 (4-4-1858)
Haywood, Mary Ann to Richardson Haywood 1-4-1858 (1-14-1858)
Hedge (Hodge), Sarah A. to Andrew Moore 4-13-1852
Hedpeth, Emeline to John P. Taylor 10-8-1864 (10-9-1864)
Helm, S. Poca to Adam R. Halls 10-11-1854 (10-12-1854)
Helm, Sallie P. to John G. Anderson 3-11-1861 (8-18-1861)
Henderson, Annie to James B. Scott 11-21-1866 (11-22-1866)
Henderson, Fannie to Henry B. Davis 11-21-1866 (11-22-1866)
Henderson, Harriet E. to Calvin L. McConnell 1-18-1859 (1-19-1859)
Henderson, Mary Jane to Rufus Thomas 10-30-1856
Henderson, Nannie J. to Wm. M. Price 9-8-1865 (9-12-1865)
Henderson, S. A. to J. E. Barnes 1-6-1854 (1-10-1854)
Henderson, Sarah J. G. to Addison H. Spain 3-13-1854
Hendley, Mary C. to Joshua G. Bailey 3-7-1859
Hendricks, Sarah to Sylvang Gardner 11-21-1857 (11-22-1857)
Hendricks, Sarah to Thomas Worsham 4-15-1864 (4-16-1864)
Henley, Mary J. to John W. Harris 3-26-1866 (3-25?-1866)
Heralson, Martha to Robert Watson 12-20-1866 (12-23-1866)
Hereford, Eliza to Thomas Clark 11-19-1855 (12-31-1855)
Herrington, Mary A. M. to Henry Gaskill 7-25-1853 (7-26-1853)
Hervey, Nancy A. to James A. Ford 3-10-1865
Hewdly, Margaret Ann to James N. Mangrum 9-12-1857 (9-13-1857)
Hewett, Martha J. to George R. Williamson 11-13-1854 (11-14-1854)
Hickman, Edy A. to Zebulan A. Murphey 6-8-1861 (6-9-1861)
Hickman, Martha Jane to James H. Foster 10-18-1866
Hicks, Catherine T. to Joseph J. Moore 2-28-1852 (2-29-1852)
Hicks, Nancy A. to Charles N. Smith 9-3-1860 (9-4-1860)
Hicks, Sarelda M. to Thomas P. Smith 12-14-1858 (12-15-1858)
Higdon, Paralee to John Warden 8-17-1860 (8-19-1860)
Hight, Naomi J. to William B. Walters 1-23-1864 (1-24-1864)
Hill (Mary J.?), Emily J. to James W. Hudson 1-18-1854 (1-19-1854)
Hill, Amanda C. to Jesse B. Hill 5-3-1865 (no return)
Hill, E. C. to Robert Cross 3-15-1855
Hill, Elizabeth P. to John V. McKibbin 11-29-1854 (11-30-1854)
Hill, Georgia Ann to G. B. McKennon 9-17-1866 (9-19-1866)
Hill, Harvey H. to America Gray 1-30-1865 (2-2-1865)
Hill, Jennie Ann to William E. Daugherty 3-26-1866
Hill, Louisa M. to David C. Brown 10-3-1859 (10-4-1859)
Hill, Manerva A. to James A. Sparkman 10-19-1854
Hill, Margaret A. to Thomas H. Henderson 2-5-1866 (2-7-1866)
Hill, Margaret E. to Joseph A. Vestal 1-5-1853 (1-6-1853)
Hill, Margaret F. to Benjamin F. Turner 12-11-1865 (12-13-1865)
Hill, Martha J. P. to James F. Henderson 4-28-1859
Hill, Mary J. to James Y. Sellars 5-2-1853
Hill, Mary to John Day 7-29-1865 (7-30-1865)
Hill, Permelia R. to Robert W. Andrews 2-28-1867
Hill, Rebecca to Christopher B. Hadly 6-18-1856
Hill, Sallie E. to E. T. Murphey 10-9-1867 (10-10-1867)
Hill, Sarah A. to John N. Swan 3-15-1858 (3-17-1858)
Hill, Sarah W. to Andrew D. Bryant 1-3-1852 (1-4-1852)
Hill, Susan to Rily H. Nickens 12-27-1856 (21-28-1856)
Hilliard, Mrs. Mary E. to Clark M. Comstock 12-13-1858  *
Hilliard, Sarh M. to Robert H. Jamison 10-31-1855
Hines, Frances J. to Elijah J. Forsche 7-31-1865
Hines, Frances S. to N. W. Currey 6-18-1867 (6-20-1867)
Hines, Jinsy to Robert Potts 6-20-1866 (6-24-1866)
Hines, Martha to John W. Pogue 7-3-1858 (7-4-1858)
Hines, Mary Jane to John A. Love 3-13-1867 (3-14-1867)
Hines, Medea Ann to Joseph Chambers 10-13-1855 (10-16-1855)
Hines, Sarah C. to Josiah H. Loftin 3-31-1865 (not endrsd)
Hines, Tennessee to Frank O. Potts 12-21-1866 (12-23-1866)
Hinson, Harriet to J. F. Jeffreys 7-3-1865 (7-23-1865)
Hinson, Nancy J. to Lawson Isbell 7-30-1859 (7-31-1859)
Hobbs, Martha E. to Newton A. Thompson 11-21-1866

Hobson, L. W. H. to John R. Smith 12-19-1857 (12-20-1857)
Hobson, Lucy C. to Curtis Hooks 1-1-1854
Hobson, Lucy to George W. Batton 3-19-1853 (no return)
Hodge, A. G. to Wilson E. Richardson 1-6-1863 (1-7-1863)
Hodge, Amanda A. to Charles Clear 2-6-1860 (3-8-1860)
Hodge, Louisa Jane to Marcus L. Martin 10-1-1862 (10-2-1862)
Hodge, Mary E. to Thomas J. Pickett 9-19-1865 (9-20-1865)
Hodge, Virginia E. to Edmond A. Oneel 12-23-1862
Hodge, Virginia E. to Edward A. Oneill 2-16-1861 (3-20-1861)
Hoffman, Matilda E. to Nicholas Schlimmer 12-20-1855
Hogan, Annie E. to Noah R. Morrow 9-19-1855
Hogan, Cynthia J. to James M. Mitchell 12-27-1865 (12-28-1865)
Hogan, Mary A. to W. B. Fry 9-4-1866 (9-5-1866)
Hogan, Nancy to Noah S. Hickman 8-19-1858
Hogans, Margaret to Henry H. Fry 11-30-1865 (12-7-1865)
Hoge, Mary E. to John W. Terass 11-1-1852 (no return)
Hoge, Mary E. to John W. Terass 11-15-1852
Hogwood, Helen W. to Joseph D. Runions 8-29-1861
Hogwood, Victoria B. to John W. Fotty 9-25-1866 (9-30-1866)
Holcem, Catharine to Marshall Johnson 6-26-1852 (6-27-1852)
Holcomb, Nancy to Wm. Holcomb 2-15-1854 (2-19-1854)
Holcum, Catherine to Marshall Johnson 6-26-1852 (6-27-1852)
Holden, Callie to Alfred Cathey 8-29-1864 (9-1-1864)
Holden, Laura to George Garner 11-4-1865 (11-5-1865)
Holden, Mary E. to John Cothran 11-4-1864 (11-6-1864)
Holden, Mary Jane to John H. Farley 5-3-1852
Holden, Mary to Alexander Cathey 2-28-1867
Holden, Sallie to John M. Lyles 5-19-1864 (5-22-1864)
Holden, Sarah E. to John E. Chumbly 10-7-1867 (10-13-1867)
Holder, Mary E. to John S. Henley 9-24-1857 (9-28-1857)
Holland, Harriet F. to F. O. Daniel 9-9-1858 (9-14-1858)
Holloway, Mary Ann to James W. Ford 5-13-1865 (5-17-1865)
Holloway, Nancy to Isaac Sarver 8-16-1865 (8-17-1865)
Holly, Frances to Gabriel T. Rutledge 4-13-1857 (4-16-1857)
Holman, Susan E. to Benjamin F. Davis 3-6-1856
Holmes, Mary L. to James P. Yarborough 7-11-1867 (7-14-1867)
Holmes, Sarah to Michael Luckett 5-21-1853 (5-22-1853)
Holt, Izora to John L. Brandon 3-17-1852
Holt, Mary C. to John H. Inman 10-30-1866 (11-1-1866)
Holt, Sarah to Valantine Allen 4-20-1863 (no return)
Hood, Delia to Samuel D. Sealy 3-2-1863 (3-3-1863)
Hood, Elizabeth to Edmond B. Sleight 4-10-1867 (4-12-1867)
Hood, Margaret to Thomas C. Gidcomb 2-2-1852
Hood, Ophelia E. to Wm. H. Hywood 11-22-1864 (11-24-1864)
Hoofman, Mary to Titus M. Edwards 6-6-1853 (6-9-1853)
Hopper, Sarah M. to James D. Rich 10-18-1865 (10-19-1865)
Hord, Martha to Ashburn Johnson 8-18-1855 (8-19-1855)
Horsford, Maey to James H. Reynolds 1-18-1858 (12-19-1858)
Hough, Mary J. to Edward Harris 4-3-1865 (4-4-1865)
Howard, Eliza J. to Anderson J. Cockrell 12-26-1860 (12-29-1860)
Howard, Emily J. to Thomas H. Bryant 1-3-1866
Howard, Eveline to Alfred F. Williams 2-15-1867 (2-17-1867)
Howard, Louisa D. to James t. Hunt 12-12-1855
Howard, Mary Ruth to Isaac J. Howlett 3-27-1861 (3-28-1861)
Howard, Melindar to Samuel R. Cecil 11-1-1866
Howard, Mollie F. to James Geddens 1-21-1867 (1-24-1867)
Howard, Nancy Ann to William M. Smith 12-30-1857 (12-31-1857)
Howard, Naomi to Theophilus Coburn 9-28-1852 (9-29-1852)
Howard, Portia T. to John D. Blakeley 3-25-1863 (3-26-1863)
Howard, Regina E. to William A. Harris 10-31-1853 (11-3-1853)
Howell, Eliz. to Hampton M. Freeman 1-16-1856 (2-1-1856)
Howell, Frances E. to J. H. Cooper 11-22-1866
Howell, Frances E. to Nathan McManis 10-23-1861
Howser, Mollie T. to James Hill 8-11-1866 (8-15-1866)
Hubble, Mariah F. to Josephus M. Haley 7-29-1857
Hubble, Sarah A. to Henry Deal 3-7-1865 (3-12-1865)
Hubble, Sarah Ann to Frank M. Poore 10-27-1865 (10-28-1865)
Huckaby, Martha D. to Neal McMinnis 12-29-1866 (1-3-1866)
Huckaby, Martha to Thomas J. Dooley 2-22-1865 (2-26-1865)
Huckaby, Mary E. to John A. Dean 11-14-1854
Huckaby, Tennie to J. W. Sealey 5-1-1866
Huckely, Martha to Wm. Estes 10-31-1857 (11-1-1857)
Hudgens, Rebecca J. to Felix Lunn 12-25-1865 (no return)
Hudspeth, Julia N. to John J. Brims 1-30-1858 (1-31-1858)
Hudspeth, Margaret E. to Wm. H. Ladd 9-8-1866 (9-9-1866)
Hudspeth, Nancy M. to Wm. R. Hill 7-17-1856
Huey, Annie L. to J. H. Sharber 12-28-1858
Huey, Cyntha to Elijah Baucom 8-11-1855 (8-12-1855)
Huey, Laura B. to William E. Brazier 9-18-1867
Huey, Nancy E. to Richard B. Anderson 10-9-1867 (10-8?-1867)
Huey, Susan J. to Orean P. Cheek 8-17-1854
Huff, Elizabeth to Rufus H. Peyton 11-3-1859
Huggins, Mary Ann to Henry Vond 11-3-1858 (11-4-1858)
Hughes, Mary E. to Samuel W. Scales 11-21-1857 (12-1-1857)
Hughes, Mary N. to George H. Brown 2-24-1858 (2-25-1858)
Hughes, Rachael V. to William P. Wilkerson 9-29-1859 (10-4-1859)
Hughes, Sara M. to Gideon W. Gifford 1-15-1866 (1-16-1866)

Hull, A. E. to W. H. Pilkinton 12-3-1864 (12-4-1864)
Humphrey, Caroline to Wilbott Kelley 3-10-1854 (no return)
Humphrey, Elizabeth E. to H. H. Nickens 11-20-1861 (11-21-1861)
Humphrey, Lucinda J. to H. J. Dorton 8-29-1855 (no return)
Humphrey, Sarah to John C. Kelley 3-15-1867 (3-16-1867)
Humphrey, Virgia E. to Thomas A. Dodson 9-26-1854 (10-4-1854)
Hunt, Frances J. to Joseph Moore 1-19-1858
Hunt, Lucinda J. to John D. Bennett 6-20-1865
Hunt, Lucretia A. to John D. Bennett 4-8-1861 (4-9-1861)
Hunt, Mary A. to William C. Richardson 3-10-1852 (3-11-1852)
Hunter, Mary E. to Andrew C. Harris 12-5-1865
Hussey, Francy C. to H. M. Ray 12-26-1865
Hutcherson, Matilda Caroline to Wm. Lee Slate 12-26-1866 (1-2-1867)
Hutchison, Sarah E. to James P. Jenkins 1-21-1858 (1-23-1858)
Ikd, Eliza A. to Marshal E. Hardison 10-24-1853 (11-2-1853)
Ingram, Mary J. to James F. Moore 1-17-1853 (1-20-1853)
Ingram, Nancy J. to Martin Garrett 3-5-1856
Irvine, Mary D. to Thomas Barton 4-16-1853 (4-7-1853)
Irwin, Rachael E. to Augustus Sims 3-17-1864 (no return)
Isbell, Sarah to Wilson Coleman 10-18-1853 (10-20-1853)
Isbell, Tabitha E. to William H. Clark 1-12-1857 (1-20-1857)
Isom, Frances A. to Andrew J. Stanfill 8-30-1864 (8-31-1864)
Ivey, Caroline to Wiley Goad 5-31-1866
Ivey, Elizabeth to William H. Crowell 8-16-1865
Jackson, Elizabeth to John T. Martin 2-27-1867 (2-28-1867)
Jackson, Leanna A. to Joseph W. Sewall 1-10-1866 (1-16-1866)
Jackson, Leanna W. to Thomas W. Gray 10-19-1852
Jackson, Leavina W. to Thomas W. Gray 10-19-1852
Jackson, Mary F. to Wm. Primm 7-23-1867
Jackson, Musadorah P. to Lewis M. Adkins 7-20-1854
Jackson, Susan E. to Thomas H. Helmick 3-3-1854 (3-4-1854)
Jackson, Susan J. to Benjamin F. Hobbs 10-22-1857
Jacobs, Emily J. to George S. L. Green 1-18-1854
Jacobs, Mary A. E. to William B. Green 1-29-1852
Jagger, Dilla E. to Johnson Davis 10-16-1855
Jague, Jane to Thomas H. B. Johnson 9-19-1860 (9-20-1860)
James, Mary F. to George W. C. Patten 10-23-1866 (10-24-1866)
James, Rachael R. to John R. Putman 2-1-1867 (2-3-1867)
James, Rebecca P. to John H. Stauderman 6-12-1858 (6-13-1858)
Jameson, Talitha E. to Joseph M. Foster 7-20-1865
Jamison, Emily E. to John W. Parks 5-12-1858
Jamison, Emily to Joseph N. Walker 5-30-1855 (5-31-1855)
Jamison, Rhoda K. to Samuel Wiley 2-5-1866 (2-6-1866)
Jenkins, Eliza A. to Wm. H. Thompson 2-12-1867 (2-19-1867)
Jenkins, Martha F. to James W. Alford 2-5-1856
Jenkins, Martha J. to Hillary Moseley 4-28-1866 (4-30-1866)
Jiggers, Mary to Thomas J. Rumbo 12-17-1866 (12-18-1866)
Job, Ellen to Simpson Holcomb 11-8-1853
Johnson (Smith), Elizabeth J. to Caswell C. Martin 4-27-1852
Johnson, Alabama D. to William Charter 11-8-1866
Johnson, Amanda F. to Wily J. Rieves 12-23-1856
Johnson, Ann E. to Eli Cothran 3-4-1867 (3-6-1867)
Johnson, E. S. to Wm. A. Quarterman 6-20-1865
Johnson, Elizabeth J. to Jasper Woody 6-30-1855 (7-1-1855)
Johnson, Elizabeth to Samuel Mills 10-31-1863 (11-1-1863)
Johnson, Emily Jane to Carlton D. Brien 3-14-1854 (3-15-1854)
Johnson, Frances A. to Joseph T. Miller 8-14-1860 (8-16-1860)
Johnson, Frances Ann to Jamas B. Kidd 1-30-1855 (1-31-1855)
Johnson, Lizzie C. to Wm. M. Street 6-12-1855 (6-14-1855)
Johnson, Louisa to William D. Fitzgerald 9-25-1861 (9-28-1861)
Johnson, Lucy to Irvin Brown 7-7-1866 (7-8-1866)
Johnson, Margaret E. to Joseph H. Dew 4-25-1866 (4-26-1866)
Johnson, Margaret to Wm. R. Reaves 6-4-1855 (no return)
Johnson, Martha J. to James T. Watson 9-10-1859 (9-11-1859)
Johnson, Martha Jane to James Douglass 8-15-1859 (8-18-1859)
Johnson, Martha P. to L. C. Blackburn 5-5-1856 (5-6-1856)
Johnson, Martha to Georgee Mayberry 3-15-1856 (no return)
Johnson, Mary E. to A. G. W. Thomas 9-18-1865
Johnson, Mary E. to Barcly Martin Johnson 4-22-1867 (5-5-1867)
Johnson, Mary E. to Rufus R. Renfro 10-2-1852 (10-3-1852)
Johnson, Mary E. to William R. Seaton 1-26-1860 (1-26-1860)
Johnson, Mary Elizabeth to D. M. Forsythe 4-17-1867
Johnson, Mary L. to Watson P. Cook 8-3-1866 (8-5-1866)
Johnson, Nancy A. to Harvey M. Flanikin 8-9-1854
Johnson, Nannie to Richard A. Longhurst 3-4-1856 (3-5-1856)
Johnson, Sallie E. to Furman C. S. Parr 9-19-1861
Jones, Bettie A. to Wm. S. Moses 11-24-1866 (11-29-1866)
Jones, Cintha E. to William N. Wilbanks 10-20-1857 (10-23-1857)
Jones, Elizabeth A. to Flavius J. Hendley 10-31-1859 (11-1-1859)
Jones, Elizabeth F. to James A. Dodson 2-15-1864 (2-18-1864)
Jones, Elvira F. to Wm. W. Joyce 9-9-1853 (9-11-1853)
Jones, Jane L. M. to John T. Bingham 1-11-1862 (1-14-1862)
Jones, Julia C. to John H. Gilliam 1-5-1867 (1-6-1867)
Jones, Lucretia A. to James H. Hoge 10-14-1856 (exec. no date)
Jones, Margaret E. to James K. P. Spencer 4-3-1866 (4-4-1866)
Jones, Mary E. to Hartwell Duvall 8-21-1857 (8-26-1857)
Jones, Mary E. to Michael Cannon 3-7-1860 (3-8-1860)

Jones, Mary Jane to James L. Jones 7-27-1861 (7-28-1861)
Jones, Nancy J. to Thomas A. Sharpe 1-7-1865 (1-10-1865)
Jones, Nancy S. to Andrew J. B. Foster 9-14-1852 (9-15-1852)
Jones, O. J. to Henry T. Chunn 6-6-1865 (6-7-1865)
Jones, Polly to Wm. T. Parker 9-21-1855 (no return)
Jones, Ruth D. to Solomon H. Bunch 10-6-1858
Jones, Sallie E. to William A. Sharp 8-22-1864 (9-4-1864)
Jones, Sarah E. to Patrick A. Cook 11-30-1857 (12-1-1857)
Jones, Sarah L. to Isaac Grissom 12-12-1857 (12-13-1857)
Jones, Sarah W. to John Holmes 8-29-1865 (8-31-1865)
Jones, Sarah to A. N. Akin 8-29-1867
Jones, Susan E. to Charles A. Putnam 12-18-1866 (12-20-1866)
Jones?, Nancy S. to Andrew J. B. Foster 9-14-1852 (9-15-1852)
Jordan, Amanda to J. M. Clymore 9-10-1866 (9-13-1866)
Jordan, Elizabeth A. M. to David H. Robison 6-21-1859 (6-23-1859)
Jordan, Julia to Arstead Bond 8-18-1856
Jordan, Lucy A. to John A. Brooks 10-2-1856
Jordan, Virginia T. to James H. Brooks 1-16-1860 (1-19-1860)
Jordon, Martha M. to Rev. Jno. S. Frierson 1-9-1855 (no return)
Journey, Hester Ann to Arthur H. Cranford 6-23-1859
Judd, Harriet J. to William Vestel 3-29-1856 (3-30-1856)
Judkins, Maggie L. to Joseph W. Brown 8-30-1859 (8-31-1859)
Kannon, Nancy S. to Lucian J. Embry 2-15-1854 (2-16-1854)
Keeble, Mary E. to Felix R. Rains 8-18-1858
Keer, Sallie to Powell P. Graves 11-30-1865
Keirsey, Sarah C. to Francis B. Sparkman 6-15-1854
Kellam, Sarah E. to James B. Cabler 10-13-1863 (no return)
Kelley, Nancy P. to Wiley Kelley 5-7-1860 (5-8-1860)
Kellum, Francesa to John T. Follis 5-12-1859
Kellum, Isabella J. to Wm. King 8-23-1853
Kelly, Emaline to Alfred Kelly 11-5-1862 (no return)
Kelly, Mary to Patrick D. OLeary 11-3-1866
Kelpatrick, Margaret A. to Isaac F. Mitchner 1-13-1857 (2-13-1857)
Keltner, Hannah E. to Wm. H. H. Tindle 4-29-1861
Keltner, Hetty A. to Benjamin W. P. Gullett 7-15-1864 (7-17-1864)
Keltner, Susan R. to Thompson Wright 1-5-1853
Kemp, Jane W. to William Jr. Perry 8-29-1853 (no return)
Kennedy, Allice A. to David C. Green 9-6-1865 (9-8-1865)
Kennedy, Annie Lou to Emanuel Roth 6-25-1866 (7-4-1866)
Kennedy, Martha S. to William Cathey 9-4-1853
Kennedy, Martha S. to William H. Cathey 12-9-1852 (12-14-1852)
Kennedy, Mary E. to John L. McMann 1-25-1861 (1-27-1861)
Kennedy, Mary F. to Lucius P. Voss 12-21-1858 (12-22-1858)
Kennedy, Nancy F. to Oliver W. Williams 11-20-1865 (11-21-1865)
Kennon, Lucretia P. to Lucien J. Embry 12-14-1855 (12-28-1855)
Kercheval, Hattie A. to Robert C. Williams 1-28-1852 (1-29-1852)
Kernell, Marilda E. to John g. Cross 11-22-1864 (no return)
Kerr, Caledonia F. to Riley W. Dodson 5-17-1854 (5-18-1854)
Kerr, Clotilda E. to George W. Kerr 12-21-1858 (12-22-1858)
Kerr, Louisa G. to Richard C. Walker 12-22-1853
Kerr, Louisa J. to Samuel F. Evans 5-29-1858 (5-30-1858)
Kerr, Maria E. to T. H. B. Hockeday 1-12-1858
Kerr, Mary J. to John J. Cowsert 12-5-1860 (12-6-1860)
Kerr, Mary J. to Thomas J. Wells 12-18-1866
Kerr, Meece to Joe McReadey 11-5-1857 (11-7-1857)
Kerr, Priscilla to David Wells 8-10-1863 (8-13-1863)
Kerr, Sallie A. to Robert S. Cowsert 11-11-1857 (11-12-1857)
Kerr, Susan C. to Wm. Parker 9-18-1861 (9-19-1861)
Kessell, Mary Ann to Wm. B. Hobson 1-8-1855
Killcrease, Harriet S. to Isaac M. Foster 11-11-1862 (11-12-1862)
Killingsworth, Mary Ann to Geo. Marshall Cayce 12-5-1855 (12-6-1855)
Killingsworth, Ophelia J. to James L. Winchester 12-18-1866 (12-20-1866)
Kilpatrick, Susan to Milton Ricketts 10-12-1857 (10-15-1857)
Kincaid, Eliza to Thomas R. Howard 5-19-1863 (5-20-1863)
Kincaide, Mrs. Sarah J. to Green T. Chaffin 8-15-1867
Kindel, Ophelia A. to John H. Ellett 8-14-1861 (8-15-1861)
Kindle, Cordelia M. to Walter S. Jennings 12-1-1866 (12-4-1866)
King, Lety D. to Augustine Bumpass 11-22-1855 (11-25-1855)
King, Mrs. Eliza to Young S. Pickard 1-9-1867 (1-20-1867)
King, Sarah to Layfayette Paul 11-5-1859 (11-7-1859)
Kinger, Mary A. to James A. Sedberry 2-8-1854 (2-9-1854)
Kinnard, Cynthia A. to Patrick H. Southall 9-4-1861 (9-5-1861)
Kinnard, Kate C. to T. J. Dixon 5-7-1855 (5-8-1855)
Kinsey, Martha to James M. Paul 4-9-1867 (no return)
Kinzer, Allice E. to Wm. R. Lofton 1-3-1866
Kinzer, Catharine E. to Ben F. Fly 2-4-1861 (2-5-1861)
Kinzer, E. Frances to James L. Davis 12-22-1859 (no return)
Kinzer, Emarintha C. to James C. Cooper 9-11-1856 (no return)
Kinzer, Lusy A. M. to Francis M. Easley 5-11-1854
Kinzer, Malinda R. to Wm. O. Roberts 7-19-1860 (7-22-1860)
Kinzer, Mary E. to George B. Marshall 7-11-1864 (not exec.)
Kinzer, Mary E. to Joseph M. Dodson 9-30-1867 (10-3-1867)
Kinzer, Mary L. to George N. McKennon 12-9-1858
Kinzer, Permelia C. to James N. Miller 12-8-1853 (no return)
Kinzer, Sarah C. to Elijah P. Parsons 5-15-1856
Kirby, Harriet to Bennett A. Nichol 12-18-1854 (12-20-1854)
Kirby, Mrs. Margaret A. to Hosea E. Willard 2-27-1866

Kirk, Harriet E. to Newton C. Gilliam 11-6-1865 (11-16-1865)
Kirk, Helena to Stephen C. Cavender 11-13-1857 (no return)
Kirk, Whig C. to Samuel H. Davis 8-12-1863 (8-18-1863)
Kirkpatrick, Sarah L. to James N. Cuney 1-25-1853
Kirks, Elizabeth A. to Stephen M. Box 3-14-1859
Kirks, Mary A. to Benjamin F. Jordan 10-13-1863 (no return)
Kirks, Mary V. to Marion McDonald 3-21-1859 (3-23-1859)
Kish, Almed to Thomas B. Patton 10-29-1857
Kite, Seleta to Thomas S. J. Lankford 2-22-1866 (2-23-1866)
Kittrell, Larissa A. to Thomas G. Martin 11-21-1860 (11-22-1860)
Kittrell, Susan E. to James T. L. Cochran 9-22-1853
Knight, Esther to William Harris 10-12-1859
Knowles, Allice B. to William J. Saunders 12-27-1860
Knowles, Sarah A. to Thomas S. Obrien 10-9-1862
Knowles, Sarah E. to John R. Cooper 12-24-1858 (12-26-1858)
Ladd, Mary C. to Dabney C. Byrd 7-5-1860
Lainey, Barbara to Wm. Rhoades 9-19-1865
Lainey, Emma to Baxter Phillips 9-16-1865 (9-18-1865)
Lamb, Mary E. to Gabriel E. Garrett 12-25-1866
Lambert, Martha to Michael Yankey 4-18-1864
Lambert, Rutha to James Whitworth 9-23-1865 (9-29-1865)
Lancaster, A. C. to G. W. Park 8-27-1866
Lancaster, Elmira to James B. Hill 10-25-1854 (10-26-1854)
Lane, Martha C. to James N. Carpenter 5-30-1855 (5-31-1855)
Lane, Olivia P. to Wesley D. Lockridge 4-13-1852 (4-15-1852)
Langston, Mary to Noah Meadows 7-27-1853 (no return)
Lasserter, Sarah T. to John A. Nicks 7-13-1867 (7-14-1867)
Latta, Eliza A. to A. K. Standrige 9-9-1867 (no return)
Latta, Elizabeth to Joseph E. Slaydon 10-16-1858 (10-19-1858)
Latta, Martha to Thomas J. Stewart 12-19-1866 (12-20-1866)
Latta, Mary C. to Pinkney C. Sanders 9-19-1857 (10-20-1857)
Latta, Nancy to L. J. Huddleston 1-11-1862 (1-12-1862)
Latta, Sophia Ann to William M. Ham 9-10-1859 (9-11-1859)
Latta, Susan to Marion Ham 2-24-1866 (2-25-1866)
Latty, Mary E. to Lewis J. Hutcheson 10-11-1858 (not exec.)
Laughlin, Bridgett O. to Austin OConnell 5-4-1859 (no return)
Lauhorn, Mary E. to Robert P. Shulsky 2-7-1860 (2-8-1860)
Lavender, Lucy to Calvin Potts 11-24-1852 (11-25-1852)
Lavender, Missouri to Milas Potts 3-26-1864 (3-27-1864)
Law, Frances E. M. to Jesse C. Howell 10-30-1866 (11-6-1866)
Lawhorn, Caroline to George Dodson 6-8-1861 (6-9-1861)
Lawhorn, Mahalla S. to George B. Dodson 7-19-1854 (exec. no date)
Lawhorn, Rebecca to Andrew S. Hodge 11-28-1865
Lawrence, Harriet to Washington Wright 2-18-1852 (2-19-1852)
Laws, Mary Ann to Francis M. Bishop 7-31-1865 (8-12-1865)
Lawson, Delila to Joseph C. Allen 10-17-1857 (10-18-1857)
Lawson, Hester J. to Enon T. Estes 5-5-1853
Lazenby, Mary F. to James D. Morrow 7-19-1860
Ledbetter, Anna to John A. Kinzer 9-14-1867 (9-16-1867)
Lee, Harriet A. to Thomas H. Sims 11-12-1856
Lee, Jane to Lucius Liles 2-3-1853
Lee, Margaret A. to John W. Johnson 11-14-1855
Lee, Rebecca to Thomas M. McCrory 8-23-1862 (9-12-1862)
Leetch, Sarah P. to Addison Satterfield 9-1-1852
Leftwick, Amanda E. to Wm. D. Jones 4-16-1866 (4-17-1866)
Leftwick, Ann Eliza to John A. Grubb 7-26-1865 (7-27-1865)
Leftwick, Mary V. to Wm. C. Reynolds 5-22-1854 (5-24-1854)
Leftwick, Permelia E. to James F. Stratton 9-11-1854 (9-13-1854)
Lessley, Ann to James D. Sanders 3-22-1853
Lester, Ellen E. T. to James J. Nolen 11-27-1855
Lester, Mary P. to Mark T. Cartwright 10-4-1860 (no return)
Lester, Mary to Emandus C. Cotton 4-10-1854 (no date)
Lewis, Amanda to Frank B. Hilliard 10-11-1866
Liggett, Amanda P. to James C. Cundiff 1-29-1856 (1-30-1856)
Lindsey, Elizabeth to Henderson Pugh 2-26-1853
Lindsey, Mary E. to John C. Weaver 12-31-1856 (1-1-1857)
Lindsley, Lovinia to John Sneed 11-1-1858 (11-2-1858)
Linn, Alexy J. to A. F. McKennon 1-3-1866
Linn, Nancy O. to Johh H. McKannon 12-22-1857
Lipscomb, Emma F. to Wm. H. McFall 12-24-1861
Little, Ann E. to Wm. M. Dooley 5-21-1864 (6-6-1864)
Litton, Nancy M. to Henry B. Hay 12-22-1866 (12-23-1866)
Litton, Sarah E. J. to Henry B. Hay 12-28-1858
Lockhart, Margaret M. to James M. Whitaker 4-20-1858 (no return)
Lockhart, Priscilla E. to Joseph Nichol 3-30-1865
Lockridge, M. L. to Columbus Merritt 7-23-1862 (7-31-1862)
Lockridge, Margaret V. to Josephus C. Parks 12-9-1857 (12-10-1857)
Lockridge, Mrs. Eliz. H. to Ed. A.H.T. Foster 1-15-1855 (1-17-1855)
Loftin, Elizabeth to Wm. J. McCrady 1-27-1858
Loftin, Mary to Peter J. Dooley 7-19-1866 (1-19-1867)
London, Nancy D. to Andrew J. Clemons 10-22-1856 (no return)
Long, Almira B. to James T. Waterhouse 2-24-1852 (2-25-1852)
Long, Eliza to James Holden 6-6-1860 (6-7-1860)
Long, Laura C. to Samuel R. Reading 5-8-1852 (5-12-1852)
Long, Martha A. to James M. Goodloe 10-26-1857 (10-27-1857)
Long, Martha Ann to James W. Pugh 5-14-1855 (5-15-1855)
Long, Mollie to Thomas J. Treppard 2-12-1859 (2-14-1859)

Long, Susanah R. to John B. Craig 3-31-1864
Love, Amanda V. to James H. Conner 6-29-1858
Love, Anna to John W. Hines 12-13-1860
Love, Sarah Ann to Henry Ritchie 10-10-1867
Lovell, Jerusha C. to W. P. Mullins 12-2-1863 (12-5-1863)
Lovell, Joice to Wm. Embler 8-25-1835 (8-17?-1855)
Lowe, Allice R. to John W. Marr 1-2-1867 (1-4-1867)
Luna, Sarah A. to Francis M. Dooly 12-22-1855 (exec. no date)
Lunn, Elizabeth J. to Radford M. Kincaid 12-15-1862 (12-18-1862)
Lunn, Jane to William C. Pewett 10-10-1857 (10-15-1857)
Lush, Margaret E. to Robert Harvey 7-11-1867 (7-12-1867)
Lusk, Mary A. to Charles B. Peery 12-2-1852 (no return)
Lusk, Mary A. to Charles B. Perry 12-2-1852
Mack, Anna to Henry B. Scott 9-3-1866 (9-4-1866)
Mackey, Mary L. to James R. Hodge 7-19-1864 (7-20-1864)
Madden, Sarah D. to Latchlin T. Dew 12-10-1853
Madden, Sarah E. to Drury Wheatly 11-27-1855
Maguire, Susan B. to Thomas W. Preston 9-21-1852
Mahar, Ellen to Jerry Murphey 7-3-1867 (no return)
Majors, Susannah to Robert G. Kennedy 11-6-1858 (11-7-1858)
Maneer, Martha K. to James McKissack 2-24-1865 (2-28-1865)
Mangrem, L. T. to P. T. West 8-4-1862 (8-7-1862)
Mangrem, Martha E. to William K. Foxall 1-27-1855 (1-28-1855)
Mangren, Frances T. to Henry V. Haley 1-16-1856 (1-17-1856)
Mangrum, Eliza L. to William R. Smith 2-24-1859
Mangrum, Jane B. to William N. Haly 2-3-1852 (2-4-1852)
Mangrum, Martha a. to Wm. B. Toad 10-29-1857
Mantle, Elizabeth to Daniel A. McCoy 5-25-1855 (no return)
Mantle, Frances to Younger Pimon 8-16-1855 (9-12-1855)
Mantle, Martha to Uriah Wilkins 1-22-1866
Mareen, Alice L. to Wm. J. Duke 11-23-1865 (11-25-1865)
Marine, Sallie to John Quinn 4-22-1863
Martin, Eliz. J. to Wm. H. Wilkes 1-4-1861 (1-8-1861)
Martin, Lavinia W. to John Alston 6-7-1859
Martin, Mahala T. to William J. Scott 4-29-1856 (5-1-1856)
Martin, Margaret C. to William B. Chaffin 11-27-1855 (11-28-1855)
Martin, Margie T. to Augustus T. Sowell 10-22-1867 (10-24-1867)
Martin, Martha Ann to Fletcher H. Cheatham 4-30-1856 (5-1-1856)
Martin, Rebecca to Dr. Henry S. Cox 12-4-1866
Martin, Sallie E. to William J. Armstrong 5-6-1857 (5-7-1857)
Martin, Sarah E. to Samuel J. Moses 12-9-1863 (12-20-1863)
Martin, Susan P. to John B. Copeland 10-25-1854
Massey, Mary Ann to William J. Willis 2-21-1866 (2-22-1866)
Mathews, Caledonia to Robert R. Phelps 12-20-1865 (12-21-1865)
Mathews, Elizabeth J. to Wm. J. Davis 9-13-1858 (9-14-1858)
Mathews, Fannie O. to Wm. M. McKissack 9-29-1857
Mathews, Narcissa J. E. to G. C. Garratt 7-7-1856 (7-9-1856)
Matthews, Ann to William Matthews 12-9-1858
Matthews, Josephene T. to James H. McCandless 3-4-1861
Matthews, M. Isabella to George H. Matthews 7-11-1866 (7-12-1866)
Matthews, Maggie A. to R. E. Craig 11-27-1866
Matthews, Mary E. to William R. C. Mack 1-28-1867 (1-30-1867)
Matthews, Mary O. to John B. Morgan 11-16-1865
Matthews, Sarah Jane to Francis M. Ragen 8-24-1865
Maxwell, Elizabeth to James P. Morris 3-6-1867 (3-8-1867)
Maxwell, Martha E. to Jarad E. Patterson 1-10-1859
Maxwell, Sarah A. to Robert Willett 1-11-1860 (1-15-1860)
Mayberry, Alice E. to Samuel J. McBride 10-13-1853
Mayberry, Martha to James H. Nance 10-23-1860 (10-25-1860)
Mayberry, Mary Jane to James F. Howser 2-27-1861 (2-28-1861)
Mayes, Alabama S. to Dr. Thos. B. Blackburn 1-10-1853 (1-13-1853)
Mayes, Emarintha to Alexander Blackbern 3-23-1857 (3-26-1857)
Mayes, Martha Ann to John Frierson 4-21-1857
Mayes, Mary Frances to J. Tilman Hendrick 1-13-1859
Mayes, Ophelia to Robert Orr 5-7-1866 (5-8-1866)
Mayes, Sarah e. to Andrew M. Prowell 2-9-1860 (2-10-1860)
Mayes, Virginia to Saml. R. Watkins 9-5-1865
Mayfield, Mary J. to J. A. McMillan 8-17-1852
Mayfield, Mary J. to J. A. McMillian 8-17-1852
Mays, Alabama to Robert Jarrett 1-15-1866 (1-18-1866)
Mays, Martha E. to F. M. Kitchen 9-12-1866 (9-16-1866)
Maywood, Nancy to John B. Smith 10-25-1853 (10-26-1853)
McAlister, Rebecca S. to Sterling Davis 9-6-1855
McBride, Alice E. to Francis O. Howser 1-24-1861 (no return)
McBride, Henrietta S. to Wm. T. Brooks 12-22-1862 (12-23-1862)
McBride, Martha to Wm. D. McKannon 1-13-1855 (1-14-1855)
McBride, Mary T. to Overton Saunders 6-29-1855 (7-3-1855)
McBride, Mrs. Mary to Henry C. Bond 1-23-1866 (1-25-1866)
McCain, Ellen W. to Andrew J. Scott 2-23-1854
McCain, Jane E. to Calvin K. Warden 11-8-1864
McCalpin, Elizabeth J. to John L. Robinson 4-16-1855 (no return)
McCandless, Martha A. to Robert Craig 6-11-1866 (6-12-1866)
McCandless, Mrs. Jos. T. to Howell T. Spain 2-1-1866 (2-5-1866)
McClain, Eliza M. to Wm. Roan 8-3-1859
McClain, Lavonia to Thomas S. Cooper 8-21-1860
McClain, Malinda to John Mullins 3-31-1865
McClain, Mynan to Aaron McManus 1-17-1852 (1-18-1852)

McClain, Rosanah to Benjamin Bolton 10-10-1854
McClanahan, Mary E. to Thomas J. Stephenson 12-23-1862 (no return)
McCloud, Ann A. to Ira A. Piper 9-22-1851
McClure, Leecy Ann to George Henderson 9-20-1858 (9-23-1858)
McClure, Nancy A. to Milton B. Derryberry 4-4-1867
McClure, Sarah to Samuel Limenstall 7-3-1865 (7-6-1865)
McConick, J. Fannie to G. W. Stanfill 10-24-1866
McConnico, Josephene V. to Josiah H. Foster 9-28-1859
McConnico, Lucinda C. to Wm. J. Jones 1-17-1859 (1-19-1859)
McConnico, Susan C. to Abdon J. Alexander 12-12-1857 (12-13-1857)
McConnico, T. K. to James P. Crutcher 7-1-1867 (7-4-1867)
McCormick, Jane C. to David N. McMeen 1-21-1857
McCormick, Mrs. Bridget to James Frail 8-4-1866 (8-5-1866)
McCrady, Ann R. to Richard M. Daughtry 2-6-1858 (2-7-1858)
McCrary, Martha A. to James Mansfield 8-10-1865 (8-12-1865)
McCrory, Sarah W. to Wm. D. Farris 2-20-1866 (2-21-1866)
McCullick, M. J. to W. A. Oden 1-16-1867 (1-24-1867)
McDaniel, Margaret to Wm. Roan 8-13-1857
McDaniel, Mary to Woodruff P. Hall 10-30-1858 (10-31-1858)
McDolton, Martha to James McKechan 8-8-1857 (8-9-1857)
McDonald, Elizabeth M. to Tarleton A. Renfro 3-7-1864 (3-15-1864)
McDonald, Mary Frances to Benjamin W. Ferguson 10-30-1861
McDonald, Roxana to George H. Bean 9-19-1866 (9-20-1866)
McDoudd, Nancy R. to Wm. D. Duke 5-21-1864 (not endrsd)
McDougal, Ruth to George W. Fryer? 12-27-1865
McDougle, Elizabeth to Mark C. Gibson 5-25-1867 (5-26-1867)
McEwen, Sallie J. to Thos. J. Caruthers 10-30-1866
McEwen, Susan E. to James H. Gregory 5-30-1860
McFadden, George Ann to William B. Cooper 1-15-1866 (1-17-1866)
McFadden, Martha Ann to Lemuel M. Smith 12-2-1866 (12-12-1866)
McFall, Nancy A. to Wm. G. Duke 12-24-1853 (12-26-1853)
McFarland, Hannah M. to Robert Warren 7-2-1854 (7-27-1854)
McGolrick, Tennessee C. to Samuel S. Campbell 9-26-1862 (9-30-1862)
McGraw, Leanne to Thomas A. Harbison 11-3-1853 (11-10-1853)
McIntosh, Margaret E. to Joseph J. Davis 12-26-1859 (12-27-1859)
McKee, Mary to John Rountree 10-25-1852 (10-28-1852)
McKee, Mary to John Rountree 10-26-1852 (10-28-1852)
McKennon, Elizabeth A. to Samuel C. Pillow 5-14-1853 (5-15-1853)
McKennon, Keezee to George W. Bailey 8-25-1865 (no return)
McKennon, Mary to Thomas S. Cooper 11-23-1863 (no return)
McKenzie, Mary E. to James W. Mathews 2-11-1867 (2-13-1867)
McKenzie, Mary J. to Isaac K. Cowsert 12-19-1859 (9?-20-1859)
McKey, Martha Jane to George D. Colquitt 1-28-1858
McKinser, Sarah to William F. Paul 12-1-1855 (12-2-1855)
McKissack, Jessie H. to George B. Peters 5-31-1858 (6-1-1858)
McKissack, Lena B. to Robert Irwin Moore 4-27-1865 (4-17?-1865)
McKissack, Lucie to Wm. P. Parham 2-4-1853 (no return)
McKissack, M. E. to Milton K. Morrow 2-13-1865 (2-19-1865)
McKnight, Martha M. to James M. Whitaker 10-10-1862 (no return)
McKnight, Mary A. to Thomas G. Stacy 2-6-1865 (2-8-1865)
McKormack, Helen M. to T. C. Shirley 2-17-1866 (2-20-1866)
McLean, Margaret M. to Wm. J. Jr. Dale 11-20-1866 (11-24-1866)
McLemore, Addie G. to Robert Akin 11-19-1866 (11-20-1866)
McLemore, Eliz. M. to James F. Alexander 9-26-1865 (9-28-1865)
McLemore, Figure A. to Benjamin A. Rogers 12-31-1866 (1-1-1867)
McMannon, Elizabeth to Collin A. Shelton 10-5-1853 (no return)
McManus, Elizabeth M. to W. F. Brown 2-23-1853 (2-24-1853)
McMeen, Louisa J. to George W. Nichols 3-3-1859
McMeen, Margaret R. to Robert C. Jamison 12-19-1866 (12-20-1866)
McMeen, Martha L. to Morgan E. Fitzgerald 12-13-1865 (12-14-1865)
McMeen, Mary E. to William P. Young 6-8-1857 (6-11-1857)
McMeen, Nancy A. to Carroll G. Fitzgerald 11-28-1857 (11-29-1857)
McMenis, Elizabeth J. to Alexander S. Spain 3-9-1853 (3-10-1853)
McMillan, Emerine H. to Johnson Rowe 9-4-1856 (9-23-1856)
McMillan, L. J. A. to Ebenezer Shaw 2-26-1855 (2-27-1855)
McMinnis, Myra to Adolphus Norman 1-2-1867
McMurry, Matildy D. to Wm. McMurry 4-22-1854 (no return)
McPherson, Rutha E. to Coleman W. York 8-23-1865
McRae, Martha R. H. to John M. Crowe 10-7-1865 (10-10-1865)
Meece, Mary Frances to Robert D. Clark 12-20-1866
Miles, Cynthia A. to John Jackson 2-3-1864 (2-7-1864)
Miller, Amanda to Wm. Johnson 9-27-1860
Miller, Ann Eliza to Beverly W. Jones 9-23-1867 (9-26-1867)
Miller, Esther L. to Elijah Hanks 7-17-1855 (7-19-1855)
Miller, F. F. to Samuel W. Jones 2-5-1866 (2-8-1866)
Miller, Hariet J. to Gabriel Brown 12-20-1852 (12-23-1852)
Miller, Laura J. to James H. Sowell 1-9-1865 (1-10-1865)
Miller, Mary Charlotte to William Campbell 9-26-1865 (9-27-1865)
Miller, Nancy J. to George P. Norvell 3-17-1858
Miller, Narcissa to George W. Garnder 12-28-1864
Miller, Norveline to E. F. Akin 2-21-1862 (2-23-1862)
Miller, Virginia F. to William C. Blanton 12-7-1858 (12-8-1858)
Milliken, Sarah A. to Handel C. Spencer 2-14-1866 (5-15-1866)
Mills, Amanda C. to Evan S. Moon 9-23-1857 (no return)
Mills, Mary F. to Wm. H. Jones 4-5-1864 (4-22-1864)
Mills, Mary Jane to James P. Booker 1-29-1861
Mills, Mary to George Stamps 10-15-1854

Mills, Nancy to Thomas Denham 2-7-1852
Mills, Nancy to Thomas Durham (Denham?) 2-7-1852
Mills, Susan A. to George W. Henderson 10-15-1864 (10-16-1864)
Minor, Mary E. to Stephen B. Crane 11-23-1863
Mitchell, Elizabeth S. to Anber H. Snell 9-2-1854
Mitchell, Margaret J. to John F. Wright 12-18-1854 (12-19-1854)
Mitchell, Martha F. to John W. Whitworth 11-7-1855
Mitchell, Mary to William L. Rumbo 1-18-1866
Montgomery, Adaline to Thomas Duke 11-10-1856 (no return)
Montgomery, Adaline to Thomas Duke 6-18-1858
Moody, Mary E. to James J. McCaul 11-28-1859 (12-1-1859)
Moody, Mary Jane to William D. Wear 9-25-1854 (9-26-1854)
Mooney, Martha L. to Robert H. Bard 11-9-1858
Moore, Caroline to Mortimore Fitzpatrick 2-22-1866 (no return)
Moore, Cordelia P. to James W. Pillow 3-23-1853
Moore, Eliza A. to Robert W. Cavin 8-12-1863 (8-20-1863)
Moore, Eliza J. to John M. Cabler 10-22-1852 (date not given
Moore, Eliza J. to John M. Cobler? 10-22-1852
Moore, Elizabeth J. to Jonathan H. Dugger 4-24-1852 (4-25-1852)
Moore, Elizabeth to Evander King 1-12-1860 (1-13-1860)
Moore, Elizabeth to Wm. K. Luckett 9-17-1860
Moore, Elvira O. to Richard S. Wilkes 10-25-1852 (no return)
Moore, Elvira O. to Richard Wilkes 10-25-1852
Moore, Fannie L. to Luther W. Black 9-1-1865 (9-4-1865)
Moore, Maria to Alexander Farris 9-14-1857
Moore, Mary E. to Andrew D. Smith 7-15-1852
Moore, Mary E. to George W. Jones 4-26-1854
Moore, Mary E. to William J. Buchanan 3-9-1858 (3-?-1858)
Moore, Mary F. to James J. West 1-11-1859 (1-13-1859)
Moore, Mary J. to George W. Maddox 5-1-1852 (5-2-1852)
Moore, Nancy Eliz. to Charles S. Ragin 7-31-1866
Moore, Nancy L. to Thomas A. Scott 9-1-1854 (9-6-1854)
Moore, Rachel to William Clanton 10-20-1864 (10-23-1864)
Moore, Sallie J. to Thomas M. Smith 1-18-1866
Moore, Saphrona G. to Wiley F. Puckett 5-27-1852 (no return)
Moore, Sarah E. to Benjamin L. Wilkes 1-15-1855 (1-16-1855)
Moore, Sarah E. to Miles L. Hutchison 3-12-1861
Moore, Sarah to Luther A. Grimes 12-18-1865 (12-19-1865)
Moore, Sophrona G. to Wiley F. Puckett 5-27-1852
Moreen, Margaret J. to Gabriel B. Brown 6-14-1860
Morgan, Emily F. to James H. Bryson 3-15-1854 (3-16-1854)
Morgan, Pernecia C. to John F. Haley 2-28-1867
Morgan, Sarah Ann to Thomas V. McKee 3-29-1860
Morris, Mary to James Collins 3-7-1863 (no return)
Morris, Sarah W. to James P. Lovell 9-11-1866 (9-18-1866)
Morrison, Mary S. to Edom Love 2-26-1867 (no return)
Morrow, Emily E. to Absalom M. Gilbreath 11-27-1852 (12-1-1852)
Morrow, Mary E. B. to Davis N. Coffy 11-1-1855 (11-8-1855)
Morrow, Minerva J. to Robert B. Craig 1-1-1856 (1-2-1856)
Morrow, Nancy L. to George W. Coffee 8-4-1857 (no return)
Morrow, Rachel A. to John A. Owens 3-31-1852 (4-1-1852)
Morrow?, Nancy D. to John R. Foster 9-28-1866 (9-31?-1866)
Morton, Nancy Jane to Wayman Pearson 12-21-1857 (12-23-1857)
Moseley, Elizabeth to David S. Owens 4-2-1855
Moseley, Sarah F. to Hillary W. Moseley 4-16-1866 (not endrsd)
Moses, Charlotte to Freeman J. Basham 3-24-1860 (3-25-1860)
Mosley, Sarah to Lish Brooks 3-24-1860 (4-10-1860)
Moss, A. P. to John R. Patterson 10-18-1860
Moss, Fracnes A. to Wm. M. Irwin 11-30-1852
Moss, Frances A. to William M. Irwin 11-30-1852
Moss, Louisa V. to Wm. D. Nelson 10-9-1862 (10-16-1862)
Moss, Mildred A. to John A. Grimes 5-14-1866 (5-17-1866)
Mullens, Dolley Ann to Charles M. Church 8-18-1859
Mullens, Martha A. F. to Wm. C. Litton 1-12-1866 (1-11?-1866)
Mullins, Adaline M. to James M. Clymore 11-24-1856 (11-27-1856)
Mullins, Louisa P. to Joshua T. Witherspoon 4-3-1858 (4-4-1858)
Murphey, Amanda to James C. McGaw 2-1-1860 (2-2-1860)
Murphey, Louisa to John W. Dillehay 3-31-1852 (3-4?-1852)
Murphey, Mary to R. B. Wantland 9-16-1854 (9-17-1854)
Murphey, Sarah C. E. to Andrew A. Morrow 7-26-1861 (8-28-1861)
Murphey, Sarah Jane to Henry M. Peyton 11-22-1860
Murphey, Sarah L. to Joseph M. Agnew 4-29-1864 (no return)
Murphy, Mary J. T. to James B. Harris 9-27-1862 (no return)
Murphy, Sarah to George L. Stacy 8-24-1853 (8-25-1853)
Myers, Margaret to Lewis J. Hodge 6-19-1865 (6-20-1865)
Nall, Mary N. to Joseph Kelly 11-24-1862 (11-25-1862)
Nance, Manerva to John Barracks 11-23-1854 (no return)
Nance, Nancy E. to Freaylenhuyson Wood 4-3-1866 (4-5-1866)
Nance, Sarah S. to Amos R. Lindsey 9-25-1856? (9-27-1866)
Neeley, Eugenia B. to Wyatt C. Harrison 12-18-1865
Neeley, Martha J. to Robert G. Harris 9-13-1862 (9-14-1862)
Neeley, Mary Jane to Wm. Tizner 9-25-1860
Neely, F. C. C. to Green M. Akin 5-7-1863 (5-10-1863)
Neely, Mary A. to John J. Sellars 4-23-1867 (4-25-1867)
Nellums, Naoma to Flemming W. Whitley 1-30-1866 (2-1-1866)
Nelms, Eliza J. to Thomas Forguson 9-17-1867
Nelson, Jane to James W. Jennings 9-21-1852

Nelson, Margaret C. to James M. Anderson 11-8-1852 (11-9-1852)
Nevils, Catharine J. to Andrew J. Bynum 12-15-1863 (12-17-1863)
Nevils, Eliza J. to Henry C. Alley 1-11-1853 (1-12-1853)
Nevils, Sallie J. to William D. Scott 6-28-1865
Newcomb, Mary Ann to Armstrong R. Collins 12-13-1859 (12-5?-1859)
Newcomb, Melvina C. to James C. Furlow 3-21-1859 (3-22-1859)
Newcomb, Sophia W. to Edward P. Baright? 2-15-1858 (2-17-1858)
Nichelz, S. E. to Robert P. Brown 11-17-1857 (11-18-1857)
Nicholls, Louisa J. to Charles W. Rountree 1-21-1867 (2-7-1867)
Nichols, Mary E. to John N. Spain 5-12-1864 (no return)
Nichols, Minerva A. to Robert S. Kerr 6-19-1863 (6-25-1863)
Nicholson, Elizabeth to James N. Williams 12-26-1855
Nicholson, Louisa to Napoleon B. Lester 11-16-1859 (11-23-1859)
Nicholson, Mary G. to George S. Martin 11-12-1862 (11-13-1862)
Nicholson, Nancy to Robert Jones 12-29-1862 (12-31-1862)
Nicholson, Sarah F. to A. C. C. Wheatley 1-15-1853 (1-18-1853)
Nicholson, Susan G. to William H. Hardison 11-6-1862
Nicholson, Susan P. to George P. Whitaker 9-11-1865
Nicholson, W. A. to John D. Thomas 12-21-1858
Nicholsonn, Sarah D. to John S. Perry 9-8-1864 (9-14-1864)
Nickens, Eliza to Robert Akers 2-16-1864 (2-18-1864)
Nicks, Eliza Jane to Peyton T. Russell 7-7-1860 (7-10-1860)
Nolen, Elizabeth to James Duke 12-18-1855
Nolen, Julia Ann to John W. Lewis 11-23-1864
Noles, C. E. to J. J. Patton 2-19-1859 (2-20-1859)
Noles, Caroline to S. E. Briley 1-3-1865
Noles, Delia Frances to Seaton P. Briley 2-6-1865 (2-7-1865)
Noles, Josephine to John H. Kennedy 10-24-1866 (10-25-1866)
Noles, Louisa F. to Stanton Slaughter 12-13-1858 (12-14-1858)
Noles, Margaret to John Cox 12-22-1857 (2-5-1858)
Noles, Rosina to Robert B. Kirk 9-12-1865
Norman, Elizabeth to Huey Norman 7-5-1864 (7-26-1864)
Norman, Ellen to Erastus D. White 12-5-1854
Norman, Frances C. to Henry Stephens 7-12-1864 (7-14-1864)
Norman, Martha to John L. Johnson 2-21-1860
Norman, Mary C. to Madison M. Alford 9-10-1859 (9-14-1859)
Norman, Narcissa to Peter Green 8-11-1865 (8-14-1865)
Norriss, Rebecca to Henry Crawford 6-1-1857
Norwood, Mrs. Ellen to Isaaiah E. Workman 11-20-1865
Notgrass, Louisa to Wm. H. McIntosh 8-16-1865 (8-17-1865)
O'Nell, Ellen J. to S. R. Alexander 5-14-1852 (5-16-1852)
O'reilley, Margaret F. to Wm. T. Porter 10-10-1853 (10-11-1853)
Oakeley, Mary Ann to Willis T. Johnson 4-20-1853
Oakley, Ann to Alexander C. Hamilton 2-12-1864
Oakley, Eliza A. to Samuel T. Sparkman 11-12-1859 (11-13-1859)
Oakley, Jeanette K. B. to Samuel Witerspoon 1-27-1855 (1-30-1855)
Oakley, Jeanie to J. W. Kelley 2-17-1864 (2-21-1864)
Oakley, Martha J. to John L. C. Puckett 11-7-1859 (11-10-1859)
Oakley, Mary Ann to Perry G. Baker 11-7-1853 (11-9-1853)
Oakley, Mary T. to Thomas S. Harbison 9-30-1867 (10-1-1867)
Oakley, Nancy E. to Cader P. Johnson 9-15-1860 (9-16-1860)
Oakley, S. S. to J. P. Church 8-20-1866 (8-21-1866)
Oakly, Martha to James Potts 4-17-1856 (4-18-1856)
Oatman, Addie to Augustus Flemming 2-14-1867 (2-18-1867)
Oatman, Margaret E. to James E. Johnson 7-2-1860 (7-3-1860)
Odel, Rachel J. to A. G. Dinwoody 11-18-1861 (11-19-1861)
Odell, Kate M. to William A. Wilson 12-19-1865
Odil, Mary to Samuel H. Armstrong 12-7-1863 (12-8-1863)
Oliphant, Mary A. to Joseph T. Stallings 10-1-1858 (no return)
Oliphant, Mary H. to John Duncan 4-4-1856 (4-6-1856)
Ordon, Mattie E. to Hiram B. Titcomb 5-29-1860
Orman, Martha to Judson J. M. Morgan 10-8-1857
Orman, Olivia C. to Thomas A. Harman 12-19-1865 (12-24-1865)
Orr, Martha W. to Wm. Shires 9-2-1867 (9-5-1867)
Orr, Mary M. to James P. Harris 7-15-1856 (7-17-1856)
Orr, Sarah Adeline to Lewis J. Ring 1-4-1859 (1-11-1859)
Orsborn, Mary M. to John S. West 7-31-1856
Orton, Cornelia C. to Samuel M. Arnell 11-15-1855
Orton, Nancy E. to Wm. W. Potts 10-23-1860
Orton, Sarah L. to S. M. Pinneo 5-7-1858 (5-9-1858)
Overstreet, Matilda Ann to John B. Logue 12-12-1866 (12-13-1866)
Overstreet, Nancy to David Brackenridge 9-15-1852
Overstreet, Nancy to Davis Brackenridge 9-15-1852
Owen, Elizabeth J. to John H. McKennon 3-15-1856 (no return)
Owen, Elizabeth to George W. Pigge 8-31-1854 (no return)
Owen, Martha Ann to Edward E. Russell 9-17-1857 (no date)
Owen, Mary E. to Josua J. Mooney 4-29-1867 (4-31?-1867)
Owens, Mary A. P. to G. M. Booker 12-23-1865 (12-24-1865)
Owens, Sabra to Thomas E. Kingston 3-24-1853 (3-31-1853)
Pankey, Susan L. to Nathan Adams 1-9-1854 (1-10-1854)
Pannell, Earsley M. to Andrew J. Bishop 10-5-1866 (10-7-1866)
Parham, Ann E. to Wm. J. Jacobs 10-13-1860 (10-14-1860)
Parish, Clara C. A. to John Ashton 6-24-1852 (7-1-1852)
Parish, Clara C. A. to John Ashton 6-24-1852 (7-7-1852)
Parish, Martha to Lewis Pinion 10-9-1856
Parish, Mary E. to James J. Funderburke 10-8-1853 (10-9-1853)
Parish, Sallie E. to James K. Hughes 4-4-1865

Parish, Sarah L. to E. H. Wilkes 9-6-1862 (9-16-1862)
Park, Jenevia Tenn. to Lucius S. Freeland 1-7-1867 (1-8-1867)
Park, Mary L. to Miles P. Murphey 7-29-1865 (8-1-1865)
Parkison, Pemelia to Thomas L. Coleburn 10-6-1866 (10-12-1866)
Partee, D. L. to Robert J. Bauguss 7-15-1852
Parten, Sarah M. to Wiley Roler 9-1-1852
Partett, Martha Jane to James T. Garner 4-9-1860
Partin, Sarah M. to Wiley Rolen 9-1-1852
Paschael, Mary A. to John L. Dunlap 11-8-1854 (11-9-1854)
Passmore, Edney to John A. Oliver 8-6-1853 (8-11-1853)
Passmore, Saccie W. to John C. Goad 7-7-1864 (7-8-1864)
Patten, Julia to John P. McFerrin 6-22-1867 (6-23-1867)
Patterson, Anna J. to James W. Sowell 10-23-1865 (10-261-1865)
Patterson, Mary D. to James L. Drake 10-6-1852 (10-7-1852)
Patterson, Rebecca to Wm. H. Lewis 11-7-1857
Patton, Alice A. to William H. Wheeler 11-27-1852 (11-29-1852)
Patton, Martha E. to John M. Blackwell 9-13-1865 (9-14-1865)
Patton, Mary C. to James W. Pugh 10-29-1866 (10-30-1866)
Patton, Mary Ella to Poindexter Dunn 6-13-1855 (6-14-1855)
Patton, Sarah O. to George W. Noles 12-12-1857 (no return)
Paul, Mary E. to James M. Smith 1-7-1867 (1-8-1867)
Payne, Mary E. to Thomas K. Patton 4-27-1859 (4-28-1859)
Payton, Catherine to Lyn Noles 9-16-1854 (9-21-1854)
Payton, Eliza S. to William M. Chaffin 3-23-1855
Payton, Semantha to Andrew Hamilton 7-6-1853
Peery, Sarah P. to Samuel S. Caldwell 3-19-1855 (no return)
Perkins, Eliza Ann to Andrew J. Dycus 1-12-1867 (1-13-1867)
Perkins, Mary H. to Abram P. Maury 6-18-1865
Perkinson, Mary E. to George B. Dishough 5-4-1858 (no return)
Perkinson, Sarah E. to James F. Moreton 9-16-1857 (9-17-1857)
Perry, Alice C. to Marquis L. Perry 9-20-1867 (9-22-1867)
Perry, Caroline to Neil S. Kelly 1-29-1857 (2-3-1857)
Perry, Julia A. to Henry C. Mack 12-19-1866 (12-20-1866)
Perry, Lucy W. to Bertin A. Renfro 4-19-1867 (4-21-1867)
Perry, Martha E. F. to James M. Warr 8-9-1866
Perry, Martha to Alfred R. Donaldson 6-19-1852 (6-20-1852)
Perry, Sarah to Wm. L. Davis 6-5-1860
Pettillo, Harriett W. to John D. Blakely 4-7-1852 (4-8-1852)
Pewett, Susan L. to Atlas W. Haywood 5-11-1866 (5-15?-1866)
Peyton, Darcas C.? to George A. Hale 1-29-1867 (1-30-1867)
Peyton, Margaret L. to Houston Adcock 6-30-1859
Peyton, Mary to Martin Hough 1-9-1861 (1-10-1861)
Peyton, Ophelia M. to James B. Chaffin 1-10-1861 (1-10-1861)
Peyton, Sarah to Thomas Mitchell 3-31-1866 (4-1-1866)
Phelps, Henrietta A. to Wiley B. Brown 5-16-1866 (5-17-1866)
Philips, Mary M. to L. A. Sullivan 10-17-1867
Phillipps, Emily to Gray P. Webb 4-18-1867 (4-19-1867)
Phillips, Caledonia to Willis H. Wood 1-14-1861
Phillips, Eliza to Abraham Meece 9-16-1863 (9-18-1863)
Phillips, Lucinda to Thomas Lawrence 1-28-1860 (1-29-1860)
Phillips, Mary T. to John S. Green 7-29-1867
Phillips, Rebecca O. to John B. Padgett 6-22-1853
Pickard, Ruth S. to George Martin 11-17-1859
Pickett, Frances to Thomas Allmond 9-1-1856
Pigg, Cilia to Young McKee 8-23-1865 (9-17-1865)
Pigg, L. D. J. to B. M. Johnson? 9-24-1867 (9-28-1867)
Pigg, Mrs. Martha J. to Terrence McCabe 7-17-1865 (7-20-1865)
Pigg, Rachel J. to John C. Dockery 10-6-1859 (10-9-1859)
Pigge, Elizabeth to John Johnson 9-15-1863 (9-16-1863)
Pigge, Nancy Ann to Norvell S. Johnson 2-22-1864 (2-25-1864)
Pigge, Nancy E. to Wm. H. Hutchinson 1-24-1865 (1-25-1865)
Pigge, Rebeca A. to Robert J. Alderson 10-21-1865 (10-24-1865)
Pilkenton, Sarah A. to Joseph A. McDonald 2-14-1856
Pilkinton, Mary E. to Robert N. Straughan 12-26-1859 (12-27-1859)
Pilkinton, Susan F. to James S. Perry 12-29-1865 (12-31-1865)
Pillow, Ann L. to J. W. S. Ridley 11-13-1854 (no return)
Pillow, Codelia P. to Jonas N. Erwin 5-15-1856 (5-18-1856)
Pillow, Cyntha S. to William D. Bethel 6-27-1860 (6-28-1860)
Pillow, Eliza L. to E. N. Pillow 11-1-1856 (11-2-1856)
Pillow, Elvira D. to J. M. Gray 2-12-1867
Pillow, Julia Ann to Jeremiah Temple 2-19-1865
Pillow, Lucy E. to Wm. C. Jaggers 12-14-1853
Pillow, Martha W. to Lemuel Long 2-18-1857 (3-2-1857)
Pillow, Mary A. to Thos. G. Sealey 3-25-1853
Pillow, Mary Amanda to Thomas J. Brown 4-20-1859 (4-21-1859)
Pillow, Mary to Wm. T. Porter 2-16-1857 (2-17-1857)
Pillow, Matilda N. to John F. Erwin 9-28-1854
Pillow, Narcissa C. to John D. Mitchell 10-23-1866 (10-28-1866)
Pillow, Sue A. to Frank Jay McLean 8-22-1860
Pillow, Susan A. to Hugh Martin 9-6-1853 (9-7-1853)
Pillow, Susan C. to James Vaughan 3-18-1859 (no return)
Pingleton, Susannah to John J. Woodward 3-29-1866
Pinkleton, Elizabeth S. to Wm. J. Reeves 2-12-1861 (2-13-1861)
Pinkston, Eliza L. to Stophen J. Moore 2-28-1860 (3-6-1860)
Pinkston, Fannie K. to John Wilsoin 6-13-1867 (6-16-1867)
Pinkston, Mary J. to Harrison O. Gilliam 12-19-1856 (12-23-1856)
Pinkston, Sarah E. to George W. Little 8-26-1857 (8-27-1857)

Pinkston, Susan E. to Joseph W. Dillskey 8-30-1854
Pinkston, Viney T. to Thomas J. Gilliam 8-21-1856 (8-26-1856)
Pinston, Mary J. to T. J. Seekers 7-5-1866
Pipkin, Mary E. to George W. White 7-15-1856 (7-17-1856)
Pipkin, Tempe to Wm. House 8-9-1855
Pogue, Cassandra P. to David Dycus 4-3-1858 (4-4-1858)
Pogue, Cinthia E. to Arthur S. Hensley 6-20-1866 (no return)
Pogue, Rebecca A. C. D. to Jesse J. Cox 2-11-1852 (2-12-1852)
Pointer, Bitta W. to James H. McGavock 7-18-1867 (7-22-1867)
Polk, Elizabeth to David F. Ellison 3-17-1855 (3-21-1855)
Polk, Emily D. to Joseph M. Williams 11-12-1860 (11-13-1860)
Polk, Fannie A. to Edward Dillon 11-27-1866 (11-29-1866)
Polk, Frances D. to P. H. Skipworth 11-12-1866 (11-13-1866)
Polk, Lucie? R. to Campbell Brown 9-11-1866
Polk, Maria W. to William W. Cherry 4-6-1858
Polk, Mary Brown to Henry C. Yeatman 9-1-1858 (9-2-1858)
Polk, Mary Jane to George Mason 3-2-1858
Polk, Mary Jones to Joseph Branch 11-27-1858 (11-29-1858)
Polk, Sallie A. to William C. A. Foster 12-18-1854 (12-21-1854)
Polk, Sallie H. to Frank D. Blake 4-23-1866 (5-1-1866)
Polk, Sallie L. to William C. A. Aydelotte 11-19-1866 (11-21-1866)
Polk, Sarah E. to Jesse Moore 8-7-1856
Polk, Sarah R. to Robert C. Jones 4-24-1855 (no return)
Polk, Virginia O. to Wm. L. Murphy 10-8-1867 (10-8-1867)
Pope, Mary E. to William J. Smith 12-14-1858 (12-16-1858)
Porter, Frances to Ephraim H. McLean 3-1-1852 (3-3-1852)
Porter, Josephine Z. to Henry C. Harlan 3-19-1867 (3-20-1867)
Porter, Mary H. to George M. Martin 5-10-1852 (5-11-1852)
Porter, Roxina V. to David M. Hunter 9-10-1859 (9-13-1859)
Porter, Sarah E. to William H. Brown 1-16-1866
Porter, Tennessee P. to Henry T. Osborne 1-30-1862
Potter, Sallie H. to Robert H. Foster 1-15-1862 (1-16-1862)
Potts, Margaret Elizabeth to William H. Marlin 4-19-1867 (4-24-1867)
Potts, Martha Jane to Abijah Byers 1-31-1856 (no return)
Potts, Mary to John Lavender 1-5-1867 (1-8-1867)
Potts, Mary to Nicholas Lavender 3-30-1852
Powell, Ellen to James P. Wells 1-7-1861 (1-8-1861)
Powell, Henrietta E. to John F. Wilber 7-3-1865 (7-6-1865)
Powell, Louisa A. to John R. Dowell 10-1-1858 (10-5-1858)
Powell, Mahala to William A. Stewart 6-12-1852
Powell, Mazee V. to James Olds 12-29-1858 (no return)
Powell, Nancy A. to A. M. P. Sykes 10-27-1866 (10-29-1866)
Powell, Nancy A. to Joel J. Mills 8-10-1860 (8-16-1860)
Powell, Rebecca E. to Wm. Rives 12-1-1855 (12-2-1855)
Poyner, Elizabeth to Wilson Overbey 8-29-1865 (8-31-1865)
Poyner, Mildred B. to Thomas W. Wrenn 7-22-1865 (7-27-1865)
Pratt, Mary Lavinia to Zaccheus D. Loyd 9-5-1866 (9-6-1866)
Prewett, Nancy T. to Zachariah Y. West 11-20-1860 (11-29-1860)
Priest, Cintha A. to Fuston Mays 9-1-1857 (no return)
Priest, Sallie Ann to Leonida A. Boyd 10-13-1859
Priest, Tennessee to Orean McGoldrick 11-6-1858 (11-7-1858)
Pryor, Esther to John C. Miliken 5-16-1860 (5-17-1860)
Puckett, Rebeca Ann to John P. Walker 3-24-1857 (no return)
Pugh, Lucinda E. to Nenniah Vincent 7-15-1858
Pugh, Nancy to Joseph W. Nance 11-25-1857 (11-29-1857)
Pugh, Nelly C. to William G. Gibson 7-30-1853 (7-31-1853)
Pugh, Pricilla Ann to Robert W. Vincent 7-15-1858
Pugh, Sarah J. to John Ricketts 10-16-1854 (10-17-1854)
Pullin, Martha Jane to M. L. Seagraves 2-16-1865 (2-17-1865)
Pullin, Susan A. to Simeon F. Sands 2-10-1858 (2-11-1858)
Purgerson, Lucy Ann to Rufus F. Craig 8-30-1865 (8-31-1865)
Purty, Eliza A. to Nathaniel Green 5-6-1858 (5-9-1858)
Putman, Sarah Ann G. to Edmund S. Cooper 3-23-1867 (3-24-1867)
Rachdael, Rachel to Thomas Patrick 4-21-1864 (4-22-1864)
Ragan, Sarah L. to Richard Brown 7-15-1861 (7-16-1861)
Ragen, Louisa Frances to Eli Lunn 3-29-1866
Ragsdale, Bercia Ann to Daniel Shae 12-26-1862 (12-28-1862)
Ragsdale, Elizabeth to Robert Alderson 8-19-1861 (8-20-1861)
Ragsdale, Lucinda to John Sughruo? 4-7-1865
Ragsdale, Sarah L. to Edward McCoy 7-6-1853 (no return)
Rail, Linda E. to Thomas J. Rail 10-1-1861 (10-2-1861)
Rail, Louisa to John Braddon 10-10-1859 (10-11-1859)
Rail, Martha Ann to Rufus B. Oakley 9-11-1854 (9-23-1854)
Raines, Mary W. to Charles M. Edwards 6-24-1857 (7-5-1857)
Rainey, Penelope E. to Jacob Garton 7-12-1855 (7-15-1855)
Rainey, Sarah to Alexander Thompson 9-11-1854 (9-14-1854)
Rains, Helena J. to Tyra Noles 1-30-1865 (2-1-1865)
Rains, Julia M. E. to James Brashear 2-4-1861 (2-5-1861)
Rains, Lizzie E. to Alexander Williams 11-29-1865 (11-30-1865)
Ralston, Calbernia S. to Charles S. Scott 7-21-1859
Ralston, Martha to John P. Prewett 8-30-1864 (9-1-1864)
Ramsey, Deanna F. to John Hannah 4-21-1853
Ramsey, Elizabeth to Nathan Garner 3-12-1864 (3-20-1864)
Ramsey, Harreit P. to John J. Jones 2-10-1866 (2-11-1866)
Ramsey, Luina? A. to Gilbert D. Matthews 12-12-1866
Ramsey, Margaret A. to Thomas J. Dickson 9-6-1853
Ramsey, Martha Ann to Wm. J. Lowrance 10-17-1860 (10-18-1860)

Ramsey, Mary E. to James N. Bradshaw 2-10-1866 (2-11-1866)
Ramsy, Mary A. to James Wardin 5-8-1856
Raney, Bridgett to Charles McCormack 12-22-1860 (no return)
Rankin, Martha E. to Frances H. Purcell 8-18-1855 (no return)
Rankin, Martha E. to John R. McDonald 11-3-1855 (11-4-1855)
Rawsey, Barberry A. to Phillip A. Owen 1-12-1852 (1-13-1852)
Ray, Evaline F. to John T. Woolverton 8-14-1867 (no return)
Ray, Liddy to Butler Woods 2-20-1867 (2-25-1867)
Ray, Permelia E. to Andrew Crawford 1-17-1855
Reaves, Lucy Ann to Rufus H. Hite 12-20-1854 (12-21-1854)
Reaves, Martha E. to John Griffin 12-28-1853 (12-29-1853)
Reaves, Mary E. to Wm. G. Lee 12-25-1854 (12-26-1854)
Reaves, Nancy America to James L. Toombs 11-29-1859
Reaves, Tempy A. to George E. Davidson 7-23-1856 (7-24-1856)
Reed, Nancy A. S. to James C. Stamps 3-31-1866 (4-1-1866)
Reed, Sarah Jane to Samuel Black 3-27-1855 (3-29-1855)
Reeves, Mary J. to Hugh Jr. Griffin 3-29-1860
Region, Elizabeth to James J. Savage 2-11-1857 (no return)
Renfro, Elizabeth to Gardiner Madden 11-3-1852
Renfro, Elizabeth to Gardner Madden 11-3-1852 (11-4-1852)
Renfro, Mary A. E. to William F. A. Shaw 11-13-1865 (11-15-1865)
Renfro, Nancy C. to George W. Clanton 10-12-1865 (10-15-1865)
Reveer, Louisa P. to Griffith C. Walker 3-22-1853 (3-24-1853)
Revier, Caledonia to Fines E. Brien 11-25-1858 (11-28-1858)
Reynolds, Martha F. to Robert W. Townson 3-28-1859 (3-30-1859)
Reynolds, Mary V. to William L. Birney 6-21-1865 (6-22-1865)
Rhoades, Rachael R. W. to Henry W. Rhoades 3-26-1866 (no return)
Rhodes, Nancy E. to Milton Whitesides 6-19-1862
Rich, Mary to Henderson Estes 11-19-1857
Richards, Elvira to Leonidas Neal 5-26-1859
Richardson, Mahaley to Gideon L. Goodman 11-3-1856
Richardson, Mary Frances to Jacob Bennett 10-1-1867 (10-2-1867)
Richardson, Nancy J. to McCoy C. McGee 10-3-1865 (10-4-1865)
Richarson, Ann M. to John R. Bugg 11-18-1865 (11-23-1865)
Ricketts, Eliza A. to John C. Cavender 1-2-1854 (1-5-1854)
Ricketts, Melissa J. to Anderson J. Akin 12-17-1866 (12-18-1866)
Rickman, Martha to Noble Reaves 7-29-1865 (7-30-1865)
Rickman, S. C. to Fred Adams 7-29-1865 (7-30-1865)
Ridley, Helen M. to W. J. Cooper 3-11-1854 (3-15-1854)
Riggins, Elizabeth to Edmund P. Fitzgerald 2-8-1865 (no return)
Riggins, Martha J. to Soverign G. Robison 12-21-1857 (12-22-1857)
Riggins, Nancy B. to Wm. B. Isbell 12-29-1863 (12-30-1863)
Riggs, Margaret I. to George W. Rountree 6-22-1853
Ritchell, Emma to Stephen M. Haslen 2-23-1860
Ritchie, Sarah Jane to Jeremiah Hardin 10-16-1865 (11-6-1865)
Rivers, Cynthia to B. Frank Carter 4-6-1852
Rivers, Mary E. to George A. Sykes 10-27-1856 (10-28-1856)
Roan, Elizabeth to Wm. Johnson 2-4-1861
Roan, Emily to James A. Smotherman 4-24-1863
Roan, Martha A. to Daniel A. Nellums 6-11-1859 (6-15-1859)
Roan, Martha V. to John F. Roan 3-9-1860
Roan, Mary E. to James M. Williams 3-1-1863 (3-11-1863)
Roan, Mary to Henry Johnson 12-26-1857
Roan, Sarah to Wm. Hicks 12-23-1865
Roan, Tennessee A. to Wm. J. Hullins 3-29-1863
Roane, Rebecca Frances to James M. Taylor 11-28-1866
Robason, Margaret Jane to James A. Harman 12-27-1858 (12-18?-1858)
Roberson, Alabama to Eli T. Trotter 10-9-1856
Roberson, Sarah E. to Moses D. Lovett 1-13-1864 (1-17-1864)
Roberts, Dora to E. W. Gambill 8-29-1865 (9-4-1865)
Roberts, Margaret to Sterling R. Porter 11-12-1856
Roberts, Martha A. to James W. Norton 4-14-1863
Roberts, Martha A. to John H. Searnase 9-23-1865 (9-24-1865)
Roberts, Martha E. to Enoch C. Kirby 12-23-1858
Roberts, Mary A. to M. C. Roberts 3-3-1854 (3-5-1854)
Roberts, Mary E. to David G. Gregory 11-28-1855
Roberts, Rebecca E. to James P. Parten 1-6-1853
Robertson, Aramitta M. to Joseph J. Adkisson 9-3-1862 (9-7-1862)
Robertson, Eliza Jane to William Brown 7-16-1864 (7-17-1864)
Robertson, Elizabeth to William H. Beasley 12-22-1852 (12-23-1852)
Robertson, Elizabeth to Wm. H. Beasely 12-22-1852 (12-23-1852)
Robertson, Mary Ann to Noah B. Owens 6-2-1855 (6-7-1855)
Robertson, Mary Eliz. to William K. Cook 3-31-1855 (3-4?-1855)
Robertson, Mary to Wm. L. Trewitt 12-18-1862
Robertson, Oly to Tennessee Thomas 8-15-1857 (8-16-1857)
Robertson, Sarah M. to William F. Cooper 1-14-1858
Robinson, Arriet to James Tucker 10-23-1862 (10-26-1862)
Robinson, Elizabeth A. to James H. Kersey 5-31-1866
Robison, Lucy Ann to Jeremiah F. Tucker 2-15-1858 (2-17-1858)
Robison, Mary M. to William D. Skelly 2-19-1856
Roche, Susan P. to Jacob R. Groves 10-15-1856 (10-15-1856)
Rock, Martha to William D. Arnold 3-24-1857
Roller, Sallie E. to John J. Jaco 5-15-1866
Ross, Martha E. to Edward E. Skipworth 3-24-1853 (3-29-1853)
Roundtree, Martha J. to Terry Smith 9-22-1859 (9-23-1859)
Rowe, Emerine to Burrell M. Thomas 1-27-1859 (1-29-1859)
Roy, Amanda H. to Albert C. Alexander 2-16-1853

Roy, Mary Elizabeth to Peter C. Cole 12-14-1865
Rucker, Helen A. to Lycurgus Collins 7-25-1864 (no return)
Rumage, Frances to John C. McFadden 3-19-1864
Rumage, Martha to Simeon Johnson 8-4-1857
Rumbo, Mary A. to James Barrett 8-26-1867 (no return)
Rummage, Susan E. to John A. Johnson 2-10-1866 (2-15-1866)
Runnion, Mary F. to James Pope 4-26-1866
Russell, Mary J. to E. C. Hofman 11-23-1852
Russell, Mary J. to E. C. Hofmann 11-23-1852
Russell, Mary J. to Wm. T. Porter 9-15-1866 (9-18-1866)
Russell, Mary to James Clark 5-30-1864
Russell, Nancy W. to Thomas H. Little 8-24-1865
Russell, Sarah to Jesse Tatum 2-8-1855 (no return)
Russell, Susan A. M. to Amos C. Sealy 9-25-1856 (9-26-1856)
Rust, Mira Ann to Elihu S. Compton 10-21-1852
Rust, Mira Ann to Elisha S. Compton 10-21-1852
Rusten, Mrs. Margaret E. to William M. Willis 11-1-1866 (11-4-1866)
Rustin, Elizabeth J. to Drury Lamb 7-6-1852
Rustin, Elizabeth P. to Drury Lamb 7-6-1852
Rutledge, Amanda to Benjamin F. Satterfield 8-7-1864
Sanders, Mary A. E. to John B. Bunch 3-2-1853 (3-3-1853)
Sanders, Mary D. to William Sellars 7-12-1864 (7-14-1864)
Sands, Missouri C. to Nimrod P. Fry 5-28-1863 (no return)
Sands, Susan Ann to Joseph T. Redding 10-25-1864 (10-26-1864)
Sanford, Eliza B. to John Y. Jordan 5-21-1857
Sanford, Madora to Samuel J. Kerr 5-1-1858 (5-3-1858)
Sargeant, Susan to James M. Allen 2-22-1858 (2-23-1858)
Satterfield, Matilda J. to Wm. W. McConnico 1-5-1858 (1-6-1858)
Satterfield, Rebecca A. to James Jones 8-6-1853 (8-7-1853)
Satterfield, Sarah P. to Edmund F. Church 9-24-1860 (9-26-1860)
Scheltler, Ellen A. to J. H. M. C. Blair 12-22-1858 (12-30-1858)
Scott, Elizabeth A. to Christopher C. Hudspeth 1-1-1866 (1-7-1866)
Scott, Hanna M. to W. D. Bryant 7-6-1853
Scott, Luceilly to George B. Nevils 5-20-1852
Scott, Lucilly to George B. Nevils 5-20-1852
Scott, Margaret J. to Wm. H. Ramsey 6-19-1860 (6-20-1860)
Scott, Martha to Allen Brown 1-2-1854
Scott, Mary M. to Elisha W. Hanks 12-22-1853
Scott, Sallie E. to J. W. Kerr 3-15-1859 (3-17-1859)
Scott, Sarah to David M. Callahan 12-22-1857
Scribner, Penie E. to Robert W. Westmoreland 3-11-1867 (3-12-1867)
Seagraves, Amanda to James E. Wright 6-1-1865
Sealey, Ellen F. to Wm. H. Johnson 8-22-1866
Sealey, Julia A. to Richard T. Willis 1-24-1865 (2-25-1865)
Sealey, Martha L. to John A. Huckaby 2-14-1866 (2-15-1866)
Seargent, Elizabeth H. to Edward B. McKennon 2-27-1854 (2-28-1854)
Seaton, Elizabeth to Carrol M. Johnson 8-1-1867 (8-2-1867)
Sedberry, Sallie A. to G. W. Irvine 5-7-1867 (5-9-1867)
Sedbury, Rebecca to Aaron T. Vestal 1-6-1857 (1-8-1857)
Sellar, Susan A. to Wm. S. Blackburn 5-7-1855 (no date)
Sellars, Margaret to W. P. Fitzgerald 9-27-1853 (9-28-1853)
Sellars, Mary to Hellman Emler 10-16-1856 (10-26-1856)
Sellars, Nancy T. to Robert C. Purett 9-6-1855 (9-7-1855)
Sellars, Sarah J. to David J. Fitzgerald 6-21-1854 (6-22-1854)
Sellers, Mary P. to James Leigh 1-5-1852 (1-8-1852)
Sewell, Eudora P. to William G. Clouston 9-25-1865 (9-28-1865)
Sewell, Molley L. to John T. Agnew 1-15-1866 (1-16-1866)
Shading, Alsenia to Wm. R. Roan 4-5-1864
Shae, Mrs. Honora to John Lynch 8-1-1858
Shal, Mary to John Foly 12-24-1857 (12-27-1857)
Shannon, Eliza to David W. Dobbins 2-28-1865 (3-2-1865)
Sharber, Mary Ann to Stephen S. Craig 1-24-1859 (1-26-1859)
Sharber, Mrs. Mary J. to James L. Hayes 5-30-1864 (6-1-1864)
Sharp, Annie C. to David S. Jones 10-20-1863 (10-21-1863)
Sharp, Nancy R. to Thomas H. Jones 5-20-1863 (5-21-1863)
Shaw, E. M. to W. G. Melugin 12-22-1866 (no return)
Shaw, Mary A. to Henry A. Grimes 11-23-1853 (no return)
Shea, Catharine to Dennis Sullivan 5-18-1860 (5-19-1860)
Shelby, Mary E. to David R. Lane 2-17-1865 (no return)
Shelly, Amanda C. to Bluford H. Fitzgerald 6-3-1858
Sheppard, Jossie A. to Thomas B. Steepleton 12-18-1865
Sheppard, Marietta Ida to John H. Holt 4-30-1856
Shires, Lucinda to William R. Brown 10-17-1856 (10-19-1856)
Shires, Mira to Jesse Harris 2-21-1854 (no return)
Shires, Sarah A. to Samuel J. Doyle 9-18-1857 (no return)
Shull, Rebecca A. to Edward E. Smith 4-27-1852 (4-28-1852)
Simmons, Manerva A. to Wm. D. Hill 8-12-1853
Sims, Margaret A. to James C. Matthews 11-13-1861 (11-14-1861)
Sims, Sallie A. to Druz Smith Cosby 3-21-1860 (3-22-1860)
Sims, Victoria J. to James H. Lewis 7-29-1861 (7-30-1861)
Skelley, Nancy C. to Rolley N. Dodson 10-19-1858 (no return)
Skelly, Leasey P. to George H. Dodson 4-1-1865 (4-2-1865)
Skillerton, Mary A. C. to Richard Finch 8-8-1867 (8-12-1867)
Slate, Amanda to Alexander Head 6-11-1859 (6-13-1859)
Slayden, Amanda to Abel Fitzgerald 6-27-1865
Slayden, Amanda to Marcus L. Chaney 1-16-1865 (ret,no endors.
Sloan, Milly to Daniel Wright 8-9-1852

Smith, Anne P. to John Brooks 2-25-1861 (2-26-1861)
Smith, Caroline B. to Ira Shires 3-5-1861 (3-6-1861)
Smith, Catharine to Meredith D. King 10-8-1867 (10-9-1867)
Smith, Eliza J. to Snowden K. Hathaway 7-22-1865 (7-31-1865)
Smith, Elizabeth J. to Caswell C. Martin 4-27-1852 (4-28-1852)
Smith, Elizabeth R. to William T. Galloway 2-3-1866 (2-6-1866)
Smith, Elizabeth to John Fuller 9-18-1860
Smith, Elizabeth to Thomas J. Williams 1-26-1854 (1-27-1854)
Smith, Essabella to Joseph Polk 12-31-1856 (1-1-1856?)
Smith, Fannie Polk to L. M. Hosea 7-20-1865
Smith, Flora D. to Edward Kuhn 4-9-1866 (4-10-1866)
Smith, Flora O. to Andrew J. Martin 7-30-1857
Smith, Louceana B. to John A. Tilford 12-13-1860 (12-16-1860)
Smith, Lucinda to James M. Nolen 10-11-1853 (10-13-1853)
Smith, Lucy J. to A. T. Blankenship 5-6-1853 (5-10-1853)
Smith, Margaret A. to F. M. Thomason 8-26-1862 (8-28-1862)
Smith, Margaret to James Hodge 6-20-1857 (6-21-1857)
Smith, Martha Jane to Joseph Shires 7-22-1854 (7-30-1854)
Smith, Mary E. to William H. Browning 10-8-1853 (10-10-1853)
Smith, Mary J. A. to John Simmons 3-12-1866 (3-20-1866)
Smith, Minerva B. to James Kannon 3-11-1862
Smith, Nancy J. to William J. Cooper 11-6-1861 (11-7-1861)
Smith, Nancy to John Kerr 3-6-1857
Smith, Octavia O. to William L. Warning 12-8-1866 (12-12-1866)
Smith, Rebecca M. to W. H. Tye 1-14-1867 (1-15-1867)
Smith, Sallie D. to Wm. J. Roberts 2-21-1866 (2-22-1866)
Smith, Sallie W. to Frederick W. Gustine 1-20-1852
Smith, Sallie to Edward Kuhn 1-16-1856 (1-17-1856)
Smith, Susan to Jackson Cox 1-30-1863 (2-1-1863)
Smith, Susan to Joseph W. White 5-17-1862 (5-18-1862)
Smith, Tennie E. to Alexander B. Cathey 9-26-1859 (9-27-1859)
Smithson, Eliza Jane to James P. Hayes 12-26-1857 (12-27-1857)
Smithson, Helen Amanda to William T. Criswell 1-1-1867
Smithson, Malinda to George Kinzer 2-18-1862 (2-20-1862)
Smithson, Martha to Frederick Wright 11-3-1853
Smithson, Sarah E. to Mathias White 1-19-1863 (2-6-1863)
Smoot, Ann to James S. Perry 1-6-1859
Sneed, Louisa to Thomas Bradon 5-3-1862 (5-12-1862)
Sneed, Margaret to Jackson Thomason 6-5-1865 (6-11-1865)
Snell, Elizabeth to Thomas A. Strange 10-17-1865 (10-19-1865)
Snipe, Jane A. to John W. S. Stone 12-22-1860 (12-24-1860)
Sowell, Hariet W. to John W. Loftin 1-30-1854
Sowell, Helen A. to James H. Rucker 7-18-1853 (8-16-1853)
Sowell, Laura C. to James R. Casky 7-25-1867 (7-28-1867)
Sowell, Martha T. to Wm. T. Owen 8-20-1866 (8-25-1866)
Sowell, Mary A. to Allen V. Tatum 8-4-1858 (no return)
Sowell, Mary A. to Elisha J. Baucome 1-13-1853
Sowell, Mary A. to Thomas J. Walker 2-20-1860 (2-21-1860)
Sowell, Nancy C. to Richard B. Hardison 12-13-1853
Sowell, Sarah C. P. to Abner Brooks 7-16-1856 (no return)
Sowell, Sarah M. to Thomas S. Stallings 1-19-1857 (no return)
Spain, Martha Frances to James M. Burkett 10-16-1855 (10-17-1855)
Spain, Mary Jane to William P. Barnette 1-31-1855 (2-1-1855)
Sparkman, Edna to S. B. Kinzer 9-30-1854 (10-1-1854)
Sparkman, Elizabeth to John Estes 12-22-1855 (exec. no date)
Sparkman, Mary M. to Alexander Trimble 9-2-1854 (no return)
Sparkman, Nancy J. to Luke S. White 12-25-1852 (12-27-1852)
Sparkman, Narcissa W. to John A. Godwin 1-12-1854
Speed, Mary Jackson to Wm. Offutt 11-16-1855 (11-18-1855)
Spencer, Isadora O. to L. Mino Rently 12-28-1857 (12-31-1857)
Spencer, Mary M. J. to Porter L. Thomasson 8-5-1867 (8-27-1867)
Spencer, Sarah J. to John N. Swan 2-6-1865 (2-7-1865)
Sprinkle, Susan to William Sprinkle 7-8-1852
Sprinkles, Mary Jane to Green B. Hill 12-29-1866 (1-1-1867)
Sprinkles, Sarah E. to A. M. Chumbly 7-18-1862 (7-27-1862)
Stallings, Mary R. to Henry Tidwell 10-15-1859 (10-16-1859)
Stallings, Mary to Joseph M. Choate 2-10-1857 (no return)
Stamps, Margaret to Benjamin Patrick 8-7-1863
Stamps, Mariah L. to Chris. C. Amick 10-20-1864 (11-20-1864)
Stamps, Mary J. to C. Workman 5-10-1864 (no return)
Stamps, Mary to Alfred Shephard 2-24-1864 (2-25-1864)
Stanfield, Adie to Preston Sandifer 8-11-1862
Stanfield, Avarilla M. to David B. Pickard 2-14-1855
Stanfield, Permelia c. to James W. Rucker 8-13-1853 (8-16-1853)
Stanfield, Sinia E. to James A. Parks 4-11-1856 (4-13-1856)
Steele, Sarah E. to William Yarbrough 8-20-1860 (8-21-1860)
Stephenon, M. J. E. to Calvin J. Shan 1-19-1858 (1-24-1858)
Stephenson, Alice E. to John W. Frierson 4-15-1852
Stephenson, Felicia A. to John C. Briggs 10-20-1863
Stephenson, Inda to Thomas Willis 6-2-1866 (6-3-1866)
Stephenson, Mary F. to Hiram Vance Thompson 11-5-1857
Stephenson, Rachel J. to Hiram H. Dodson 2-5-1856 (2-16-1856)
Stephenson, Susan M. to Francis M. Bain 10-12-1853
Stephenson, Tennessee to Spencer W. Buford 9-12-1865 (9-13-1865)
Stevens, Elizabeth J. to Addison S. Thurmond 6-20-1855 (no return)
Stevens, Martha R. A. to Joshua W. Dodson 8-27-1857 (9-1-1857)
Stewart, Elizabeth J. to Wm. W. Gordon 2-4-1853 (2-6-1853)

Stewart, Elizabeth to James K. Grimes 4-4-1867
Stewart, Gillacy A. E. to Franklin B. Cummings 3-12-1867 (3-14-1867)
Stewart, Jeannie to James A. Williams 11-27-1863
Stewart, Sarah J. to William H. Wood 8-15-1860
Stinson, Eliza to Robert Bugger 6-22-1867 (6-23-1867)
Stockard, Caroline E. to John R. Debow 10-13-1856 (exec. no date)
Stockard, Elizabeth J. to Thomas A. Harris 12-6-1858 (12-?-1858)
Stockard, Ruth to Newton J. Matthews 1-10-1867
Stockard, Sarah A. to Americus B. Buch 7-14-1856 (7-15-1856)
Stone, Mary A. to James Sneed 5-3-1862 (5-5-1861?)
Stone, S. A. to Wm. M. Neeley 2-1-1866
Strange, Mary V. to John L. Sandefer 12-27-1862 (12-28-1862)
Strange, Virginia to Samuel D. Sealy 12-23-1862 (no endorsement
Strayhorn?, Caledonia to Richard Compton 7-21-1866 (7-25-1866)
Stricklin, Malinda L. to William Burr 10-23-1860
Stricklin, Margaret J. to Wm. Hood 1-7-1854 (no return)
Strong, Martha M. to Samuel A. Worley 12-13-1865 (12-15-1865)
Sullivan, Ellen to James Sullivan 2-7-1861
Sullivan, Mary to Cornelius Lynch 1-16-1860
Sutton, Margaret to John R. Jones 4-25-1859 (no return)
Sutton, Sarah A. to Green B. Coffee 5-8-1854
Talley, Lotty to Wm. Johnson 6-30-1855
Tankersly, Mary H. to George K. Erwin 11-21-1861
Tankersly, Sarah L. to James P. White 10-10-1866
Tanner, Mary to William Aldridge 11-22-1858 (11-24-1858)
Tanner, Matilda L. to Edmund H. Aldridge 6-26-1852 (6-27-1852)
Tanner, Sarah F. M. to John C. Haynes 10-26-1854
Tanner?, Elizabeth P. to Richard C. Campbell 2-11-1867 (2-12-1867)
Tarpley, Minerva E. to Wm. F. Hewatt 1-30-1866 (2-7-1866)
Tarwater, Mary to Milton Garrett 12-3-1852 (12-4-1852)
Tatum, Sarah (Susan?) Ann to Thomas Sowell 6-5-1852 (6-6-1852)
Tatum, Sarah A. to Thomas Sowell 6-5-1852 (6-6-1852)
Taylor, Emily to Thomas Potelo 9-12-1862
Taylor, Eveline to Hugh L. W. Hickman 8-15-1855
Taylor, Frances to Washington P. Walker 1-26-1852
Taylor, Martha Ann to James M. Johnson 11-23-1858
Taylor, Martha Jane to Joshua Hobbs 8-20-1853 (8-25-1853)
Taylor, Mary to Campbell Nichols 9-21-1853 (9-22-1853)
Taylor, Sallie Ann to Andrew Morgan 9-19-1857 (9-20-1857)
Taylor, Sallie P. to Thomas P. Marsh 4-4-1864 (4-6-1864)
Terry, Martha P. to Egbert G. Wright 2-22-1864 (2-24-1864)
Thernnot?, Sallie E. to John N. Neely 3-9-1858 (3-10-1858)
Thomas, Amanda C. to Jefferson P. Morris 11-6-1860 (11-8-1860)
Thomas, Clarissa A. to Major Howell 1-13-1857 (no return)
Thomas, Emeline to Erwin Thoms 8-9-1860
Thomas, Emma E. to Thomas H. McKinney 4-20-1867 (4-23-1867)
Thomas, Lizzie to Granville T. Hearn 11-1-1865 (11-2-1865)
Thomas, Lucy to George W. Pearson 1-18-1864
Thomas, Margaret D. to James R. Rushton 8-14-1861 (8-15-1861)
Thomas, Margaret J. to Robert Davis Smith 4-20-1867 (4-23-1867)
Thomas, Margaret M. to Jos. Rob. Chapman 8-6-1859 (no return)
Thomas, Martha W. to James Kennedy 10-23-1854 (10-24-1854)
Thomas, Mary M. to Robert Stephens 6-29-1860 (7-1-1860)
Thomas, Mollie J. to Zadock R. Robertson 12-14-1865
Thomas, Mrs. Eliz. N. to Duncan Hastings 6-7-1858
Thomas, Palmira Ann to Swain G. Dannelley 8-2-1865 (no return)
Thomas, Rebecca E. to Thomas B. Hill 8-4-1865 (8-5-1865)
Thomas, Rebecca to John E. Amis 10-12-1857 (10-13-1857)
Thomas, S. H. to Z. Conkey 5-24-1852 (5-25-1852)
Thomas, Sarah B. to Wm. L. Jarnagan 3-9-1866 (3-28-1866)
Thomas, Sarah C. to John W. Priest 11-11-1859
Thomason, Angeline to John McClain 3-10-1862 (3-15-1862)
Thomason, Ann to William Chapman 1-22-1866 (1-23-1866)
Thomason, Caledonia to Eli King 11-6-1865 (11-10-1865)
Thomason, Lovidy A. to John B. Howell 6-2-1863 (6-4-1863)
Thomason, Mahala J. to Wm. Norman 7-4-1865 (7-6-1865)
Thomason, Malinda to James R. Thomason 7-22-1855
Thomason, Martha S. to Benjamin F. Willis 12-27-1858 (12-28-1858)
Thomason, Mary E. to James A. Grimes 11-6-1858 (11-7-1858)
Thomason, Nancy to Robert Holmes 10-31-1862 (10-3?-1862)
Thomason, Parthena to John Holmes 11-29-1863 (no return)
Thomason, Rowena J. to Thomas F. Morrow 6-2-1859 (6-3-1859)
Thomason, Trissa Ann to Joseph Frost 3-31-1865 (4-2-1865)
Thomasson, Leana P. to George F. Green 12-10-1866 (12-29-1866)
Thompson, Elizabeth to Thomas S. Gibbs 11-3-1859
Thompson, Jennie C. to Nathaniel R. Wilkes 10-20-1858 (10-21-1858)
Thompson, Lucy A. to William F. Adkison 12-19-1866 (12-20-1866)
Thompson, Lucy P. to John Lehanan 2-10-1858
Thompson, Margaret W. to James B. Patterson 5-11-1857 (5-12-1857)
Thompson, Mary A. to Rufus C. Ramsy 12-24-1855
Thompson, Mary to James C. Mullens 11-14-1866 (3-10-1867)
Thurman, Jane to John Wilkins 8-27-1853 (8-28-1853)
Thurman, Tennessee to Bluford H. Fitzgerald 9-27-1867 (not exec.)
Thurmond, Mary Jane to Joseph N. Wells 2-2-1867 (2-13-1867)
Thurmond, Mary to W. T. Johnson 3-5-1855 (3-8-1855)
Thurmond, Sarah F. to Wm. M. Pigg 1-19-1859 (1-20-1859)
Tidwell, Ann to Taswell A. Renfro 12-9-1857 (12-10-1857)

Tidwell, Louisa to Abner W. Cooper 10-10-1864 (10-11-1864)
Tidwell, Nancy to Joseph Tidwell 11-29-1852
Tidwell, Nancy to Joseph Tidwell 11-29-1852 (no return)
Tillmon, Sallie A. M. to Andrew J. Massey 7-6-1867 (7-7-1867)
Timmons, Eliza J. to William G. Sedberry 10-5-1859 (10-6-1859)
Tindle, Eliza J. to Joseph S. Birkeen 10-26-1854 (11-1-1854)
Tomlinson, Harriet A. to William A. Watkins 9-18-1865 (9-10-1865)
Tomlinson, Nancy A. to Wm. Hubbard 3-26-1867 (3-27-1867)
Toumbs, Elizabeth to Maddison M. Mitchell 12-10-1853 (12-11-1853)
Trainum, Elizabeth F. C. to Andrew Watel 10-2-1865
Trigg, Priscilla to William F. Callahan 1-17-1866 (1-25-1866)
Trigg, Susan E. to Joseph Weatherly 10-26-1863 (no return)
Trimble, Rebecca to Richard A. Rountree 1-15-1866
Troster, Josephine to John W. Robison 8-17-1857 (exec. no date)
Trousdale, Fannie L. to Patrick H. Hughes 6-12-1865 (6-14-1865)
Trousdale, Mattie E. to Edwin Harris 3-14-1860
True, Mary C. to Spencer D. Beaves 12-23-1865 (12-24-1865)
Tucker, Ann E. to Alexander O. Davis 11-1-1864 (11-2-1864)
Tucker, Eliza to Francis Speed 2-29-1853
Tucker, Emely F. to James H. Jamison 3-15-1864 (3-16-1864)
Tucker, Lucinda to Eli A. Powell 7-20-1852
Tucker, Lucinda to Eli A. Powell 7-20-1852 (exec. no date)
Tully, Bettie R. to John J. Horner 4-14-1857
Tune, Elizabeth to Mark Gibson 1-4-1854 (1-6-1854)
Turbeville, Martha J. to Joseph B. Wright 12-28-1865
Turbeville, Rebeca J. to Joseph M. Little 8-17-1852 (8-18-1852)
Turbeville, Rebeca J. to Joseph M. Little 8-15-1852 (8-18-1852)
Turnage, Mariana to Lorenzo D. Christian 3-8-1865
Turnage, Sarah E. to Reuben Franklin 1-18-1865
Turner, Amanda P. to James F. Agnew 9-4-1862 (9-18-1862)
Turner, Elvira L. to John B. Moore 10-24-1860
Turner, Emely J. to Wm. W. Dobbins 12-11-1863 (12-15-1863)
Turner, Louisa to John Watson 1-11-1858 (1-14-1858)
Turner, Martha A. to Jessee Andrews 10-24-1860 (10-25-1860)
Turner, Ophelia L. to John A. Wilson 3-21-1865 (3-22-1865)
Tyler, Delphina to Samuel J. McKnight 10-9-1866 (9?-4-1866)
Tyler, Josephine T. to James L. Allred 7-15-1865 (7-20-1865)
Underwood, Margaret to Benjamin F. Babbitt 1-25-1860 (1-26-1860)
Underwood, Mariah P. to James O. Douglas 3-6-1862
Underwood, Mary A. to James O. Cooper 8-22-1863 (8-27-1863)
Underwood, Mary E. to James C. Mills 8-27-1859 (8-28-1859)
Underwood, Nancy P. to John W. Dixon 6-23-1863 (6-24-1863)
Underwood, Priscilla to John J. Roane 12-10-1855 (12-13-1855)
Vaughan, Martha E. to Littleberry R. Owen 12-7-1864 (12-8-1864)
Vaughan, Mary A. to Wm. H. Reddin 7-11-1860
Vaughan, Mary E. to James T. Jones 12-12-1854 (12-14-1854)
Vaughn, Ruth A. to John H. Cooper 12-12-1857 (12-13-1857)
Vernon, Mary M. to John F. Eddleman 10-11-1865 (10-17-1865)
Vestal, C. N. to W. T. Foster 12-21-1858 (12-22-1858)
Vestal, Eliza S. to Joseph J. Brown 5-29-1852 (5-30-1852)
Vestal, Lamira? to William J. Vestal 10-23-1865 (10-24-1865)
Vestal, Martha J. to Andrew J. Dawson 11-2-1854
Vestal, Mary J. to Joshua P. Church 10-27-1852
Vestal, Mary J. to Joshua P. Church 10-27-1852 (no return)
Vestal, Mary Jane to Green T. Fitzgerald 8-3-1864 (8-3-1864)
Vestal, Mary P. to Benjamin F. Williams 11-24-1858
Vestal, Sarah E. to James E. Goad 10-29-1864 (11-3-1864)
Vestal, Sophia E. to Joseph T. Young 12-15-1852
Vestal, Sophia E. to Joseph T. Young 12-15-1852 (no return)
Vick, Lena C. to J. C. Gibson 5-4-1867 (5-5-1867)
Vincent, Lamyra to Robert W. Tindel 11-25-1858 (11-26-1858)
Voorhies, Laura to Jason Lee Bullock 9-13-1860
Voorhies, Robina to Charles N. Vaught 11-27-1866
Voss, Rebecca J. to John H. Mullens 12-15-1867 (1-10-1867)
Voss, Sarah P. to Frank A. Leonhard 9-12-1860
Voss, Susan Jane to Jacob Sharp 2-27-1856 (2-28-1856)
Waddle, Lousa J. to Jesse Conn 9-3-1857
Wahl, Sophia Amanda to William Berry 7-11-1859 (7-14-1859)
Waldron, Cynthia to Martin Burlison 3-11-1861
Walker, Annie M. to Lemuel H. Philip 12-26-1854
Walker, Celia P. to Robert D. Atkinson 10-4-1866
Walker, Cerena A. to Dolphin L. Fitzgerald 8-31-1852 (9-1-1852)
Walker, Cerena A. to Dolphin L. Fitzgerrald 8-31-1852 (9-1-1852)
Walker, Elizabeth to Elias J. Armstrong 12-20-1865 (12-21-1865)
Walker, Elizabeth to Lucius M. Bell 9-26-1853
Walker, Elvira to Theodoric E. Lipscomb 9-3-1867
Walker, Frances J. to Zacheus D. Wilson 1-14-1860 (no return)
Walker, Kate E. to J. A. Peden 8-27-1867
Walker, Laura L. to Austin A. Noles 6-2-1862 (6-10-1862)
Walker, M. J. to J. R. D. Williams 11-6-1865 (11-9-1865)
Walker, Margaret E. to James C. Moore 11-11-1852
Walker, Mariah P. to Frank C. Armstrong 4-23-1863 (4-27-1863)
Walker, Mary A. to Samuel L. Garner 12-29-1866 (12-30-1866)
Walker, Mary E. to Joshua J. T. Thomas 4-10-1855 (4-11-1855)
Walker, Mary T. to Anderson F. Johnson 1-3-1856
Walker, Nancy V. to Wm. Giles 10-27-1853
Walker, Sallie C. to George W. Stockerd 4-7-1862 (4-8-1862)

Walker, Sarah A. to James R. Hanna 9-14-1854
Wall, Annie to Gaskill Darton 5-11-1857 (no return)
Wallis, Malvina to John A. Roberts 9-10-1852 (9-12-1852)
Walls, Sarah to Archibald Parner 3-17-1857 3-18-1857
Walter, Tennessee to William J. Church 3-12-1857 (no return)
Walters, Parthena to David J. Church 10-16-1856
Walzon, Martha C. to G. W. Smith 4-17-1854 (4-19-1854)
Ward, Mary R. to George D. Wilson 7-26-1865 (7-30-1865)
Warden, Eliza to Isaiah T. Maxey 4-23-1855 (4-29-1855)
Warden, Priscilla M. to James T. Ramsey 12-31-1866 (1-1-1867)
Warden, Susan L. to John J. Stockard 12-31-1866 (1-1-1867)
Warfield, Artemesia to Stephen P. Nicks 12-16-1853 (12-20-1853)
Warren, Fancy E. to Newton J. Vaughn 1-12-1858 (1-13-1858)
Warren, Martha H. to David R. Corlett 11-8-1858 (11-10-1858)
Warren, Mary E. to Wm. T. Irvine 12-19-1866 (12-20-1866)
Warren, Nancy W. to Frederick Christly 11-21-1854 (11-23-1854)
Warren, Sarah M. to Russell F. McCord 11-5-1866 (11-8-1866)
Warren, Sarah M. to Russell F. McCord 11-5-1866 (no return)
Watkins, Emily C. to Joseph E. Dixon 11-7-1860 (11-8-1860)
Watkins, Martha J. to John C. Green 8-15-1860 (8-21-1860)
Watkins, Mary V. to James L. Bond 12-17-1858 (12-19-1858)
Watson, Julia to Edward T. Caldwell 5-4-1861 (5-5-1861)
Watson, Margaret E. to Washington Gilliam 3-2-1861 (3-7-1861)
Watson, Martha R. to Benjamin F. Heraldston 7-15-1856 (no return)
Watson, Martha to David Guest 8-2-1852
Watson, Martha to David Guest 8-2-1852 (no return)
Watson, Mary M. to Andrew W. Caldwell 12-29-1863 (12-30-1863)
Watson, Nancy Jane to James M. Craig 3-18-1861 (3-21-1861)
Weatherford, Martha C. to Andrew J. Hickman 10-27-1858
Weatherford, Minerva E. to Wm. A. B. Howell 1-20-1866 (1-23-1866)
Weaver, Eliza Jane to Wm. D. Lindsay 5-23-1856 (5-25-1856)
Weaver, Fanny A. to John S. Hunter 5-25-1859 (5-26-1859)
Weaver, Honor C. to James R. Boshears (Beshears?) 8-21-1852 (8-22-1852)
Weaver, Honor C. to James R. Boshears 8-21-1852 (8-22-1852)
Weaver, Margaret to John Dabbs 2-17-1865 (2-20-1865)
Weaver, Margaret to Leeander Weaver 10-19-1860 (10-21-1860)
Weaver, Sarah J. to James W. Due 2-11-1861 (2-12-1861)
Webster, Fannie P. to Thomas L. Porter 4-18-1860
Webster, Mary Camp to Richard C. Gordon 8-20-1863
Webster, Sallie W. to Jesse S. Harris 12-23-1858
Welles, Mariah to Thomas Lindsey 9-22-1859
Wells, Hannah to Joseph R. Dodson 11-16-1858 (11-?-1858)
Wells, Lucy Ann to Willis H. Renfro 1-27-1858 (1-28-1858)
Wells, Margaret E. to Pheril V. Rogers 6-1-1853 (6-2-1853)
Wells, Mary M. to John A. Miller 11-28-1866 (11-29-1866)
Wells, Nancy P. to Wiley S. Emby 10-9-1852 (10-10-1852)
Wells, Nancy P. to Wiley S. Emby 10-9-1852 (10-10?-1852)
Wells, Sarah E. to Rufus Woody 9-14-1857 (9-17-1857)
West, Fannie to John T. Davis 3-26-1863
West, Mary Jane to Alexander Cothran 3-14-1860
West, Mary Jane to George W. Smalley 8-5-1859 (8-7-1859)
West, Mary Jane to Richard Gilmon 12-18-1859 (no return)
West, Mary T. to John Stockard 11-1-1864 (11-2-1864)
Westmoreland, Eliza Ann to James B. Mash 6-3-1864 (6-5-1864)
Westmoreland, Mary C. to Josiah D. Mitchell 12-23-1863 (12-24-1863)
Westmoreland, Millicent B. to Walter Rowekeeble 2-2-1860
Westmoreland, Phoeba A. to Wm. B. Johnson 11-19-1863
Whitaker, Sarah B. to Wm. H. Dodson 2-5-1856 (2-13-1856)
White, Angeline E. to W. Calvin Boyd 12-25-1861
White, Anna C. to Thomas H. Williams 2-4-1867 (2-5-1867)
White, Arabella M. to Brinkly Harwell 12-2-1865 (12-3-1865)
White, Elizabeth J. to Henry H. Kinzer 2-6-1861 (2-7-1861)
White, Elvira to Wm. E. Goodman 12-16-1862 (12-18-1862)
White, Emma to Samuel W. Kingston 11-23-1852 (11-21-1852)
White, Emma to Samuel W. Kingston 11-23-1852 (11-21?-1852)
White, Margaret R. to James K. P. Hutchinson 4-14-1866 (4-16-1866)
White, Mary T. to William Beasly 3-24-1858
White, Mary to B. L. White 5-13-1865 (5-14-1865)
White, Mary to Boling H. Horsford 11-28-1861 (11-29-1861)
White, Mary to William L. Young 5-1-1865 (5-11-1865)
White, Phoebe to Richard Cross 10-12-1858 (10-13-1858)
White, Rebecca Jane to Soloman Edgin 4-19-1860 (4-22-1860)
White, Salina R. to Thomas P. Eskew 5-6-1857 (5-7-1857)
White, Sina Ann to William A. Wilkes 1-16-1860 (1-19-1860)
Whitehead, Ann M. to Joseph H. Duke 9-29-1859 (10-1-1859)
Whitehead, Mary E. to Y. H. Johnson 4-3-1854
Whitehead, Mary Ellen to Frank H. Purcell 9-11-1857 (9-14-1857)
Whitehead, Mary Jane to John H. Standemann 8-15-1857 (no return)
Whitehead, Sallie J. to Charles C. Hudson 10-6-1858
Whiteside, Molley J. to N. D. Garner 1-14-1867 (1-17-1867)
Whitley, Mary to Wm. H. Estes 11-27-1860
Whittaker, Betty to J. W. Kinnard 2-18-1867 (2-21-1867)
Whittaker, Sarah J. to James Brooks 11-28-1865 (12-29-1865)
Whitworth, Frances to Burzella M. Green 7-12-1856 (7-13-1856)
Whitworth, Lucinda V. to John E. Denton 2-8-1865 (2-9-1865)
Wiem, Mary Ann to John A. Thompson 8-7-1852 (8-10-1852)
Wiern (Wiser?), Mary Ann to John A. Thompson 8-7-1852 (8-10-1852)

Wigington, Nancy to Thomas Harrison 10-3-1865
Wilcox, Susan M. to William H. Wheeler 6-29-1858 (6-30-1858)
Wiley, Addie to John D. Moore 2-12-1867
Wiley, Elizabeth to J. H. Smith 3-19-1853 (3-20-1853)
Wiley, Frances C. to Jesse J. Savage 6-15-1863 (no return)
Wilkers, Mary K. to C. B. Abernathy 11-15-1866
Wilkes, E. A. to Elijah Blocker 7-7-1862 (7-8-1862)
Wilkes, Harriet M. to Henry Murphy 3-16-1853 (3-17-1853)
Wilkes, Josephine C. to John T. Steel 12-1-1853 (no return)
Wilkes, Martha E. to Joseph B. Shaw 1-17-1855
Wilkes, Mary R. to E. B. Martin 10-3-1856 (3-11-1856)
Wilkes, Sallie E. to James A. Cochran 12-16-1865 (12-19-1865)
Wilkes, Sarah F. to William Alderson 6-24-1857
Wilkins, Eliza C. to James Dyer 12-20-1858 (12-21-1858)
Wilkins, Louisa B. to William B. Wilson 5-8-1861
Wilks, Nancy to Pleasant Fitzgerald 5-18-1858
Willaford, Martha Ann to Jesse Adcock 6-4-1859 (6-5-1859)
Willett, Jane to Willis Wileford 6-29-1860 (6-30-1860)
Williams, Amanda J. to Henry L. Wilson 11-29-1856 (no endorsement
Williams, Amelia A. to John L. Biggers 12-19-1866 (12-25-1866)
Williams, Anna M. to George M. V. Kinzer 11-18-1865 (11-23-1865)
Williams, Annie to Addison S. English 12-8-1864 (12-9-1864)
Williams, Candis M. to Wm. D. Delk 10-11-1865 (10-12-1865)
Williams, Catharine to George M. Logan 1-24-1854 (1-25-1854)
Williams, Eliza A. to Williamson Y. Kirk 1-19-1866 (no return)
Williams, Eliza to John F. Grimes 9-24-1862 (9-25-1862)
Williams, Ellen to Nathaniel N. Norwood 6-2-1857 (6-3-1857)
Williams, Fannie C. to Rufus Lisenby 2-11-1861 (2-12-1861)
Williams, Josephine to W. H. Harris 9-8-1866 (9-9-1866)
Williams, Josie E. to Leroy Voss 11-27-1866 (11-29-1866)
Williams, Lucretia M. to Stephen G. Easley 4-21-1860 (4-22-1860)
Williams, Margaret P. to Wm. A. Nicholson 10-15-1855 (10-23-1855)
Williams, Mary E. to John W. Lockhart 6-1-1867 (6-2-1867)
Williams, Mary L. to William Underwood 1-1-1866 (1-4-1866)
Williams, Mary to Abraham Clanton 1-16-1854
Williams, Mary to John F. Gray 4-27-1857 (4-29-1857)
Williams, Rachael to John J. Gist 4-28-1866 (4-29-1866)
Williams, Sarah E. to John H. Bond 11-14-1854 (11-15-1854)
Williams, Sarah M. to Wm. J. Jones 4-23-1856 (4-24-1856)
Williams, Serena A. to George E. Sutton 8-20-1861 (8-22-1861)
Williamson, Anna A. to Americus R. Crutcher 2-27-1865 (3-1-1865)
Williamson, Magie E. to Henry L. Crutcher 7-27-1863 (7-28-1863)
Williamson, Mary A. to Wm. Leel 12-22-1857 (12-23-1857)
Willis, Eliza J. to George W. Harden 2-10-1866 (2-11-1866)
Willis, Fannie to William F. McClure 8-12-1865
Willis, Gennette to Andrew J. Givens 10-16-1854 (10-27-1854)
Willis, Sarah E. to James K. Holden 10-8-1862 (no return)
Wills, Mary Jane to Carson Williams 4-28-1857 (4-29-1857)
Wilmott, Helen K. to James F. Ingram 1-27-1863 (no return)
Wilson, Malinda to Harmon Roberson 12-13-1866
Wilson, Margaret E. to George S. Fain 12-17-1857
Wilson, Martha A. to Levin E. Covey 8-18-1860 (8-19-1860)
Wilson, Martha E. to Wm. O. Thompson 10-17-1853 (no return)
Wilson, Martha to David Guest 8-2-1852
Wilson, Mary A. J. to Joseph F. Hargrove 10-12-1867 (10-13-1867)
Wilson, Mary E. to David Hamilton 9-16-1854 (9-17-1854)
Wilson, Mary F. to Wm. H. Moseley 8-8-1860
Wilson, Mary H. to Wm. H. Fariss 5-21-1866 (5-22-1866)
Wilson, Matilda J. to Edward L. Lansdown 1-2-1866
Wilson, Mrs. Eliz. E. to James E. Hawthorne 8-30-1866 (9-4-1866)
Wilson, Sarah J. to John G. Adkinson 11-24-1859
Wiltsher, Sarah E. to Wm. T. Dew 10-8-1857
Wiltshon, Nancy Jame to Lewis G. Lanier 10-16-1855 (10-18-1855)
Winchester, Elizabeth J. to Andrew Regan 3-26-1867 (3-28-1867)
Wingfield, Mary M. to Thomas G. Martin 12-21-1854
Winn, Harriet C. to Edward A. Hunter 8-31-1858 (9-1-1858)
Winn, Mary Ann to John A. Thompson 8-7-1852
Winn, Mary J. to William J. Cross 4-5-1854 (4-6-1854)
Winn?, Mary M. to Wm. W. Ruston 8-28-1852 (8-29-1852)
Wisener, Angeline B. to Samuel J. Roberts 10-14-1852 (10-15-1852)
Wisener, Sarah Jane to Elijah N. Hanks 4-19-1855
Wisener, Sarah Jane to George T. Stone 6-22-1867 (6-23-1867)
Witham, Nancy E. to Joseph B. Woodside 1-31-1853
Witham, Sarah A. to David Thomas 10-19-1852 (10-20-1852)
Witherspoon, Annie E. to Crawford W. Irvine 8-15-1864 (8-16-1864)
Witherspoon, Fannie C. to Hugh W. Sanders 1-25-1866
Witherspoon, Mary E. to Sidney C. Cook 3-13-1856
Witherspoon, Sallie A. E. to Wm. P. Miller 2-20-1865 (no return)
Wollard, Margaret S. to Andrew J. Harris 12-17-1853 (12-18-1853)
Wood, Abigail to John J. White 7-19-1866 (7-25-1866)
Wood, Ann E. to John Gardner 3-8-1858
Wood, Ann to James B. Jordan 5-29-1852 (5-30-1852)
Wood, Calista to Willard Parker 10-30-1866
Wood, Cordilia N. to A. S. Robinson 2-15-1865 (no return)
Wood, Harriet F. to Thomas C. Crawford 5-5-1863
Wood, Lucy C. to Mount Levanus Stewart 11-22-1855

Wood, Martha J. to George W. Martin 11-22-1864 (11-24-1864)
Wood, Mary Ann to Elijah C. Denton 4-5-1866 (4-8-1866)
Wood, Mary P. to Jaems M. Roberson 9-16-1863
Wood, Sallie A. to Charles T. Crawford 12-16-1857 (12-17-1857)
Woodward, Lavina to John C. Huckaby 8-5-1865 (8-6-1865)
Woody, Margere to David B. Jones 10-24-1866 (10-25-1866)
Woody, Margeret to David B. Jones 10-24-1866 (10-25-1866)
Woody, Sarah Ann to James Jones 3-6-1867 (no return)
Wooldridge, Ann E. to Wm. G. Huey 9-18-1854 (9-13?-1854)
Woollard, Mary A. to Samuel Ragsdale 5-31-1853 (6-2-1853)
Worgum, Mary to Michael Snider 4-2-1860
Workman, Amanda to Thomas Yokely 9-8-1864 (9-19-1864)
Worley, Clarinda C. to George O. Kirk 8-28-1866 (8-29-1866)
Worley, Elizabeth to James A. Cathey 9-19-1866 (9-20-1866)
Worley, Mary B. to Thomas B. Brooks 10-16-1854 (10-17-1854)
Worley, Nancy Ann to Burton Warfield 2-10-1858
Worley, Sallie Ann to N. G. Ham 12-6-1859
Wortham, Mary Lee E. A. to Nathaniel G. B. Williams 2-26-1855 (2-27-1855)
Wreem, Eliz. G. to Matthew M. Harbison 7-28-1855 (8-2-1855)
Wrenn, Mary M. to William W. Ruston 8-28-1852 (8-29-1852)
Wright, Amanda to Andrew J. Rains 4-6-1863 (4-16-1863)
Wright, Carrie C. to A. C. Neeley 4-1-1867 (4-2-1867)
Wright, Elizabeth C. to Nathaniel Nicholson 1-23-1865 (1-26-1865)
Wright, Leannah to Mark L. Jackson 1-5-1858 (1-6-1858)
Wright, Louisa J. to Milton A. Wilkes 7-31-1856
Wright, Malinda Caroline to Joseph L. Crews 7-13-1864 (7-14-1864)
Wright, Malinda J. to Samuel D. Seeley 10-24-1860 (10-25-1860)
Wright, Mary E. to Pearce Wheatley 8-21-1865
Wright, Mary E.? to Rufus H. Hight 10-8-1857 (10-10-1857)
Wright, Mary to Charles A. Tuley 12-28-1855
Wright, Nancy E. to Jasper B. Cockrill 1-14-1857 (1-15-1857)
Wright, Nancy to Robert E. Davis 10-12-1867 (10-13-1867)
Wright, Rosana to Elisha J. D. Nall 4-21-1862 (4-22-1862)
Wright, Sarah N. to Thomas E. Kirkpatrick 5-29-1861 (not endrsd)
Wright, Tirza E. to Terry C. Notgrass 5-23-1861 (5-24-1861)
Wright, Unita Julia to George M. Martin 12-28-1854
Wright, Valeria to Absolum Burkett 4-9-1864 (4-12-1864)
Wylie, Mary to Moses Tanner 8-11-1858 (8-12-1858)
Yancy, Maria W. to John A. Fain 8-20-1857
Young, Elizabeth J. to Eli E. Akin 12-19-1859 (12-22-1859)
Young, Ella to Dewitt C. Helm 1-11-1858 (1-12-1858)
Young, Laura A. to William P. Gant 4-29-1857
Young, Margaret to Lycurgus Collins 5-18-1852 (5-19-1852)
Young, Sallie E. to Colin M. Campbell 10-10-1853 (10-11-1853)
Younger, Mrs. Sarah J. to Robert L. Walters 8-21-1865
Younger, Rachel E. to James M. Vestal 11-10-1852 (11-11-1852)
Younger, Sarah to John M. Church 7-16-1853 (7-17-1853)
Younger, Tennessee O. to W. B. Robertson 5-27-1865 (5-28-1865)
Zellner, Margaret to David Lipscomb 7-23-1862

9 781596 411272